MANAGING KNOWHOW

ADD VALUE . . .
BY VALUING CREATIVITY

KARL ERIK SVEIBY
TOM LLOYD

BLOOMSBURY

This book is dedicated to Ronald Fagerfjäll, our mentor and friend, who knows more about managing knowhow than both of us put together and to Mrs Lubavitch, doyenne of the 'oldest profession', who produced one of the first definitions of the knowhow company:

'Oy, yoy, is this a business . . . you got it, you sell it and you still got it!'

First published 1987. Paperback edition 1988.

Copyright © 1987 by Karl Erik Sveiby and Tom Lloyd
Forword © 1988 Wally Olins
Bloomsbury Publishing Limited, 2 Soho Square, London W1V 5DE

ISBN 0 7475 0331 1

10 9 8 7 6 5 4 3 2

Diagrams produced by Cooperdale on an Apple Macintosh computer
Typeset by Rapid Communications
Printed and bound in Great Britain by Richard Clay Ltd, Bungay, Suffolk

• Contents

• Foreword

Like Molière's Bourgeois Gentilhomme who was amazed and delighted to learn that he had been speaking prose all his life, I had no idea until I read this book that I have been managing knowhow for the last twenty odd years. I just thought I was a lousy manager trying to cope with a bunch of highly creative, well paid eccentrics.

Sveiby and Lloyd's book will make a lot of sense to those of us who are pioneering new kinds of business activity. It will also give us a warm glow. It's nice to feel that there are lots of us struggling with the same problems, making the same mistakes and now and again getting a few right answers.

It's also an optimistic book. It says that the goodies will win. So those of us with new ideas which we pursue obsessively with a manic eye for quality will get our just rewards—on earth. We won't according to this book have to wait until we reach heaven—or even make do with the USM.

The book tells us that in the post-industrial society, which we are just entering, what the authors call the information society, hard issues in management, costings, pricing, sourcing, plant location, distribution and all that will be increasingly influenced by soft issues. What is the environment like in the work place? How do people collaborate with each other? What are the core values of the company? They say that the culture of the company, its ethos and its identity, will be increasingly significant in attracting and keeping the right kind of people, in building success with customers.

Well, I agree with all that, particularly, no doubt, because that's the trade I practise.

The book is very interesting on issues of size. The last few years have seen the growth of huge advertising agencies/marketing services conglomerates which the City of London in one of its frequent rushes of blood to the head fell in love with—for about five minutes.

Sveiby and Lloyd say that large size doesn't really suit knowhow companies, they can't really cope with it. The authors think that these kind of businesses will break up—and I'm inclined to agree with them.

But what do you do about highly successful knowhow companies that do grow, not by acquisition but organically simply because people want to buy what they provide? This book doesn't have too many answers to that question. I wish it did. We have nearly 200 people and offices in Europe and the US, so we need to know—fast.

One last thing, people of advanced years will stop being called 'old'. They'll simply be thought of as 'experienced'. I love that. It's the best thing in the book.

Wally Olins
Chairman
Wolff Olins Business Ltd
London

August 1988

• Preface

This book is the product of an Anglo-Swedish collaboration. Either one of us could have explained the origins; it fell to me largely because in English, I am the 'host'.

The central concept of the book, the 'knowhow company', was born in 1983 when my co-author Karl Erik Sveiby, working as an analyst with the Swedish financial information group Affärsvärlden, was struggling with the new 'consultancy' firms that were being floated on the Stockholm Stock Exchange.

They lacked substance and so could not be analysed with the same tools developed by Affärsvärlden for analysing traditional companies. While pondering the problem Karl Erik was struck by the many similarities between these companies and Affärsvärlden itself, despite the very different business areas in which they operated.

During the following four years he concentrated his analytical efforts in this area, working closely with managers and professionals in more than 100 companies in widely varying fields employing lawyers, computer consultants, management consultants, journalists, physicians, academics, teachers, civil servants, research scientists, advertising professionals, merchant bankers, venture capitalists and financial analysts.

Though Karl Erik's work has focussed mostly on Scandinavian companies, he has also talked to managers and professionals in companies elsewhere in Europe and in the US. Altogether he has analysed the accounts of several hundred knowhow companies. In this book his research has been augmented by my own work with UK companies.

The picture that has emerged is of a whole new breed of company operating in a wide variety of industries but sharing many common characteristics. All of them are struggling with the strategic problems associated with the building of durable organisations based entirely on the knowhow of human beings.

Karl Erik and I have been friends and subsequently business colleagues since late 1984 when I had just failed in my first attempt to negotiate the management buy-out of *Financial Weekly* from Robert Maxwell's organisation.

Seven months earlier Routledge & Kegan Paul had published my book *Dinosaur & Co. Studies in corporate evolution*. Karl Erik read it and discovered that some of the ideas it contained corresponded quite closely to concepts he was developing for his book. Looking back it was inevitable that we would decide to collaborate in developing our ideas in a third book.

Dinosaur & Co. had concentrated on technology-driven companies and, as its title implied, it took an evolutionary view of business. It suggested that technological change greatly reduced the benefits of size in the corporate world. I suspected at the time that part of my argument – possibly a substantial part – could be generalised to apply to all companies but I was content to restrict the focus of my book to technology-driven companies.

Karl Erik's award-winning book *Kunskapsföretaget* contained a more generalised form of my argument, worked out in much more detail and developed in a way that made it more practical. Karl Erik and I had arrived independently at similar ideas about knowhow companies before we met. The difference was that I had approached them via a polemical, journalistic route whereas he had trod a more analytical, pragmatic path.

The present book, though relying on Karl Erik's pragmatism in its structure, represents a fusion of these two approaches. We have tried to define this new breed of company, to explain its origins, to identify the management challenges it represents, to supply the rudiments of a tool-box for managers conscious of the limitations of conventional theory in this area and, at the end of the book, to explore some of the theoretical implications of what we regard as a development in corporate evolution of the first importance.

Though we take issue with a number of the axioms of modern management theory we are not being deliberately heretical. We are conventional in placing emphasis on focus, contemporary in stressing the importance of corporate culture and positively atavistic in this age of the hired manager in giving priority to leadership and the social dynamics of company life.

Where we differ from contemporary literature is in our conception of the problem management theory is attempting to solve. The idea that changes in the speed of change in the corporate world, in the availability of capital, the scarcity of knowhow and the structures of industries are together creating a new kind of company, is central to our argument. We believe the 'problematique' of management theory has shifted. We hope this book will encourage the focus of theory to follow this shift and to devote its present vitality to solving the new problems and exploiting the new opportunities the arrival of the knowhow company creates.

The pages that follow are sprinkled liberally with case studies. They are taken from the experiences of both authors so they fall into two main categories – Swedish and British. We considered anglicising the case study portfolio completely but decided this would rob the book of what might be seen as one of its strengths – its dual cultural provenance.

The more we thought about it the more intrigued we became by the contrasts between the Swedish and British economies. The Swedish economy has been much more successful than Britain's in recent years and yet Sweden has a long tradition of what by British standards would be deemed 'leftist' government.

Sweden sports two unsubsidised, world-class car companies, a remarkable number of internationally competitive groups in such industries as engineering, consumer durable goods, telecommunications, data processing and retailing and, with a population less than a fifth of Britain's, has in recent years produced more top-class tennis players than any other country.

We believe Britain has much to learn from the success of the Swedish economy and, for reasons we explain in Chapter One, we believe Europe as a cultural unit may yet have much to teach the rest of the world about managing companies in the information society.

A detail associated with the Anglo/Swedish origins of the book that should be mentioned is that there are roughly ten Swedish Krone (SKr) to the pound sterling. We give the conversion in most places but occasionally the SKr is left to speak for itself.

Tom Lloyd
July 1987

· Introduction

A new society – some call it the **information society** – is emerging. It is bringing with it a new kind of company. This book is about the management challenges such organisations present.

How do you manage, control and develop companies employing talented, egocentric, highly qualified people engaged in complex and creative problem-solving? Though invisible their output is extremely important to our modern way of life. It enhances the quality and increases the quantity of the goods and services we consume.

We shall call these organisations **knowhow companies**. They sell their output – knowhow – to customers who, in their turn, sell goods or services to others.

There is nothing new about knowhow companies. People have been trying to market their knowhow in various ways for centuries. The recent upsurge of interest in knowhow companies and their employees, sometimes called 'gold-collar workers', is because more and more people in more and more industries are engaged in **complex problem-solving** as opposed to straightforward shop floor production.

Knowhow organisations are emerging everywhere, as exotic pockets of gold-collar employees within traditional manufacturing companies, in service companies, in the public sector as well as in the private.

The classic knowhow company is the consultancy firm. Managers of manufacturing companies and government bodies have much to learn from successful management consultancy firms and the way they have addressed their particular problems.

These lessons must be learned. A key part of the transition from the 'industrial' to the 'information' society is the progressive **transformation of traditional organisations and companies into knowhow companies**. This book includes several examples of manufacturing companies which have succeeded by focusing on their **core knowhow**. In future such policies will be necessary but not sufficient conditions for success – with them you MAY succeed; without them you WILL fail. By concentrating on knowhow management company **leaders** will gain a new and more focused view of their organisations.

One of the most important and most dramatic aspects of knowhow management in the information society is that it puts **the individual at the centre of the stage**. Of all the resources of the knowhow company the individual human being is by far and away the most important. It is for this reason that the advent of the knowhow organisation represents a revolution in the power structures of the business world.

Since the beginning of the industrial revolution and arguably during the centuries that led up to it the owners of **financial capital** have been in the driving seat.

The old order is changing. From now on the owners of **knowhow capital** will be calling the shots. It is they who have the greatest power to extend the horizons of our knowledge and to enrich our lives.

SUMMARY

- We have high-lighted above in bold type some of the key features of the new business environment.
- The **information society** is the habitat.
- The **knowhow company** is the corporate species that has begun to thrive in the new environment and which has knowhow as its life-blood.
- Its business consists of **complex problem-solving**.
- An important contemporary trend is the progressive **transformation of traditional organisations and companies into knowhow companies**.
- One key aspect of this process is a shift in the patterns of corporate power which is thrusting **the individual to the centre of the stage**.
- The resource that drives the new economics is **knowhow capital**.
- A fundamental shortage of knowhow capital is replacing the scarcity of **financial capital** as the main constraint on economic development.
- **Managing knowhow** is the new business challenge.

1

• Introducing the Knowhow Company

• The milk of knowledge

There is a world of difference between the milk of to-day and the milk our ancestors drank 100 years ago. The modern fluid is pasteurised, homogenised, enriched with vitamins, packaged and then delivered to our doorsteps by sophisticated distribution systems.

The taste is probably much the same although taste (and smell for that matter) is not a quality that is easy to record for posterity. But we would certainly recognise the milk our ancestors drank and would probably find it palatable enough. It is more or less the same fluid; the difference, and it is an enormous one, is the much **richer content of knowhow** in to-day's product.

The production and distribution of milk are highly developed knowhow areas. Modern farmers have to be mechanics, chemists, nutritionists and vets all rolled into one. They need experience in animal husbandry and a working knowledge of genetics for stock breeding. They use all this knowhow to deliver your bottle of milk. We call this varied amalgam of expertise the farmer's professional skill or **'professional knowhow'**.

The modern farmer has also developed sophisticated knowhow in the fields of business administration, tax, personnel management, distribution, marketing and the handling of perishable food products. All this knowhow is needed in our modern societies if bottles of fresh milk are to appear on our breakfast tables each morning. One might call this knowhow the farmer's **'managerial knowhow'** deployed in the production and distribution of a liquid that is more or less the same as it was in our grandfathers' day.

In those days cows produced less than 2,000 litres of milk per head each year. Modern dairy cows produce nearer 6,000 litres per head a year. Dairy farmers have exploited their knowhow to produce more milk at a lower 'real' (inflation-adjusted) cost. Accumulated knowhow can change a 'product' as basic and as simple as milk out of all recognition.

• The knowhow-dependent society

Society is becoming increasingly dependent on sophisticated knowhow. Washing-machines are filled with semiconductors and electronics which are substitutes for some of the knowhow of our grandmothers. We cannot be sure whether the machines wash any cleaner than grandmother because very few people still use her methods.

We do know that the knowledge in the washing-machine's circuitry requires the modern family to put far less effort and time into mere washing. We have been liberated from a drudgery – we can use our new freedom for 'higher' things.

The knowhow in the washing-machine is stored more visibly than it is in milk and is accumulating at a faster rate. To-day's washing-machines contain many more functions than did their precursors just five years ago. The same is true of cars, radios and many other consumer durable goods. Our life-styles and in a real sense our freedoms depend on the knowhow that permeates all we consume.

• What is a knowhow company?

A knowhow company produces and sells knowhow. Superficially it resembles the traditional conception of the 'service' company and many service companies would qualify as 'knowhow' companies.

But though all knowhow companies are service companies, **not all service companies are knowhow companies**. The service sector is not a discrete phenomenon but rather a **spectrum of company types** ranging from those organisations wholly adapted to the needs of their customers – the 'knowhow' companies – to organisations that have so refined and packaged their output that they have more in common with manufacturing companies. We call the latter **'industrial' service companies**.

The typical knowhow company finds it very hard to standardise its operations. Because it cannot force its clients to adapt to it, it must perforce adapt to them. It is hard to see how the activities of a surgeon treating a patient on an

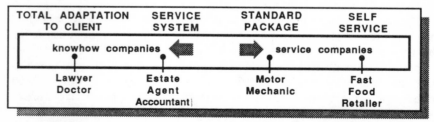

Figure 1 The service sector covers a wide spectrum, from traditional service companies on the right to knowhow companies on the left. Knowhow companies solve complex, non-standardised problems, traditional service companies solve simple ones. Companies between these two types experience problems of strategy. Should they go left or right?

operating table or of a lawyer preparing a brief for a client can be 'industrialised' to any extent.

The **complex and creative output** of the knowhow company and the more **standardised industrial production** of the service company often co-exist within the same organisation in the same way as some of the characteristics of 'lower' animals survive in their more highly evolved descendants. The banks are typical service organisations. Their branch employees take care of routine transactions over the counter at the same time as others, elsewhere in the organisation, are engaged in more complex, individual problem-solving such as large credit investigations, cash management problems, portfolio management, corporate finance and so on.

In the companies on the far right service has become industry: the key to profitability lies in efficient, industrialised, pre-programmed production aimed at a mass market. The McDonald's fast-food chain exemplifies this type. Because of the desire to achieve what economists call 'declining marginal costs' most service companies try to industrialise (make routine) as much of their business as possible. Take the banks. Right now they are busy trying to substitute teller machines and automated withdrawal equipment for the traditional cash/ ear transactions.

In contrast, the companies on the left-hand side of the diagram are engaged in much more complex, less standardised problem-solving. They call their customers 'clients' and they treat them as individuals. The extent of their adaptation to their clients is sometimes apparent in their conversation. A barrister discussing a case and a merchant banker discussing a takeover will often use the first person plural when referring to their clients; 'we decided to plead guilty' or 'we didn't believe they could raise their bid'.

Many successful service companies have succeeded in so industrialising their activities that they become more or less independent of the individuals in their organisations. McDonald's has introduced cash-registers with symbols instead of numbers enabling them to employ illiterates. Companies like McDonald's have highly developed management knowhow and almost perfectly honed business ideas. Their efforts have been devoted to making their problems so simple they can be solved by traditional industrial management methods.

Most bank employees supply relatively standardised services – only a small minority take care of client-oriented activities requiring higher levels of education.

That is why many banks should still be classified as service organisations. In some ways they are moving to the right of our diagram, towards a more 'industrialised' style of operation. At the same time they are being tugged to the left by their diversifications into fund management, corporate finance and venture capital. The more qualified, highly educated staff in these areas cause a disproportionate number of problems; so much so that they sometimes seem to be tearing their host organisations apart. The banks have entered a period of rapid evolution; they are at a stage of transition. Though many of their senior managers may not be aware of it, changes in their environment, and particularly in the needs of their customers, are transforming banks from traditional service companies into knowhow companies.

A few years ago much was being made of the concept of 'convergence' in the telecommunications and data processing industries. Technological change, it was argued, was bringing the telephone and the computer closer together. Soon, it was predicted, computer companies like IBM would be competing directly with telecommunications companies like AT&T.

This prediction has come true. The two industries, previously quite distinct from each other, are in the process of fusing together. The idea of convergence, from being the 'blue sky' speculation of visionaries, has become a fact. Nowadays it is fashionable to talk of the **'convergence'** of the service-oriented banking industry with the knowhow-dependent securities industry. Just as Information Technology was the unifying theme of the earlier fusion, so the idea of an integrated 'financial services' industry has begun to colour the strategies of banks and securities firms.

The recent Big Bang in the City of London represented a quantum jump in the evolution of the banks from service to knowhow organisations. The British banks, along with many of their foreign rivals, prepared for this abrupt convergence by indulging in a frenzy of acquisitive activity in the securities industry, paying huge sums for stockbroking firms.

Within weeks, as the skills and knowhow they thought they had acquired departed for higher-paid jobs elsewhere, they began to understand the difference between service and knowhow companies (see Chapter Eleven: 'Barclays Bank buys knowhow', pages 149 – 51). They still have much to learn.

The banks are quite well advanced in this transition. Other industries are following them. Insurance companies, hospitals and most large industrial groups have people supplying standardised services as well as people engaged in complex, creative brainwork (what we shall call the 'pro-team'). This polarisation is a special kind of problem that will grow more serious as time passes. We will return to pro-teams later.

There is thus a distinct difference between service companies and the knowhow companies which are the subject of this book.

The **four main distinguishing features** of the knowhow company's production are:

- non-standardisation
- creativity
- high dependence on individuals
- complex problem-solving

• The key resource

In the knowhow company the key resource is not the financial capital or the production process but the human being. In this respect the knowhow company is quite different from the traditional manufacturing company. The difference can be described in terms of a distinctive **knowhow company language**. The left-hand column represents the vocabulary of the knowhow company and the right-hand column the vocabulary of the industrial company:

Knowhow company	Industrial company
Information	Revenues, flow of goods
Human being	Machine
Knowhow	Capital, fixed assets
Education	Maintenance
Recruitment	Investment
Departure	Disinvestment
Data production	Production
Time	Raw material

N.B. These are extreme categories. For most companies and in most cases the words will have intermediate meanings.

INFORMATION – REVENUES, FLOW OF GOODS   The output of the knowhow company is **knowhow-enriched information** rather than tangible goods. It sometimes takes the form of words on paper but usually the main manifestation of knowhow output is an improvement in the performance of the knowhow company's customer or client.

HUMAN BEING – THE KNOWHOW MACHINE   The human being is the 'machine' of the knowhow company. The greater the number of able people there are in an organisation the greater its productive capacity.

The human being is the only productive resource in such companies. The journalist, the research engineer, the programmer, the consultant and the physician, **the knowhow professionals**, all work by exploiting their knowhow. If the doctors fall ill there are no robots to replace them. It is impossible to automate their work. And in addition to being the machines of their companies these people are also the machine managers. We shall return to the theme of self-management later. For the present it is sufficient to note that it is characteristic of the knowhow company and one of the most important keys to understanding the new management problems such companies present.

KNOWHOW – CAPITAL, FIXED ASSETS   Knowhow, or, more correctly, knowledgeable human beings, constitute the most important and sometimes the only capital of the knowhow company. **Financial capital is seldom a significant contributor to profitability.** To be sure there are knowhow companies which use financial capital such as brokers, finance companies and fund managers but even in these organisations it is the knowhow of the human beings which determines the profitability of the financial capital. (For a detailed discussion of the capital-intensive knowhow company, see Chapter Eleven, pages 139 – 61).

Many knowhow companies have strong financial balance-sheets but the equity represented by such strength is usually a result of high profits rather than a requirement of the business. The surplus cash is seldom used in the operation.

A company's knowhow capital grows as a matter of course each year as its employees become more experienced. The rate of growth can be increased by educational programmes and other measures designed to encourage personal development. On the debit side of this invisible balance-sheet, knowhow capital is lost when experienced people leave the company or when they under-perform because of poor leadership or an otherwise uncongenial environment.

EDUCATION – MAINTENANCE   Education is one way of improving and main-taining a knowhow company's 'machines' in good working order. Each em-ployee needs a certain amount of education just to keep up with developments in his or her field. The knowhow company must spend money on educating its employees. It is as essential to the preservation of knowhow capital as a maintenance budget is essential to the preservation of the value of plant and equipment. Successful knowhow companies put far more resources than mere maintenance requires into education. They may even have their own schools, run their own courses and set up their own training programmes. They use education as a management tool. For them it is more than just a maintenance cost – it is a positive investment in knowhow capital.

RECRUITMENT – INVESTMENT   Recruitment decisions are among the most important a knowhow company makes. Ensuring the applicant's professional qualifications are up to scratch is just the beginning. Personal 'chemistry' is equ-ally important if not more so. The traditional company takes great pains when investing in new machinery to ensure the equipment's specifications are adequate and that it can do the job required of it. Knowhow companies can afford to be no less thorough when adding to their own inventory of 'machinery'.

And of course recruitment is also a crucial management tool, particularly at times of strategic change when the next recruit must contribute to and, in a sense, exemplify the new direction. We shall return to the 'recruitment idea' later.

DEPARTURE – DISINVESTMENT   The threatened or actual departure of a good employee is the worst problem the leader of a knowhow company can face. It is a predicament comparable to that of a dairy manager watching a cow 'disin-vesting' a new milking machine under her hooves.

INFORMATION – PRODUCTION   The only product of the knowhow company is the processing and distribution of information.

TIME – RAW MATERIAL   Time is the knowhow company's most precious raw material whether it be its own time or bought time. Depending on the situation time can be either a cost or an investment. Time put into a properly organised R&D programme is an investment. This is very obvious in R&D-intensive in-dustries. Computer programmers and development engineers often describe the competitive position of their company in terms of their lead. 'We are at least two years ahead' means the competition needs at least two years of R&D to reach the same level of knowhow. Time is thus a competitive weapon. The pioneers of a new market or niche always have a competitive advantage by virtue of being first. The earlier into the field the more knowhow can be accumulated before the competitors catch up. A large competitor can sometimes put more man years into R&D and thereby overhaul an early entrant. That is why managers in these industries judge their competitors not by the volume of their output but by the size of their R&D departments.

• The main types of knowhow

• Professional knowhow – the business idea

Professional knowhow is the core knowledge of the knowhow company – the essence of the business idea from which all revenues flow. In the law it is legal knowhow; in accountancy it is accounting expertise; in the lab it is scientific and engineering creativity (an engineer, it is said, is someone who can make for 25p what any damn fool can make for £1 while a management consultant is someone who can do the opposite); in the circus it is the art of the clown; in book publishing it is talent spotting and project management; in architecture it is design and engineering skill.

The success of a knowhow company depends ultimately on the ability of its professionals relative to that of their counterparts in rival companies.

The task of the professional manager is to stimulate and motivate the professionals to work well together so that collectively they realise the business idea.

• Managerial knowhow – increasing the company's value

Managerial knowhow is the ability to preserve and enhance the company's value.

Managerial or organisational expertise incorporates several knowhow areas – marketing, administration, accounting and so on, but there is one overriding requirement. Top management must have the ability to increase the value of the company. And, by the same token, they must have the ability to guard effectively against decreases in the company's value. They must monitor and guide the development of the company so that it becomes an organisation robust enough to survive a change of leadership or the departure of key people.

The importance of this **responsibility for value** becomes apparent when someone asks a question like 'what is a knowhow company employing 10 professionals worth?' One might start the valuation exercise by looking at profitability but this is not much help – it is merely an imperfect record of the ability the company has shown in the past. The true value could be as little as nothing or as much as £2m. The problem in valuing knowhow companies stems from their **dependence on key people**. If a company of 10 knowhow professionals is owned and run by one person, the entrepreneur, it may be worthless however successful and profitable the accounts show it to be at the time. If the entrepreneur sells out and leaves, the new owner cannot be sure of keeping either the customers or the employees. The new acquisition may literally fall apart in his or her hands.

A company has no objectively assessable value until it is sold. Astute buyers will take great pains to assure themselves that the company they wish to acquire is likely to perform under their ownership at least as well as it has done in the past. If the management of the knowhow company is unable to demonstrate this kind of robustness, the company must be deemed to have a very low value. That it will often be possible to sell it for considerably more than its true worth is because there are many buyers of knowhow companies who are not astute, who may be dazzled by the visible profits but blind to the invisible liabilities.

Some managers are tempted to increase financial net worth by investing in property and other fixed assets. This is NOT the answer. It is extremely dangerous to try to increase net worth by venturing into other areas. Unless such investments are well-managed the weight of the new financial assets may distort the original business idea out of all recognition.

This is not to say financial assets can be ignored. On the contrary, they need, though they seldom are in knowhow companies, to be managed professionally. Cash and cash management are very important in rich knowhow companies.

• Knowhow company categories

There are at least four different categories of knowhow companies.

THE FACTORY   We reserve the label 'factory' for service companies where a low individual level of knowhow is combined with high managerial expertise.

Many successful service companies fit this description. In a typical case the management has succeeded in developing such elaborate and comprehensive support systems that the company is able to supply efficient service without being dependent on the ability of individuals. McDonald's, the fast food chain referred to above, is a good example of the type.

An example closer to the home of knowhow, so to speak, is the traditional card-punching bureau which specialises in keying in and registering data from its customers' invoices. The task is simple; the secret of success is to so standardise the punching process that there is no need to employ highly qualified personnel.

THE OFFICE   Our office category is characterised by both a low level of professional knowhow and low managerial ability. It is not free; it might even be described as a slave organisation. It is typically to be found running the administration of professional institutes and associations. It is dedicated to the service of members; those working for it have no freedom to act in their own right or on their own behalf. They are unable to develop a managerial expertise of their own and are not permitted to develop a professional expertise in the areas where members are active. The personnel are employed purely to implement the decisions of the association members.

Because the office can seldom generate a creative working environment the knowhow professionals are unable to develop and therefore tend to leave or languish. Staff turnover tends to be high in the 'office' category of knowhow companies or very low, reflecting the loss of all the talent and an inability to recruit more.

THE AGENCY   The agency is a very creative place. The professionals have a high level of knowhow and work well together. They have the freedom to develop their own professionalism and are under constant competitive pressure to do so. Their environment is both challenging and stimulating.

The plight of the clerks and managers is not so congenial. They have low status and few routines within which to develop their own expertise. They complain that the professionals take no notice of them and often the manager of the agency is quite unable to control it. This is often the case even when the top management function is rotated between professionals. The professionalism of the temporary 'managing partner' becomes tainted by menial pre-occupations. Some law firms will recognise themselves in this description.

Most new, fast growing knowhow companies are 'agencies' because most knowhow companies are founded by a few professionals. In the early stages at

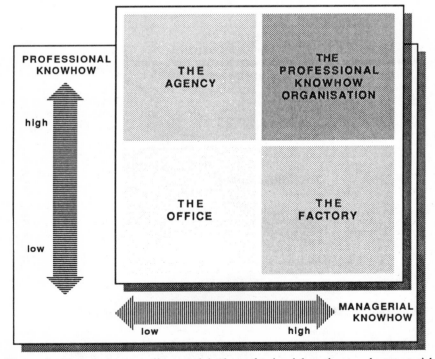

Figure 2   Knowhow companies need both professional knowhow and managerial knowhow. You need to combine a high level of both in order to achieve a solid business based on creative people and to become a 'professional knowhow organisation'.

least the organisation of the company has a low priority because there are so many purely professional problems to take care of.

An agency is unlikely to survive in the long-term. Sooner or later it will be broken up by internal rows or will go under because it has failed to develop into a professional organisation.

THE PROFESSIONAL ORGANISATION   The professional organisation is the ideal. Its hallmarks are long-term stability, long-term value growth and an ability to develop skilled professionals and new leaders. A knowhow company cannot become a 'professional organisation' until it has learned to replace key people without a decline in quality.

• Information systems and the business idea

An advertisement campaign which ran in various magazines in late 1986 seemed, at first glance, to be offering, for a mere £1.35, a red Lamborghini sports car capable of travelling 3,000,000 miles on one gallon of petrol. Imagine what effect such a schoolboy fantasy, if realised, would have on the world – on the oil, motor and transport industries to start with. It would change everything.

It was, of course, an allegory, the clue to which was the logo of the adver-

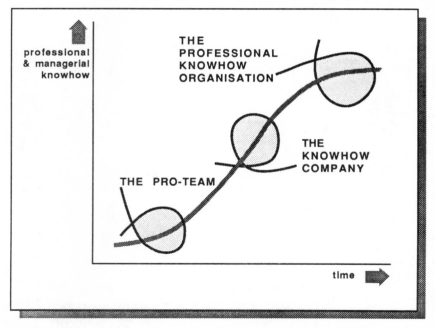

Figure 2a   The 'pro-team', an embryonic knowhow company, lacks managerial knowhow but may develop into a knowhow company by acquiring it. It normally takes many years to reach the ideal – the professional knowhow organisation.

tiser, the accountancy firm Ernst & Whinney's consultancy division, tucked away on the bottom right-hand corner of the two-page spread. The advertisement was designed to illustrate the extent to which the price:performance ratio of computers has improved since their birth 30 years ago. The super-economical, super-cheap Lamborghini is what would now be commonplace in the automotive world had the car undergone the same development.

The computer is both a creature of the information society and its most powerful driving force. It is a product in its own right but, much more important, it is an **all-purpose tool** of awesome power. And one of the few assertions about the future that can be made with any confidence is that the computers of to-morrow will make to-day's machines seem puny and hugely expensive by comparison. In the computer world the equivalent of the ten million miles per gallon, 10p Lamborghini is barely a decade away.

The computer was made for knowhow companies. As an extension of the human brain it has the potential to lever knowhow to heights undreamed of just a few years ago. Knowhow companies and computers both pre-date the advent of the information society but both exemplify it in the same way cotton mills and steam engines exemplified the industrial society.

Computers store information, help to convert it into knowhow and act as nodes in the networks and communication channels that constitute the fabric of knowhow companies. They take much of the drudgery out of knowhow working, freeing the professionals for more creative kinds of activity for which computers, as yet, have little aptitude.

There is software to help with such typical professional tasks as calculation, word-processing, design and project planning. And software for structured decision-making – another typically professional task – will be available soon.

● With a word-processing package the professionals can write their own reports as well as a trained secretary and much more quickly than if they had to write a first draft by hand.

● With the aid of the computer the professional can access databases throughout the world and, with the help of search software, can distil the information he retrieves down to the bare essentials with a few well-chosen keystrokes.

● With the aid of the computer professionals can keep track of networks, send small reminders, notes or just greetings. Database and word-processing software can reduce what were once large jobs, such as printing 100s of addresses, to routine tasks swiftly executed.

To those who work near computers the idea that these machines can improve and extend communications and actually enhance human relations will seem a mite implausible. Society seems filled with computer freaks or 'hackers' who isolate themselves from others. Computer knowhow is a knowhow area in its own right. There are those as 'as it and those 'as don't.

But the **'hackers' are a transitional species**. They are not the typical professionals of the future. They will become a small but necessary minority. They can be compared with people like Noam Chomsky and Simon Dik, the inventors of the 'transformational' and 'functional' grammars respectively. As they study language, the rest of us talk to each other. As the computer freaks study computers, the rest of us use them.

The computer is a tool of many parts. It can be used for so many different purposes that at present armies of 'hacker' professionals are still needed just to seek out new applications. But the relative multiplicity of computer freaks in the world today is a temporary phenomenon; a sign that computer technology is still in its infancy.

The example of the LASER (Light Amplification by Stimulated Emission of Radiation), a relatively trivial invention compared to the computer, illustrates how multi-purpose tools adapt to the world and force the world to adapt to them. Initially the laser, invented by the US physicist Charles Townes in 1958, was no more than a laboratory curiosity. Its coherent beam could be used to map the Moon's surface more accurately than ever before but to all practical intents and purposes it was a solution in search of a problem. It has subsequently found a whole host of problems. Lasers are the key elements in modern gyro compasses, they will soon be driving the world's fibre optic telecommunications networks, they have become domesticated in Compact Disc audio players which are about to become hugely powerful computer storage devices. They will also be driving the next generation of optical computers and they have found many applications in manufacturing, ranging from the marking of goods, metrology, alignment and the whole area of holography. For a while the laser became a famous technology as it conquered more and more fields. Nowadays it is so well established that one rarely hears of it. It has retreated into the background.

The professionals of the information society must know how to handle the computer. They have no option if they are to stay in the forefront of their respective fields. The professional who cannot handle a computer in the twenty-first century will be like a Wild West cowboy afraid of horses.

- **Computers – the factories and warehouses of the twenty-first century**
  Computers are the factories and warehouses of the twenty-first century. They play the same role in the information society as factories and warehouses played in the industrial society.

  One obvious difference is that information stored in data files is less tangible than an item of equipment stored in a warehouse, but the most important distinguishing feature of the computer is that it can not only store knowhow, it can also manipulate it and turn it into new knowhow.

  Computers can acquire, organise and store stock (data) and, by applying to it software incorporating knowhow, they can add value to the raw data. They represent, in terms of the information society, something akin to the fully automated production process traditional manufacturers dream of.

- **Opportunities for the entrepreneur**
  The business horizons of the entrepreneur are extended enormously by the computer. Knowhow can be stored, processed, refined and packaged with database, word-processing and statistical software and transmitted far and wide using the computer as a node in a communications network.

  The all-purpose nature of the computer makes it applicable to most modern industries. It is, even now, transforming many 'industrial' service organisations into knowhow companies, sometimes without the top executives of the companies concerned being aware of it.

- **Banking – a case in point**
  The banks are no longer merely brokers of capital and credit. They are being transformed into knowhow companies. The process began more than a decade ago when the computers were first brought in as banking support tools. Until 1975 they were mainly used to rationalise the work load in order to reduce the number of employees. They took over much of the paperwork and permitted the automation of a proportion of desk transactions.

  The critical point came when the computers were linked to each other through networks. Today it is hard to find a bank anywhere which is not connected, internally and externally, through computer networks. So far the network has mainly been used for 'heavy' administrative traffic like accountancy information and transactions between accounts.

  A new kind of network – **the network of the information society** – is now being installed in many banks and shops. It is used to serve clients. 'Debit' registers in shops are being connected to banks. Cash and even credit cards are becoming theoretically if not yet actually superfluous.

- # From service to knowhow

  People do not drink less milk or drive fewer cars in the information society. On the contrary, consumption of most goods is still increasing all over the world. The difference to-day is that goods are combined with knowhow in order to make them more attractive to the customer. More and more companies and organisations, ranging from large groups like General Motors and ICI to government bodies and private companies, are evolving into knowhow companies.

  The highly qualified salespeople in to-day's manufacturing companies try to help their customers develop their businesses by selling products combined with knowhow. The remarkable success of the Finnish ship-yard Wartsila illustrates the point.

  Wartsila builds various kinds of special purpose ships, such as ferries and ice-breakers. It has very deliberately built up a high degree of expertise within certain niches. By so doing it has managed to remain profitable in one of the world's most crisis-stricken industries. It has been particularly successful with its passenger ferries. A key feature of the Wartsila strategy is to build ships entirely adapted to the business idea of the customers. Through co-operation between Wartsila and its 'clients', notably the vigorously competing Silja and Viking lines, ferry traffic between Finland and Sweden has been revolutionised. To-day the 15-hour journey between Stockholm and Helsinki seems more like a night out on the town than a voyage. There are plush bars, discos, cinemas, supermarkets and several restaurants.

Wartsila has accumulated so much knowhow in the area of passenger transport that it now claims 30% of the world market for passenger ferries and has beaten off the challenge of low-cost ship-yards in Japan and Korea.

• Buy solutions not products

People in the Western world will soon be spending more on solutions to problems than on physical products. Here, as elsewhere, America is in the vanguard. Low personal taxes and the high purchasing power they have generated have helped to develop the most substantial knowhow-based service sector in the world. In America it is quite natural to have window-cleaners clean your windows, 'horticultural consultants' cultivate your garden and mechanics take care of your car.

Most of the recent growth in US employment has come from this sector. America has the most dynamic and efficient knowhow-based companies in the world.

By comparison the European service sector is very under-developed. The US are far ahead on any measure of exports from service sectors though, as we shall see, they are not exporting service itself but knowhow. Sweden is a striking illustration of the point. She has the biggest service sector in the world, measured as a percentage of GNP, and yet her service exports, again measured as a percentage of GNP, are a mere half of America's. The poor performance of the Swedish service sector is because Swedish services are produced mainly by the public sector. In contrast to their American counterparts Swedish managers of state-owned organisations have never needed to be profit-oriented and so have never developed the management skills needed to export knowhow.

In the US the trend towards the knowhow-based information society is already very clear. In a study of 4,200 public companies conducted by *Business Week* in 1985, information and knowhow companies emerged with a firm hold on the list of the '100 best' small companies in the US. About two-thirds were information companies operating in such areas as computers, telecommunications and publishing.

• Europe's challenge of the 1990s

Though Europe is presently lagging behind the US in the development of information-based industries there are some reasons to be hopeful about our relative performance in the information society. The qualities and traditions that have held the continent back during the rise of the American and Japanese superstates may give it an edge now the industrial society has run its course.

In terms of the concepts of this book, the Japanese and American business cultures have emphasised **focus** and **size** respectively whereas the European business culture has emphasised **collaboration** and **variety**. All cultures have their strengths and weaknesses and all become more or less appropriate as time passes.

Europe's lack of focus compared to Japan has been a considerable liability since the war. We have failed to establish comparative advantages in any traditional industry and we have lost comparative advantages in computers, consumer electronics, car manufacturing, shipbuilding and many other areas.

America too has been losing ground to the Japanese in recent years but has been better able to defend itself because of its size. The American market is so huge that it is relatively easy to start new businesses. This means the US corporate **gene pool** – the potential for variation in the company sector – is being constantly refreshed. One might say that the gene pool's turnover rate is relatively high.

In Europe, on the other hand, the slowness with which the various national economies are becoming integrated has prevented the larger overall size of the economic community from expanding the corporate gene pool. Instead of one large economy we still have a number of discrete, medium-sized economies.

But this is changing. Despite language differences a **collaborative culture** is slowly developing in Europe, witness such programmes as ESPRIT, EUREKA, Airbus Industrie and the European Space Agency at the national level and, at the corporate level, joint companies like Royal Dutch Shell and Unilever and more recent signs of corporate re-alignments like GEC's merger of its medical equipment business with that of Philips in Holland.

The cultural richness and variety in Europe and a generally more creative spirit which have, in the past, made concerted, focused approaches to industrial development rather difficult, have begun to appear more like strengths than weaknesses. Symbols of the change include Japan's purchase of a van Gogh painting for a record £23m and the invasion of Broadway by the British theatre.

It is, of course, extremely hard to assess the respective economic merits of different cultures in different situations and at different times. It is clear, however, that collaboration, cultural sophistication and creativity in its widest sense are advantageous in the information society.

It is also clear that in the areas where such qualities have commercial significance such as advertising, design, drama, television, financial services, legal and accountancy services, publishing, popular music and the like, European countries are already doing relatively well.

During the rest of this century knowhow in its widest sense will become all-important for success in business and management. Knowhow capital will play the same role during the 1990s as financial capital played during the age of the industrial society. But knowhow has a slippery quality. The most highly qualified 'capital' (people) will be very mobile. People are the embodiments of knowhow capital. No tax laws or foreign currency controls can stop this kind of capital from crossing any border it chooses!

• Solicitors and circuses

The modern management consultancy firm is the purest form of the knowhow company. It employs highly educated, professional and self-confident people whose knowhow other companies are willing to buy.

If the consultant does well the client has made a good investment and the consultant has been rewarded for his or her knowhow without losing it. The consultant might even gain knowhow. Most consultants prefer clients with interesting problems because they are more likely to learn something new. But though the consultancy firm is the most typical it is by no means the only kind of knowhow company. Others are:

- law firms
- accountancy firms
- computer service companies
- advertising agencies
- brokers
- universities
- R&D laboratories
- hospitals
- theatres
- government offices
- newspapers
- circuses
- high-tech companies

Does it seem far fetched to compare a circus with a law firm? We hope to show in this book that the managers of the circus, the law firm, the advertising agency and the R&D laboratory are all confronted by similar problems and that the way to solve them is to focus management attention on knowhow.

SUMMARY

● Products and processes everywhere are being progressively **enriched** by knowhow of two kinds – **professional** and **managerial**.

● Society as a whole is becoming **knowhow-dependent**.

● Human beings are **the key resource** in knowhow companies.

● In the information society **financial capital** ceases to be such a significant contributor to business success.

● **Professional knowhow** is the basis of **the business idea** in knowhow companies.

● **Managerial knowhow** is responsible for the growth in the company's **value**.

● The four basic categories of knowhow company are: The Factory, The Agency, The Office and the ideal, The Professional Organisation.

● Computers are important, **all-purpose tools** peculiarly suited to the knowhow company, offering opportunities to the knowhow entrepreneur.

● **Europe's challenge of the 1990s** is to learn how to export knowhow.

2

• Knowhow Capital = Power

• The poverty of money

It is generally assumed that in modern, 'capitalist' societies a dual power structure prevails consisting of government on the one hand and the owners of financial capital on the other. Indeed the political colour of an administration is often characterised by the freedom the former allows the latter. Power is deemed to be money. The deeper the pocket, the more powerful the person or the organisation. If governments are the 'kings' of the modern world then surely the equivalent of the old feudal barons are names like Rockefeller, Morgan, Hanson, Murdoch and more anonymous but even wealthier financial institutions such as pension funds and insurance companies.

This dual government/capital power paradigm is out-moded. In the information society the owners of financial capital are becoming progressively less sure of themselves. They no longer speak, through their money, with the brutal power to which they have grown accustomed.

The disenchantment with the idea of the 'conglomerate' – the idea behind the spate of mergers in the late 1960s and early 1970s – is strikingly illustrated by the subsequent spate of divestments and re-groupings round 'mainstream' businesses.

The death of the conglomerate idea and the periodic property booms and busts that occur in Western economies represent **failures of financial capitalism**. Money is no longer omnipotent. Ownership of financial capital makes it possible to buy businesses but it confers no ability to run them well. Managerial ability and knowhow have nothing to do with money though, as we shall see, they have much to do with ownership.

Those seeking capital today to finance new companies or projects are interested not only in the wealth of their prospective backers but also in their ability to add knowhow value to the business project in the form of marketing expertise, production skills and general managerial ability.

Financial capital has become a buyer's market; the commodity in short supply these days is not money but ability, the skill and expertise which we call **knowhow capital.**

• The rise of venture capital

One of the most significant developments in European capital markets in recent years has been the rapid growth since 1980 or thereabouts of so-called 'hands on' or 'pro-active' venture capital invested in young companies by the managers of specialist funds on behalf of the financial institutions and wealthy individuals.

The idea, pioneered in the US in the early 1960s, is that small companies with limited access to capital markets and with too little in the way of assets to be in a position to borrow much from banks, should be financed instead by equity investors prepared to accept a high risk in return for the prospect of a high reward.

The difference between the new 'hands on' style and traditional passive investment is that the former is invested by managers familiar with the special problems of young, entrepreneurially-run companies and with the new technologies that many of to-day's entrepreneurs are trying to exploit.

This special expertise is used to 'manage the risk' involved in such investment. The venture capital fund managers take an active interest in how the companies they invest in are run. They help the entrepreneurs to build up their networks of contacts, to fill in the gaps in their management knowhow in areas like finance and marketing, and to impose strict financial controls so that entrepreneurial enthusiasm does not run away with itself and plunge the company into a cash-flow crisis.

The formula has proved attractive to both institutional and personal investors, the latter attracted to this high risk form of investment by tax-breaks like those incorporated in Britain's Business Expansion Scheme.

From a standing start in 1980 there were 125 UK venture funds by the end of 1986. Venture capital, confined largely to the US and to Investors in Industry (3is) in the UK at the beginning of the decade, has grown throughout the world.

Table 1 Venture capital around the world – end 1986

Country	Number of firms	Total funds ($m)
US	530	24,000
UK	125	6,000
Canada	45	1,000
Japan	70	850
France	45	750
Netherlands	40	650
West Germany	25	500
Sweden	31	325
Norway	35	185
Denmark	14	120
Eire	10	100
Australia	11	50

Source: Venture Economics

But US-style 'hands on' venture capital has not proved easy. The trouble in Europe is that the new venture capital funds have been raised mostly by banks, finance companies, pension funds and a few industrial companies which have tended to recruit managers from the financial industry. Management knowhow remains thin on the ground in the European venture capital industry partly because, for the time being anyway, there is more to be made from being an entrepreneur than backing one. This inherent weakness notwithstanding, the European venture funds seem here to stay.

Raising money with which to invest has been easy enough. Banks, financial institutions, wealthy individuals (or 'high net worth individuals' as modern parlance has it) and even governments have been more than willing to pour money into the new, small company investment area.

Thus large quantities of financial capital, unsupported by adequate knowhow, have flooded into the 'target' companies. The performance of the initial phase of the European venture capital industry is therefore likely to be disappointing – not too bad but not nearly as good as the pioneers had hoped and as the suppliers of finance had been led to expect. Fund managers and investors alike are beginning to realise that by not investing knowhow alongside finance they are greatly reducing their chances of success.

• Knowhow capital bids for power

Knowhow capital, embedded in human brains, is both **mobile and heterogeneous**. The typical knowhow company needs relatively little financial capital. There are no fixed assets to speak of; often the only requirement is to finance current assets and initial operating losses. In companies like these the traditional 'owners' – the suppliers of finance – find their grip on the business growing progressively weaker. Those who have nothing to contribute but money may soon discover that in knowhow companies the bargaining power of the staff is so strong that they have to sell part of the company to their employees to prevent them from leaving.

Even then the traditional owners cannot be sure of their employees' loyalty. These days the best and most highly qualified employees tend to leave and form their own companies if they begin to find aspects of their employer companies, such as the power structure, a little irksome. This **corporate fission** – also known as **spin-out** – is already endemic in several knowhow-dependent industries such as management consultancy, brokerage, advertising, design, computers, insurance and technology-driven companies.

• The power shift

The Western industrial society is a sophisticated amalgam of laws and institutions evolved over a few centuries and designed to minimise the problems associated with the management of ignorant people.

The theories developed by the great thinkers of the industrial society are all based on the assumption that the workers are only one resource among others. There were said to be three 'factors of production': land, capital and labour. Karl Marx objected to a system in which workers are used with maximum efficiency to give the capital owners the best possible return on their investment, but he never doubted that that was the way capitalism really worked.

The industrial society has suffered from a **shortage of financial capital** since its very beginnings in the nineteenth century. Theories are still designed and taught a century later based on the assumption that the ultimate purpose of capitalism is to optimise the use of scarce financial capital. With the aid of the various allocative institutions such as the stock exchange, mathematical theories such as operational analysis and investment models and the price of capital (the interest rate), we have developed a socio-economic system entirely focused on optimising the use of scarce financial capital.

But there is no longer a shortage of financial capital. The topology of most Western economies (particularly the 22-nation OECD group), from being generally flat under a veneer of thinly spread because scarce financial capital, has become puckered with so-called 'cash-mountains'. Many of the contemporary industrial giants are practically bursting with cash. For lack of projects to put their money into and because they see little future in their own industries they buy each other. Financial capital revolves faster and faster. More and more money chases fewer and fewer projects.

When traditional companies find no investment opportunities in areas they know they either buy other companies or venture into other promising but unfamiliar areas. This is why so much money is lost to-day in the new 'hot' industries like biotechnology, pharmaceuticals, computers and the media. Such diversification gives the giants an entirely spurious appearance of flexibility. In reality they remain wedded to the belief, denied by their experience more forcefully each day, that finance conquers all.

Symptoms of this error are the turbulent conditions in to-day's financial markets (see Chapter Eleven: 'Barclays Bank buys knowhow', pages 149–51). The mistake is embedded in the structures, institutions and general outlook of all the world's capital markets.

Power in knowhow-based companies is derived not from the fact of ownership of the majority of the share capital but from ability and the respect of fellow professionals.

In the industrial society the capital owners had vast power compared to their employees. Countervailing political systems and unions were formed by the workers to challenge this despotism. That organised labour is engaged in a constant power struggle with capital remains the conventional view. The union movement of to-day still relies for its appeal and coherence on the alleged existence of a strong antagonist, the capital owner.

• Employees become employers

In the knowhow companies of the information society the power system is quite different from the industrial company. The **employees can seize power**. They have the knowhow; they are the 'machines' and the 'production' process. The need of knowhow companies for financial capital is low. That is why highly qualified and knowledgeable people are not particularly interested in unions these days. Union density, the proportion of the employed labour force in union membership, has dropped in the UK from 54% in 1979 to 48% and is still falling. The old confrontational style of unionism, exemplified by Arthur Scargill, president of the British National Union of Mineworkers (NUM), is being gradually replaced by a more pragmatic style, exemplified by the electricians' union, the EEPTU, that acknowledges the increase in the inherent bargaining power of members.

Even in Sweden, where union density is still 90% of the workforce, the unions are finding it hard to recruit members in knowhow industries. SIF, the white-collar union in Sweden, is engaged in an internal debate about the role of unions in the future and about what they can offer the professionals in the information society. They are likely to conclude that they cannot offer very much. Most of the concessions the unions have fought for since their formation will be wrested with ease from the capital owners by the new knowhow professionals bargaining on their own accounts.

The power of the professionals derives from their ownership of the only asset worth anything in the information society – **control over knowhow capital**. The knowhow professionals can leave at any time, defect to a competitor or form their own company. They are often the driving force behind the business idea but, except in the very short-term, they are more or less wholly **independent of their employers**. They often have larger networks outside their own companies than inside.

Individual professionals have the power to force their employers to treat them with much more respect than the brutally exploited mill-workers could demand up until the beginning of this century. For the moment this power shift remains, for the most part, latent. There are few companies, except in certain specialised areas, which have seen the way the wind is blowing and begun to grant their knowhow employees their rights.

The employees in many of to-day's knowhow companies are actually getting far **too low a proportion of the added value** they produce – a much smaller share than workers in manufacturing companies for example. This is the main reason why they tend to change jobs so often. They become frustrated and take their destinies into their own hands and leave.

The recognition that an emerging **shortage of knowhow capital** is equivalent to a power shift helps to explain the turbulence in some knowhow-intensive industries like consultancy, stockbroking and data processing.

But the turbulence is unlikely to be confined to these few industries. During the death throes of the industrial society more and more companies are being 'professionalised' and transformed into knowhow companies.

Companies in service industries like banking, newspaper publishing, accountancy and many parts of the public sector are the first of these new wave organisations. It is in these companies that we find the most heated discussion of matters to do with employee ownership and influence – matters which the owners of financial capital have traditionally shown little interest in or understanding of.

SUMMARY

- The hegemony of **financial capital** is coming to an end.
- It is being replaced by **knowhow capital** which is **mobile and heterogeneous.**
- The coming reign of knowhow capital means **employees can seize power.**
- The owners of knowhow capital are **independent of their employers.**
- The increased bargaining power of the professionals is because of a fundamental **shortage of knowhow capital.**

3

• Information Society = Knowhow Society

• The coming of the knowhow age

Far from being a vision of the distant future the information society is fast becoming a fact of modern life. Recent US statistics show that already over 50% of America's Gross National Product (GNP) is information, suggesting the US is leading the business world into the knowhow age.

The Japanese futurologist Yoneiji Masuda has forecast that by the year 2010 several countries will have reached the point where knowhow-based production accounts for more than 50% of GNP. Masuda's predictions were based on comparisons between the evolution of the transport systems of the industrial societies and the evolution of information systems. He concluded that information technologies are developing between three and six times as fast as did transport technologies. Extrapolating these trends suggests that societies based almost entirely on knowhow production will be a reality by the millenium.

• Investment in knowhow

The idea of investing in knowhow seems to be a hard concept for politicians to grasp. The conventional wisdom in most Western countries, including Britain and Sweden, is that 're-industrialisation' is the only effective cure for the industrial society's ills. Politicians constantly bemoan the declining rate of investment in buildings and equipment believing it to be a sign of a failure of will on the part of industry to keep up with the times. Some political parties, such as Britain's Labour Party, believe industry's propensity to invest is so low that government needs to step in to make good the deficiency.

But the low investment rate indicated by the official figures is an illusion. A recent investigation by a Swedish industrial association showed that if one adds investment in research and development and market research to the investment in hardware (buildings, plant and equipment) one gets quite a different picture (see Fig. 3). **Investment in knowhow,** though not measured by official statistics, is increasing all over the world as we enter the information society. Though it goes largely unrecorded in official GNP statistics and company balance sheets it is just as important if not more so than the investment in tangible, visible assets the politicians set such store by.

One could say that companies have entered a new evolutionary phase in which **growing smarter** (accumulating knowhow) has a higher priority than **growing stronger** (accumulating tangible assets). The problem for government is that business development in this respect has, to all intents and purposes, gone underground. Knowhow accumulation is difficult to detect, hard to measure by conventional methods and even harder to influence. Indeed, there is great scope here for serious policy errors.

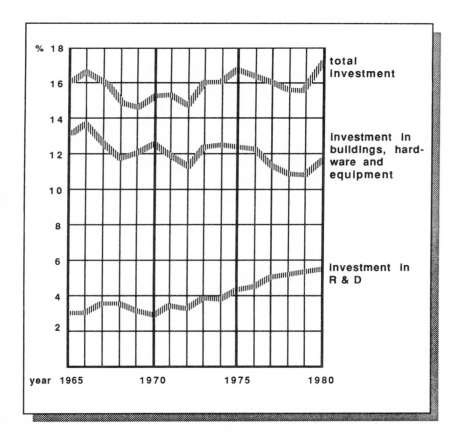

Figure 3   Swedish companies have been investing in buildings and equipment for over 20 years. Investment in R&D is a relatively new idea and indicates a change from an economy based on traditional production to one based on knowhow.

• The allure of the media industry

Forecasts like Masuda's, disseminated by modern information technology, explain why investors at large have become so interested in information and media companies in recent years. Shares in media companies are changing hands at prices indicating a value for each company of around 20 times net annual earnings. This compares to an average of about 10 times earnings for traditional manufacturing companies. The high 'price/earnings' ratios (P/Es) are evidence of a general belief on the part of investors that information and media companies have the ability to grow very rapidly over the next decade or so.

Some of these media investors come from very different industries. The Norwegian mining company Orkla bought a large, privately-owned publishing company in 1984. The British pan-African natural resources company Lonrho acquired Scottish newspaper publishing group George Outram in 1979 and later bought *The Observer* Sunday paper from the US oil group Atlantic Richfield. In 1977 the UK construction and shipping group Trafalgar House acquired the Express Newspapers publishing group.

One of the 'sexiest' companies in Norway in 1985 was MediaInvest which had expanded rapidly by acquiring a number of 'media' companies. Investors rushed to buy MediaInvest shares when the company was brought to the stock exchange.

Unfortunately neither the Norwegian investors nor the management of MediaInvest understood clearly **the difference between information and knowhow** (see Fig. 4). It is not easy to make money simply by producing information as MediaInvest and its hapless backers found out to their cost when the company ran into serious problems at the end of 1985.

The same may soon prove true of the TV satellite broadcasting industry, one of the new darlings of the media sector. Why should a TV satellite operator be any more profitable in the long-run than a newspaper printing company? There is huge over-capacity in Europe's printing industry. It can produce far more information and copies of information than its target customers have the appetite to consume.

Satellites are the printing presses of the information age. In all probability their owners will soon encounter problems of over-capacity and will have to struggle for market share.

• Databases

During the first half of the 1980s international database companies began springing up in great profusion. Today there are more than 2,000 databases of various kinds available for inspection and research to paying subscribers all over the world. Some of the original database companies quickly evolved into database 'hosts', buying stored information from magazines, newspapers, statistical organisations, libraries and so on. The data are stored in computers and accessed over and over again through gateways like telephones, telex terminals or videotex screens.

The revolution in the database industry was sparked off a decade ago by a rapid decline in the costs of computer storage and by the appearance of new software enabling users to search and edit with simple key words.

But so far the database hosts have not been conspicuously successful; indeed many have incurred heavy losses. Customers have not been willing to pay the prices the database hosts have felt obliged to charge to cover their marketing costs. The reason for the failure is simple; customers do not regard an ability merely to retrieve information as being particularly valuable. **Information 'per se' is worth very little**. It needs to be **knowhow-enriched** to be of much value.

The database host of to-day is really no more than a broker, comparable to the traditional wholesaler. Unless such companies can find ways to **add value to their data** they will find the going hard. They and their investors are beginning to learn the difference between information and knowhow.

• Knowhow is value-added information

Information is a flow of data. If one retrieves, adds and accumulates information in such a way that one can retrieve it again, it becomes enriched with knowhow. Storage, selection, analysis and the extraction of new information from existing

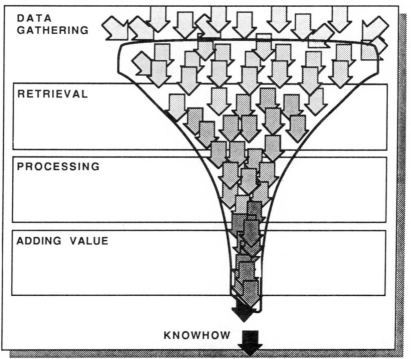

Figure 4   Only by retrieving and processing relevant information can you add value to it and produce knowhow.

information by deduction are all knowhow-enrichment processes. One can think of it in terms of a company balance sheet. **Knowhow is an asset**. An organisation which can accumulate and store information effectively will thereby increase the value of its knowhow in the balance-sheet. But though the knowhow asset is very important it remains, for the moment, virtually invisible. It cannot be measured in traditional ways. We shall suggest later ways in which this gap in accountancy technology might be bridged.

The value of knowhow is becoming more widely appreciated. There is much talk these days of 'managerial quality' and 'knowhow' when a new company is being formed or a takeover bid is being mounted. Some managers are beginning to give a higher priority to the building up of knowhow within their organisations than to building empires with huge sales forces and extensive manufacturing facilities.

● Knowhow capital as a substitute for financial capital

All over the world £billions upon £billions worth of goods are stored in warehouses. The world's production lines all have buffers, for raw materials at the input end and for finished goods at the output end. Trade is supported by stocks. There are always trucks, trains and ships filled with goods on their way from suppliers and to customers.

The factories need buffer stocks to prevent the production engineer's nightmare, the halt of the production line for lack of materials, from becoming a reality. But if suppliers had perfect knowledge of when, where and how their customers needed materials the customers would no longer need buffers. The raw materials would flow straight from suppliers to the line and straight out again as finished goods to the customers.

The Japanese, with their **'kanban'** system, regard **buffers as evidence of inefficiency**. With the help of sophisticated information systems linking customers, wholesalers and suppliers and the various production stages within the factory together they have managed to reduce stocks by astonishing amounts. The turnover to capital ratios of most Western car manufacturers range from one to three. Some Japanese car makers like Nissan have achieved levels of 20. Wholesalers in the Swedish paper industry have developed systems connecting the supplier's computers to those of the customer. This gives the customer and the supplier near perfect knowledge about each other's supply situation, enabling both to reduce drastically their buffers, their warehousing and thus their working capital. There are many other ways in which **knowhow capital can reduce the need for financial capital**.

● Alfa-Laval – a nineteenth-century knowhow company

The story of Alfa-Laval begins in 1878 with the invention by the engineer Gustav de Laval of the 'continuous separator', a device for separating cream from milk. The need for such a machine had been clear for some time and a number of companies were engaged in a desperate race to crack the problem first. De Laval went into partnership with the businessman Oscar Lamm, one of those who had realised the enormous market for such a product.

They formed a new company, Separator. They had plenty of competition. In Germany alone there were 53 companies desperately trying to develop the separator and there were over 20 in Sweden. In many ways the state of the European dairy machinery market in the late nineteenth century was similar to the present flux in the world personal computer market.

Separator opened up a winning lead over its competitors when it succeeded in acquiring the rights to a device called the 'Alfa discs', invented by a German. By dividing the milk inside the separator into several very thin layers the discs greatly increased the speed of the separation process.

The securing of the Alfa patent marked the beginning of the first life-cycle of the separator. The new company began to exploit its knowhow. Growth thereafter followed a pattern that has subsequently become a classic for the knowhow company genre (see Fig. 5).

The first customers were the dairies of course, but Separator soon found a ready market for its smaller, manual models among farmers. By the turn of the century more customers were emerging from industries as varied as engineering, power supply, shipbuilding, textiles, margarine making and petrochemicals.

The management of Alfa-Laval decided their customer base was a good market for other lines. They began to supply dairy customers and farmers with a whole range of products, mainly acting as agent for other suppliers.

They also bought in new knowhow from outside such as a heater for continuous pasteurising. When the market for the original separators became saturated in the early twentieth century Alfa-Laval's strong brand image among its existing customers helped it to maintain its competitive position.

The organisation, selling thousands of products into markets all over Europe, became increasingly complex. By the mid-twentieth century it had moved into several areas outside its original core knowhow and yet was still regarded by financial analysts in the 1970s as a high-tech group with good growth potential. Was there not a need for separators in the new and fashionable areas of biotechnology and medical equipment?

However, the management failed to deliver the expected growth. In 1984 profits were halved. Among other diversifications Alfa-Laval had gone into contracting on a large scale in the Middle East and had incurred heavy losses on some projects.

What prompted Alfa-Laval's ill-fated move into the contracting business? The answer is a cautionary tale for all companies tempted to stray too far from their core knowhow. Ten years earlier Alfa-Laval had begun, quite sensibly, to sell its knowhow about large scale dairy production. 'System sales' or 'turnkey' contracts were one of the trends of the early 1970s. Alfa-Laval sold tailor-made dairies to customers all over the world. Though the separators were essential components of the dairies, other companies did most of the construction work, acting as sub-contractors to Alfa-Laval. The latter organised the projects and so acquired a certain amount of project management knowhow. With the the group's decentralised management style it was only natural that those involved in these projects would try to make use of their knowhow in a more general way. In 1985 the cold store project in Libya produced a loss of SKr100m and the management admitted they had made a strategic mistake.

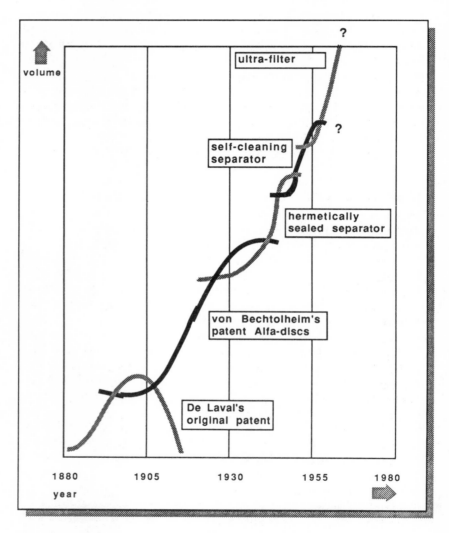

Figure 5   Alfa-Laval, a nineteenth-century knowhow company, added one knowhow area to another over a period of 100 years and followed a growth pattern that would become a classic for knowhow companies.

• Sinclair Research

Sir Clive Sinclair, pioneer of the home computer industry, made an ill-fated venture into the motor industry a few years ago when he launched a battery-powered electric tricycle. He reckoned his knowhow was in taking a collection of existing technologies, refining them and then putting them together in novel products that could be sold in large numbers. 'If I can do it with computers,' he reasoned, 'why shouldn't I be able to do it with cars?' The C5 electric trike was certainly novel but it did not sell in large numbers. Sinclair misjudged his knowhow as he had done earlier with his electronic 'Black Watch' and his mini televisions. His knowhow was much more intimately linked with calculators and computers than he realised.

There are many examples of companies diversifying, running into trouble and then retreating back to their core businesses with badly-burned fingers. There was little left of Sinclair's core business by the time the C5 fiasco became apparent but we have not seen the last of Sir Clive yet. He is on his way back with the first in a new range of computer products, though, after the sale of his computer business to Amstrad, he cannot call them Sinclair.

• Knowhow orientation – the key to success

Focus has been a key word for strategists in diversifed groups during the first half of the 1980s. Many companies have been completely re-vitalised by major 'rationalisation' programmes aimed at pruning activities not directly related to the 'mainstream' business. And the victims of the pruning knife – the former loss-making subsidiaries – have been transformed too through **management buy-out teams focussing on fewer areas of knowhow**.

Swedish Match has undergone a learning process similar to that of Alfa-Laval. The company, founded by the famous Swedish tycoon Ivar Kreuger in the early twentieth century, enjoyed rapid, world-wide expansion exploiting its knowhow in match production. Matches need to be packed and it was not long before Swedish Match had developed good knowhow here too. The packing machinery division expanded vigorously during the 1950s and moved into non-match areas such as bottling machines, carton making and fish packing. During the post-war boom in construction and building, Swedish Match also expanded into building equipment and materials. By the end of the 1970s the group was positively bristling with a host of diversified activities. But match production remained the only consistently profitable part of the group.

The new strategy for the 1980s was disinvestment. The company rapidly sold off most of its activities in areas other than match and lighter production. Several management teams were allowed to buy-out their businesses. One was led by the head of a packing company who bought parts of the packing division for a nominal SKr1 (10p) in 1982 and concentrated on making a few selected kinds of packing machines. The company went public in 1985; a year later its market value was well over £10m.

• Why buy-outs work

In May 1987 the Centre for Management Buy-Out Research at the University of Nottingham published the results of a study of UK management buy-outs that had subsequently been floated on the stockmarket. It showed that in the 1985/86 financial year MBOs accounted for over one-fifth of all flotations on the Unlisted Securities Market, London's second 'tier' market where most initial public offerings are made.

The 102 companies covered by the report were intially sold to their management teams for a combined sum of £820m. Their combined value by the time of their flotation had risen to £1.5bn. By the time the report was published this figure had risen to £2.4bn. Buy-outs in general have proved very good investments, out-performing conventional flotations very comfortably, particularly during the first two years after flotation. The report showed that buy-outs that went for a full listing on the London stockmarket in 1984, either as initial public offerings or as promotions from junior markets, had increased their aggregate market value by nearly 113% by February 1987, compared to an increase of less than 96% for the market as a whole.

British examples of successful buy-outs include First Leisure (bought out from Trusthouse Forte and Thorn EMI by Lord Delfont), the National Freight Consortium (bought by its staff from the government), Jeyes (bought out by management from Cadbury Schweppes) and Mecca Leisure (bought out by

Table 2   Management buy-outs
Total number and value of buy-outs in the UK 1967–1986

Year	No.	Value (£m)	Average value (£m)
1967–76	43	n/a	n/a
1977	13	n/a	n/a
1978	23	n/a	n/a
1979	52	26	0.50
1980	107	50	0.47
1981	124	114	0.92
1982	170	265	1.56
1983	205	315	1.54
1984	210	415	1.98
1985	229	1,150	5.02
1986	261	1,210	4.64

n/a=not available
Source *Trends in UK Buy-outs*, 1987 Edition. Venture Economics and The Centre for Management Buy-out Research.

management from Grand Metropolitan). Most buy-outs work well.

Their success is due to a high level of motivation, greater freedom and a more intense focus. One buy-out leader estimated that in any subsidiary of a group of companies there will always be, however well the group is run and however tight the financial disciplines it imposes on its subsidiaries, at least 10% of cost that can be 'sweated out' by a cost-conscious management team. Highly motivated management, obsessed with a single business idea, can turn an ailing subsidiary into an independent high-flier almost overnight.

- **The case of AGA**

  In the final decade of the nineteenth century the Swedish engineer Gustav Dahlén discovered how to produce and distribute the explosive gas acetylene. On the basis of this knowhow he formed the AGA company.

  Dahlén is best known for the gas-driven lighthouse but he was also active in many other high-tech areas which had nothing to do with gas such as radios, television, infra-red cameras and submarine periscopes.

  And though none of these new businesses spawned by AGA's engineer-dominated culture could match the success of the core gas business, the management remained firmly wedded to the diversification idea. In the mid 1960s they became even bolder and began to invest the mature gas division's rich cash-flow in medical equipment and electronics, two of the most fashionable growth markets of the day, in an attempt to build up two new 'legs' for the business.

  The result was disastrous.

  Ten years later a new management team launched the operation 'back to gas'. All the high-tech companies were collected in one company – Pharos – which was floated off on the stock exchange. AGA kept the gas and concentrated its management and engineering resources on its old core knowhow. Even the internal services were sub-contracted and all buildings not directly connected with gas production were sold.

  To-day AGA is entirely concentrated on its core gas business and is competing very successfully with the world's large international gas producers.

- **Lessons to be learned**

  Analysts said AGA's failure was because its engineers lacked market orientation. Just as plausible an explanation is that the company deployed its management resources in too many areas where it had no knowledge. The managers could not cope with all the unfamiliar new markets, suppliers and products. The same can be said of Alfa-Laval, Sinclair and Swedish Match.

  Divestment and concentration on the core business have been key management concepts during the early 1980s, not just in Sweden and the UK but all over the world. Profitability has increased and the slimmed-down, focused companies have regained much of the strength lost during the diversification binges of the previous decade. There are also many examples of successful buy-outs from old, disillusioned conglomerates. Buy-outs are regarded as among the least risky investments for venture capitalists. The lesson is clear. **Focus on core knowhow is a key success factor** whatever industry you are in.

The rapid development of the information society is affecting every business in every sector including 'traditional' industries like farming. Many chief executives have learned from bitter experience that expanding into knowhow areas where they have no competence can cost an arm and a leg. They have also learned that it is equally dangerous to deploy resources on too many knowhow fronts at once.

But though focus on core knowhow is a necessary strategy in the information society it is not a sufficient one. As we shall see, focus on core knowhow is just one of 10 key success factors in the new business environment.

SUMMARY
- To date the extent of investment in knowhow has gone largely unrecognised.
- Knowhow is not simply information – it is value-added information.
- Knowhow must be focused.
- The focus on core knowhow explains why management buy-outs work well. Lack of focus is often the reason why conglomerates fail.

4

• Putting Knowhow Companies to Work

• Business idea – personnel idea

The business idea belongs to the key people

Managers of knowhow companies can always identify a few key people without whose knowledge and ability the business idea would be in jeopardy. These are the skilled professionals – the big revenue earners and the people able to solve the most complicated problems. They have large networks outside the company and are generally well-known in their industry.

Because the loss of such skills would threaten the survival of the company, the value of these people cannot be measured in conventional ways. Investors in companies quoted on second or third 'tier' markets must keep this in mind. There are plenty of examples of profit collapses at small companies following arguments between key people and management. (More about investing in knowhow companies in Chapter 12.)

Sometimes one can trace the business idea to a single person – the entrepreneur or leader. He or she has the greatest professional skill, is the undisputed chief executive, the organiser, the marketing manager and the hirer and firer of staff. The skills of these key people and their ability to turn those skills into revenues determine the success or failure of the knowhow company. In some cases the link between the person and the business is so intimate as to make the two virtually indistinguishable.

• Personnel idea

The personnel idea of a company can be described as a general opinion about **what kind of people are to be employed**, how old they should be, how well educated and what attitudes they should have if they are to fit in with the organisation. The **recruitment strategy** and the subsequent **education and**

development of the people are parts of the personnel idea and are comparable in some ways to the 'personnel policy' of a traditional company.

But because people are so important and have such an influence on a knowhow company's ability to solve problems, the personnel idea must be a much broader concept than the personnel policy. For managers of professional organisations **the personnel idea is an integral part of strategy**. It contains four basic elements:

- recruitment idea
- personnel development
- personnel motivation
- personnel departure

An essential requirement of the personnel idea is that it should recognise that **people mature, develop and change**. Human beings, the constituent parts

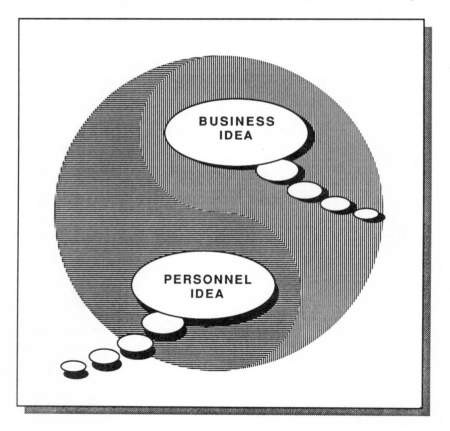

Figure 6   There is no knowhow business without people. The business idea is so closely linked to the personnel idea that the two may be almost indistinguishable.

of a knowhow company's invisible balance sheet, are not constant. They strengthen in some ways at some times and in other ways and at other times they weaken.

• The laminated business – the onion

A successful media entrepreneur was once asked to describe his company. He thought for a while and then said:

> 'I see before me an onion. When you believe you've reached the core of the company there is another layer. Sometimes I wonder what I will find at the centre. Is it the business idea or perhaps the idea about how to develop our people?'

Let us look at the onion in cross-section. At the core are the business and personnel ideas **intimately connected** with each other (perhaps two aspects of the same thing). Around the core are several layers containing the various parts of the company. Each layer is connected with the adjacent layers and must not be separated. If the layers break apart the structure splits and the organisation dies.

Which layers come closest to the core depends on the kind of organisation. In private sector companies operating in competitive markets the marketing func-

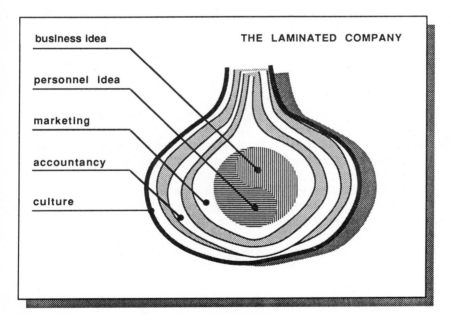

business idea

personnel idea

marketing

accountancy

culture

THE LAMINATED COMPANY

Figure 7   The knowhow company is a laminated business. It consists of many layers. At the core are the business and personnel ideas, surrounded by layers of supportive functions like marketing and accountancy. The culture of the company forms the thin, transparent skin that binds the organisation together.

tion is obviously crucial. That is why we have put it closest to the core in our diagram. We have named only one other layer – the **accounting function** – the sad neglect of which is one reason why some knowhow companies never develop into professional organisations.

- **The marketing function**

  The marketing function is the layer closest to the core of the onion. In this respect the knowhow company is no different from the service company. But in contrast to traditional companies, in knowhow or service companies it is not possible to delegate marketing to functional specialists. This has been demonstrated by, amongst others, Christian Gronroos and Richard Normann (see Chapter 11, page 148).

  In knowhow companies **the professionals themselves are the best salespeople**. They are in constant contact with clients and it is their knowledge clients are buying and their reputations which are winning new business.

- **The accounting function**

  The accounting function plays a special role in the knowhow company because the book-keeping and its associated reporting systems constitute **one of the very few firm structures** that can be built up in a knowhow company.

  In a sense it represents the unchanging 'germ line' linking the new corporate model of the knowhow company to the old industrial model from which it is evolving.

  Traditionally the power of the accounting department has stemmed from its ability to mirror and monitor the company's performance. It acts as the monitor of top management. It is easy to see how this role could become rather difficult in a knowhow company where, as we shall see in Chapter 5, conventional performance yardsticks like profitability and return on capital are of limited use. Partly because of a weakness in the accountancy profession itself – its failure so far to get to grips with the concept of the **invisible balance-sheet** – conventional accountancy skills are a mis-match with the accounting requirements of the knowhow company.

  In these circumstances it is no wonder frustrated accountants are commonplace, almost clichés, in knowhow companies. They lack the tools and the knowledge to play the normal role of financial guru to the chief executive or leader. And the leaders, who may have a feel for the importance of the invisible balance sheet, usually lack both the technical knowledge and the interest in accountancy to enlighten their benighted allies.

- **Structures**

  The professional organisation **needs few tangible fixed assets**. There are no machines or warehouses and no visible inward and outward flows of raw materials on the one hand and finished goods on the other. The organisation might not even own its own premises. This lack of tangible substance has encouraged many analysts to conclude that knowhow companies are **inherently weak organisations,** always at the mercy of the whims of a few individuals.

Knowhow companies themselves often fall into the same conceptual error. The finance director of one such company we know explained the decision to buy rather than rent a new office building in terms of a wish 'to put some guts into the balance-sheet'.

But professional organisations (successful knowhow companies) are able to erect structures, consisting of human relations, shared values and attitudes, networks and collaborative arrangements between people inside and outside the company, that are quite as 'gutsy' as the bricks and mortar of a mortgaged building or a depreciating stock of goods.

Let us look at a few of these structures:

- **The network**
The 'network' concept first emerged in management literature during the 1970s, inspired partly by developments in computer technology. The advent of Local Area Networks (LANs) and developments in wider communications technology such as digital data exchanges, packet-switching, high-speed optical fibre cables and cellular radio, focussed attention on a new paradigm – the company as **a communicating organisation.**

But there is another kind of network more often described in psychological and sociological literature. Everyone lives and works within **a network of other people** consisting of close friends, colleagues, clients and acquaintances. The business of a knowhow company, in whatever industry it operates, is based to a large extent on the intensive use of such human relationships. Network theory is no part of this book but it is important to recognise that networks of this kind are one of the most important types of firm structure that can be built in professional organisations.

Top managements of professional organisations learn to use the portfolio of networks contributed by members of staff. In practice they range from the trivial, such as a computerised client register, to the more sophisticated, such as 'the old boys' network' existing between former school friends. Such **commercially significant systems of 'contacts'** exist everywhere. A professional organisation with a strong network system, that is to say many relationships of high quality with important people outside the company, has a strong, firm structure.

The professional organisation is adept at forming and using networks. The methods are similar to those employed in the old industrial and farming communities of long ago, the main difference being that in those days the networks were circumscribed by geography and time. These days the networks of knowhow companies have no such constraints. The computer networks – 'mailboxes' – of today give immediate access to everybody in the net irrespective of when and where in the world they happen to be.

So far **computer nets** are used mainly by computer professionals within large companies. Their potential for establishing, maintaining and cementing relationships is thus not yet widely recognised. It is interesting, however, that some of the large computer companies are actively using their internal computer nets for the purpose of strengthening and developing their internal cultures.

Personal relationships outside the computer nets are very important, of course. Computer nets are no substitute for human contact but they do strengthen existing relationships and they give the people working in such organisations the potential to create and maintain much wider networks than has been possible in the past.

In a way networks of both the digital and personal kinds are what professional organisations are all about. The old-fashioned charts showing parent companies and subsidiaries arranged in tree-like diagrams describe legal relationships but give no indication of how business ideas and knowhow interact within and outside professional organisations. The personal contacts of the professionals are much more important for the development of the knowhow and thus the business than the relationships of ownership.

There are many examples of knowhow companies which have no relationship at all with their parent organisations but frequent contact with other companies. If we were to draw up the organisation charts of such companies in terms of their networks the parent organisation would be written out of the script entirely. In such cases ownership links have become so attenuated that it may be just a question of time before the knowhow subsidiary divests itself and restarts as an independent operation (see Fig. 8).

- **The accounting system**

If properly used, the accounting system can be one of the most important stable structures within a professional organisation. In just the same way as in traditional companies it enables the management, through a continuous flow of reports, to monitor and control the organisation's activities.

But the knowhow company lacks the enormous flow of paperwork and all the administrative routines associated in traditional companies with the flow of goods. Because so few invoices are raised and there are so few suppliers there is **no need for a large administrative organisation**. Superficially anyway the accounting system of the knowhow company is very simple – too simple to have become the subject of much research.

- **Co-operation agreements**

Another way of endowing a professional organisation with substance, structural strength and security is to enter into **contracts and co-operation agreements** with partners, clients, suppliers and other companies operating in complementary areas. These kinds of relationships reduce risk by reducing the organisation's isolation. You feel less alone although no less independent.

- **Property**

The 'home' of the company, often used as a symbol in the corporate livery or logo, is an important part of the organisation's structure. How the space or the rooms are distributed between departments and precisely who sits where help to determine how and between whom relationships develop. The office must be planned with great care. The proximities created will determine much of the organisation's internal structure and many of the important information channels.

Buying the office is a way of creating substance as well as structure but **beware the lure of property**. If the company limits its investments to its own

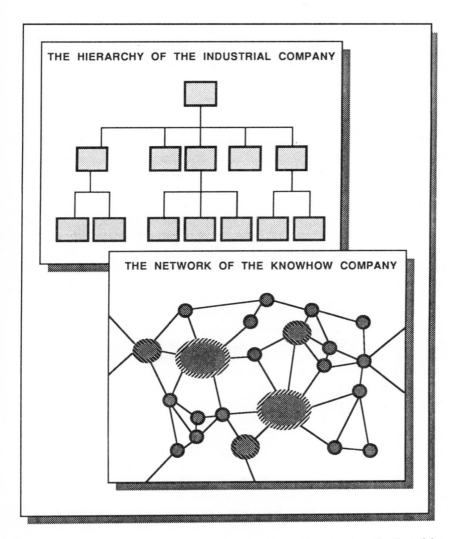

Figure 8   The knowhow company does not have a hierarchical structure like that of the industrial company.

office the business idea remains intact but as soon as it starts to invest in other property or starts a finance company the business idea is in jeopardy. It may slip away without the management noticing. **Investment in property reduces flexibility** and ties the structure to the past. If managements are aware of these risks there is no reason why property should not play a part in a portfolio for managing surplus cash but a knowhow company lets property considerations influence strategy at its peril.

- **Culture and ethics**
  Every successful company has its own culture. IBM employees know it, the Hewlett-Packard people know it and so do ICI managers when they travel to the other side of the world to visit one the group's remote outposts. It is the spirit of the organisation. It permeates everything and affects every employee.

  An onion has no shell, just a thin, dry outer layer. But cutting through the outer layer never causes the onion to fall apart. It contains an invisible cement that binds the layers together. Culture is that strong, invisible cement binding an organisation together.

  Corporate culture has become a very fashionable concept in management theory over the past few years but so far consultants and researchers have failed to shed much light on what constitutes a culture, how it works and the ways in which it can be grown. Many books have been written about corporate culture and many definitions offered. Perhaps the simplest and least unsatisfactory is that of Marvin Bower, head of the McKinsey consultancy firm. He described corporate culture as: '**The way we do things around here.**'

  If a knowhow company has succeeded in developing into a professional organisation it has, by definition, developed a very strong culture. The architects have been the founders and early pioneers whose trail blazing has left in its wake a jumble of precedent, incident, anecdote and apocrypha which together constitute a style – a kind of operating manual for the whole organisation to which managers and staff at all levels unconsciously adhere.

  A culture that is both strong and adaptable and capable of regular refreshment by injections of new blood and new ideas is **an extremely powerful management tool**. The highly qualified employees of professional organisations are used to abstract thinking and are thus prone to create, understand and be guided by strong cultures.

- # Dramatis personae
  In the first chapter we encountered the corporate hero of this book: the professional knowhow organisation. It represents the form to which all knowhow companies should aspire. It is the knowhow company's role model. We will now meet the main players, the four categories of employees, who must learn to work together efficiently and harmoniously if the knowhow company is to develop into a professional organisation.

- **'The professional'**

It goes without saying that the professionals are the **most important resource of all**. The exploitation of their knowhow is the company's only source
of revenue. Inevitably the professionals have the **highest status**. One might
even say – though it is advisable not to say it too often or too loudly – that the
sole function of the rest of the personnel is to act as a dedicated support staff for
the professionals.

This is in the natural order of things and it shows in the way the professionals
behave towards lesser mortals. One only has to think of the omnipotence of the
doctor in the hospital or the easy, patrician self-confidence that radiates from
successful lawyers, actors and consultants. The professionals know their
status, are proud of it and quite naturally they often try to exploit it for their own
ends.

But typical professionals are both **unable and unwilling to manage
other people**. They are interested only in **the freedom to develop their
professional skills**. And neither are they in need of much management themselves. They know what is expected of them and because of their often intimate
relationships with their clients they act as self-salespeople. A high degree of

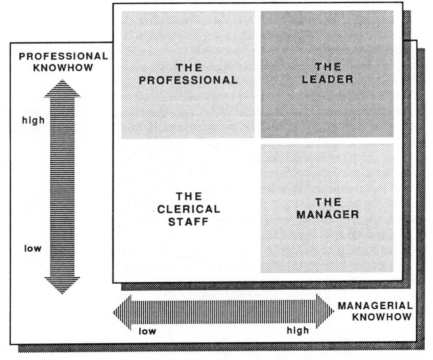

Figure 9   There are at least four categories of personnel in knowhow companies. The
PROFESSIONAL is the production 'machine' and only revenue source and is supported
by the CLERICAL STAFF. The MANAGER lacks professional knowhow but is strong
in managing the business. The LEADER is the prime mover and combines both skills.

professional self-management is an important feature of the knowhow company.

Above all, good professionals are rare. They are hard to find, hard to keep and difficult to replace. The constant lamentations of chief executives about the lack of skilled people shows clearly that in this part of the labour market the professionals – the 'sellers' – hold the whip hand.

They are also **difficult to integrate** into an organisation. The good ones will have developed styles of their own and may be unwilling to accept new rules. If a knowhow company is to develop into a professional organisation it must find ways and means to accommodate and **adapt to the 'difficult' professionals**. The old industrial stereotype of 'hard' managers who upbraid their staff for failing to adapt are liabilities in knowhow companies. Hard managers destroy knowhow capital by demoralising people and thus hastening their departure. A knowhow company must persuade professionals to commit because it cannot force them to submit.

• The Knot – a cautionary tale

The true story of a talented professional we shall call Knot will serve to illustrate the kind of problems that knowhow companies have to deal with.

He was called 'the knot' from his cradle. His father (who later disappeared with another woman) thought him a knotty and wrinkled baby. It was an appropriate nickname for other reasons because sometimes he would get knotted up inside and would rage in a fury, kicking and lashing out at anyone or anything within reach. In his teens Knot was a lonely boy.

He was a problem for his teachers at school. His maths master described him in his term reports as 'extremely clever' because Knot never made a mistake in tests – if he showed up for them. 'A monster' was his English teacher's verdict when instead of writing the English essay he had been assigned he scribbled a computer program on toilet-paper.

Knot won a place at university to read maths and information processing. At the beginning of his first year he pocketed his grant and as much extra money as he could beg and borrow and disappeared to France for a year. He returned penniless and 100,000 francs in debt, took all the courses, passed all the exams and was awarded his degree in just over 18 months.

He and a group of university colleagues decided to go into computer consultancy together. In 1981 they bought a used computer with three terminals and won an assignment from another computer consultancy to write a database processing package. Knot had to join later because he was recovering from concussion sustained when he slid down the bannisters from a second floor party. He crashed into the stone floor in the hall and they had to take him away in an ambulance.

His colleagues took care of all the practical details of the start-up but the new consultancy only really came alive when Knot appeared, bursting with energy and ideas. He infected everyone with such enthusiasm that together they produced a revolutionary new kind of database structure which put the young company on the computer consultancy map and began to generate substantial royalty revenues.

Knot had laboured night and day, doing the work of three men according to his colleagues. He was the one who solved most of the bugs in the programs and maintained the momentum when others began to tire or become dispirited.

When the work was finished and the revenues began pouring in Knot and a few other amateur speculators bought a futures contract on 30 tonnes of Nigerian peanuts. On the cargo's arrival in London it was impounded by the customs because of serious contamination. Knot ended up with losses of £50,000 which he covered by borrowing from a loan shark. To meet the heavy interest payments he began to write computer programs which he invoiced from his own private company. His absences from the company became frequent and prolonged and after a few years of quarrelling he left. With no Knot the spark deserted his erstwhile colleagues. They broke up soon afterwards and took jobs in large companies.

Knot was a 'superpro' when he functioned but became a distracting and subversive influence when his bad judgement took over. He was both the young company's greatest asset and its greatest liability. He made it and he broke it. How does an ordinary organisation handle such extraordinary people?

One could say that to accommodate extraordinary people – in fact they crop up quite often in knowhow companies – the organisation needs to be extraordinary too but that is not much help. There are **no simple solutions**. All that can be said is that if leaders wish to take advantage of such gifted mavericks they must adapt the organisation to them and be very flexible. Standard labour market rules do not apply.

- ### 'The manager'
The traditional manager has a high level of organisational knowhow but a low level of professional knowhow. They are typically to be found in the conventional industrial company as head of a division or department at middle management level. They are rare birds in knowhow companies because their skills are more suited to large organisations.

They find it hard to make headway in small, unstructured knowhow companies because it is more or less impossible for them even to aspire to, let alone achieve, the status of the professionals. Without that status – or something equivalent to it – **the top positions are out of reach**.

The manager is normally to be found in knowhow companies leading small support teams in such areas as accounting and marketing. For young knowhow companies managers are luxuries they cannot afford. They only need 'ordinary' managers when they reach a certain size, say 30–50 employees.

And though managers as a breed are more plentiful in the marketplace than professionals some are more suitable than others. Of the few who have had experience of knowhow companies a large proportion will say with some feeling 'never again!'. And yet if they are not used to knowhow companies it is hard for them to win the acceptance of the professionals.

- **'The clerical staff'**

  The clerical staff (mainly women) handle the support services, the secretarial tasks, the accounting and other office work. Their prime task is **to support the professionals** so they, the breadwinners, can function efficiently.

  Office work in the knowhow company differs little from that in other companies. Accounting, administration and secretarial work is fairly standard throughout the industrial spectrum. Those who can do it competently are relatively easy to find and can be paid relatively standard salaries – there is usually **a 'going rate' for the job**.

  But clerical staff can be **a dangerous source of discontent**. They are often very conscious of their lowly positions in the pecking order. They resent being at the bottom of the heap or the back of the office. They feel like 'skivvies' whose interests are constantly ignored. There is at least something that can be done about this sense of inferiority. It must be handled with care. One cosmetic convention we use, adapting a stockbroking term, is to call the clerical staff collectively the 'front office' rather than the more usual and unnecessarily pejorative 'back office'.

- **'The leader'**

  The 'leader' is **the driving force** of the knowhow company and is more or less irreplaceable. He or she has often founded the company and the organisation is usually run along the lines the leader lays down. In small organisations the leader's role is very much that of the team coach – the chief motivator. In larger operations it is that of the chief organiser and the one responsible for growth and development.

  The leader is **almost always an ex-professional** who has developed an ability to organise. It is very rare to find an accountancy firm, advertising agency or theatre company not led by an ex-professional.

  Leaders seldom need to be appointed formally. In contrast to managers who receive their status from a board of directors, leaders receive their mandate from their colleagues. A striking feature of the leaders of professional organisations is their lack of titles or overt accoutrements of power. They have no need of them. Their position is accepted by the rest of the personnel because they have 'conquered' it themselves. Managers need status symbols because their internal position remains equivocal while it is seen as merely the result of a dispensation by a higher authority such as the board.

  A knowhow company can manage without a leader but can never be more than either an agency or 'factory'. If it is to develop into a professional organisation it must have more than one leader. But it is not a question of the more the merrier – having too many leaders and potential leaders is asking for trouble.

  The challenge for the knowhow company is to **develop new leaders**, capable of carrying the business idea into the future. A company cannot be described as a true 'professional organisation' until it has survived the emergence of a new generation of leaders.

  The **balance between professionalism and leadership** is crucial. Since the professionals are the core of the company, leaders need their full support to be effective. They must earn it in the first place and retain it subsequently by ensuring the professionals continue to find their work challenging. The leader must, at the same time, be able to carry the business idea forward. We shall look more closely at the role of the leader in Chapter Seven (pages 88–97).

• Unprofessional professionals

Why is it that successful computer consultancies almost always employ old-fashioned, manual invoicing systems and that accountancy firms are frequently several months behind in their book-keeping? Those who have worked in such organisations know the answer only too well: helping to run one's own company is boring and what's more it is low status work. In modern parlance such corporate house-keeping is too remote from the 'sharp end' for the professional's taste.

This perceived division between 'real', 'professional' work – the stuff of the business idea – and the hum-drum activity of keeping the books and ensuring the stationery cupboard is adequately stocked can cause serious conflicts in knowhow companies between professionals on the one hand and managers and other 'support' staff on the other. Consider the relationship between the editorial and the advertising departments on a newspaper. The journalists more or less consciously look down on the advertising salespeople. They see them as daubers of vulgar slogans on pages that might otherwise have been filled with gripping news stories or impassioned polemic. In view of the fact that advertising sales normally account for upwards of 60% of a newspaper's revenues this kind of prejudice would appear to be singularly inappropriate.

Similar conflicts arise in most other kinds of knowhow organisations, especially those in the state sector such as hospitals and universities, though it must be said that in contrast to newspapers – where the journalists have the advantage – the administrators usually seem to end up on top, at least in terms of the power they wield if not in terms of status.

• The personnel mix

A typical knowhow company with 50 employees might have:

- 25–35 professionals
- 10–15 clerical staff
- 1–5 managers
- 1–3 leaders

These proportions will differ between industries, of course, and between organisations depending on how well they are run. In a badly managed law firm or government department, for example, the ratio between professionals and clerical staff might be 1:2 – there may be twice as many secretaries and administrators as lawyers or executive civil servants.

It is normal in private knowhow companies to **look after the professionals** well. It is important that the development of the people in the organisation proceeds according to the wishes of the professionals and leaders otherwise the business idea will be diluted. There are numerous cases in government where this and other basic principles of good knowhow management are routinely flouted.

• The dilemma – the need for dual expertise

Departmental class-consciousness is a major problem for knowhow companies. The professionals are seldom very interested in the development of their 'places of work' as companies or organisations. They are much more concerned with the **development of their own expertise** in their specialist fields. Indeed it is commonplace, in areas like medicine and journalism for example, for the professionals to display considerably more loyalty to their professions than to the organisations that employ them.

The truth is that competent organisers, capable of developing effective administrative systems, are rarities in knowhow companies. It is almost as if, in some quite fundamental way, an atmosphere of professional knowhow is inimical to the development of good, entrepreneurial managers.

The need for this blend of professional and managerial ability – what we call **'dual expertise'** – is so great and its occurrence in a single person so rare that many knowhow organisations have learned to **separate the functions** between two top managers. Thus one finds pairs of managers like the editor/publisher pair in newspapers or the director/producer pair in films and the theatre. It is usually the professional manager, the editor or the director, who has the highest status and the most visible profile. The publisher and the producer appear, at any rate, to play minor roles. It is interesting to note, however, that in television the highest status – as indicated by the name that ends the credits – is afforded to the producer rather than the director. This suggests power has shifted from the latter to the former as the content of the TV product – quiz games, chat shows, soap operas etc – has become degraded, compared to feature films, as its production has become more industrialised.

The lot of the chief executive in a knowhow company is not an easy one. He

Figure 10 The dilemma of the knowhow company is that the same people seldom combine both professional and managerial knowhow. You rarely find a good lawyer or consultant who is also a good manager.

normally gets landed with the most menial of the administrative jobs. As one CEO of a consultancy firm put it: 'I'm something between a cleaner and a shoulder to cry on.' He was responsible, amongst other things, for invoicing and personnel matters, tasks which the professionals find at best insufficiently rewarding and at worst, downright boring.

This tendency for the chief executive to 'fill in' the boring administrative tasks that the other professionals feel are beneath them should be vigorously resisted. There is always a risk that the chief executive will become so involved in his service role that he **loses his grip on the professional reins**. This can be very dangerous. The chief executive is normally one of the few with a real overview of the organisation and it is he who is mainly responsible for the development of the company. It is essential that his power and influence amongst the professionals be preserved.

Both kinds of leadership, professional and managerial, must be combined in a knowhow company's top management. Some companies solve the problem by having two or more people at the top with no single chief executive. Others combine all the roles in one man. Many knowhow company collapses can be attributed to a failure to resolve the leadership conflicts inherent in the need for dual expertise. Successful companies have resolved the dilemma in various ways. It is likely, in the future, that **collective leadership**, usually pairs, will emerge as the most successful model.

• The hospital

Most Swedes and Britons begin to suspect, after many hours spent in crowded waiting rooms, that their health service does not work very well. This would be surprising if it was not so familiar because the patient is ostensibly the hospital's client. In any normal company the client is being constantly courted and pampered because if he is dissatisfied he may not return. Can you imagine a lecturer at a medical school impressing upon his students the principle that 'the customer', i.e. the patient, 'is always right'?

It is very hard for a patient in a hospital to feel he is being treated as a very important person – as the client without whom the company or organisation could not prosper. A visitor to a hospital soon realises that the most important person around is not the patient/client but the doctor.

The whole organisation of the hospital and the rhythm of its working day are built around the doctors. They take all the important medical decisions and if for some reason they are unable to function, perhaps because of illness or overwork, the rest of the organisation tends to grind to a halt. And in a general hospital there are emergency cases to deal with. When the ambulance arrives, blue lights flashing, the 'flu patients just have to wait.

There is very little the hospital personnel can do about it. They need to keep a 'stock' of patients in the waiting room to ensure that not a minute of the overworked doctor's precious time is wasted. Because of a chronic shortage of both money and doctors the surgeries are under-staffed. Since the doctor is the only one allowed to make a diagnosis, even when the case seems clear, everyone – patients and support staff alike – are forced to dance to the doctor's tune.

Production is the top priority in hospitals and in most other public bodies. The aim is to maximise production efficiency i.e. the throughput of patients.

Hospitals demonstrate very clearly what happens in a knowhow company when the management, instead of concentrating on solving the problems of individual clients, gives the highest priority to 'production'. When production is the imperative, the producer – in this case the doctor – must perforce be king. The hospital's business idea demands it.

The almost god-like quality of the doctor is reinforced by the fact that one very rarely sees him. Within Swedish health care to-day there are about 15,000 doctors and almost 300,000 other personnel. To put it another way there are upwards of 20 nurses, cleaners, cooks, technicians, receptionists and secretaries for each doctor. There is a 95% chance that the next person you see in a hospital will not be a doctor.

The people the patient encounters most frequently are usually the ones with lowest status – the clerical assistants and cleaners. Status in a hospital is determined entirely by the level of medical knowhow. The patient is generally the least knowledgeable in this area and so he or she, the hospital's client, is required to sit 'patiently' and respectfully on the bottom rung of the status ladder.

The specialisation of the Swedish medical profession into discrete knowhow areas began more than 200 years ago when what was then the largest hospital in Sweden was divided into one medical and one surgical clinic. To-day, in the big hospitals, there are at least 40 different specialities. Each doctor has medical responsibility for his patients and each consultant takes overall responsibility in his district or hospital for his own specialist area.

But this organised, coherent and rigid medical/productive hierarchy is in sharp contrast to the equivocation and illogicality of the administrative/managerial structures common in most hospitals and health services.

The chief physicians have budgets – discretion to spend – amounting to tens of millions of pounds per head. They have the right to prescribe treatment, employ expensive diagnostic equipment, order admissions, refer to specialists, instruct staff and make a host of other decisions, almost all of which involve spending of some kind or another.

And yet their responsibilities are in no way comparable to those of private sector managers. The doctor is not allowed to recruit his own personnel, even though staff costs account for about 70% of his budget. Senior physicians cannot even order the hiring of temporary personnel during holiday periods. Such matters are in the hands of the personnel department of the hospital.

This lack of managerial discretion does not bother the doctors at all. They like it that way. Since work of this kind involves mostly low status paper-pushing they are more than happy to leave it to others. In his heart of hearts the doctor scorns mere management. The uncompromisingly élitist attitude of doctors is exemplified in their unofficial oath of professional allegiance: 'No-one spends seven years at medical school to become an administrator.'

The result of this widespread prejudice is that doctors and the hospital's administrators are in a state of more or less permanent war with each other. The doctors feel hounded by paperwork and hobbled by bureaucratic rules and regulations. The administrators, hounded in their turn by politicians and civil servants to reduce costs, are constantly frustrated in their search for efficiency and economy by doctors who know little and care less about the economics of health care. The tension is the opposite of constructive. The administrators have the responsibility for efficiency and cost-effectiveness but no power to improve either; the doctors, who have the power, have neither the responsibility nor the inclination to prefer the 'cheap' solution to a medical problem.

Dual expertise in hospitals is everywhere conspicuous by its absence. The doctors have no education in and no appetite for business administration and the managers know precious little about medicine. There is no common ground – no meeting place. And the incessant conflict between the two opposing camps precludes any possibility that some accommodation, in the form of an effective collective leadership, might be reached.

The situation is further aggravated by the fact that doctors, despite their heavy responsibilities, are not allowed to take investment decisions either. This is the prerogative of politicians chairing committees on which the doctors seldom have more than token representation.

The dilemma for the administrators and politicians is that they have no means of control other than by written rules, regulations and systems most of which the doctors find exceedingly irksome. The administrators, hungry for power, try to ensure every decision of 'importance' is taken by one of their members. This is why the personnel department tries to take recruitment away from the doctors and why the politicians claim the right to take investment decisions which should really be the responsibility of the specialists.

In these circumstances it is not surprising that the administrative staff in Swedish hospitals has outgrown the professionals. According to one investigation the number of administrative personnel grew by 7.7% between 1974 and 1981, whereas total employment in hospitals increased by only 5.7%. The Swedish hospitals are caught in a typical dilemma for knowhow organisations – the dual expertise problem. The professional and the organisational managements are distinct from and deeply suspicious of each other.

Modern hospitals appear from the outside to be rather typical 'factories'. The priority is production and the organisational style is industrial. The professionals, who play the role of expensive machines around which the production process is designed, have power within the system but no power to change it.

But internally hospitals are typical knowhow organisations. Those with the highest knowhow level have the highest status. In fact knowhow orientation in hospitals is extremely strong – there are even sharp divisions between the various specialities. One finds in hospitals islands of expertise, equivalent to what we call 'pro-teams', consisting of groups of highly qualified specialists (surgical units for example) which work together with great skill, dedication and efficiency. But they are always isolated. It is rare for their professionalism to infect the rest of the organisation.

How did it get like this? Why has the client/patient, who in a normal business would be at the centre of things, been relegated to the role of raw material, of less consequence than the humblest cleaner? One answer is that hospitals in Britain and Sweden are monopolies. Dissatisfied customers cannot go elsewhere. Another answer is that the state, in its caring wisdom, has robbed the patient of the essential client prerogative – the right to pay or withold the fee.

SUMMARY

- The **business idea belongs to the key people**. It **incorporates the personnel idea** which contains four basic elements; **recruitment, development, motivation and departure**.
- A professional organisation is a **laminated business** with interdependent layers including the marketing and accounting functions.
- There are five basic structures in a professional organisation: **networks** which make the company a **communicating organisation; the accounting system; co-operation agreements; property** and **culture**.
- Knowhow companies have four categories of personnel: the **professional** who is hard to manage and operates largely under a system of self-management; the **manager** who has skills which are more suited to large organisations; the **clerk** whose main role is to support the professionals; the **leader** who is normally **the driving force** of the company and the one responsible for expansion and development.
- Leaders receive their mandate from their colleagues.
- A professional organisation needs more than one leader.
- Knowhow companies need **dual expertise**; professional and managerial. This is hard to achieve because the **class-consciousness** in knowhow companies affords the highest status to the professionals.
- There is a need for **collective leadership**.

5

• Measuring Knowhow

• Towards a new accounting system

Few modern knowhow companies have accounting systems capable of **measuring the development of the knowhow capital**. This is because there are no easily measurable criteria of changes in knowhow capital. The most common object of measurement in knowhow companies is time. Consultancy, law and accountancy firms and advertising agencies have all developed highly sophisticated **time accounting** systems. Clients and the managers typically receive detailed information about how much time the professionals have spent on cases and client assignments.

But this kind of **input-related information**, which is clearly necessary for billing purposes, is not much help to managers. They need **output-related information**. The fact is that the accounting systems of most knowhow companies are in such bad shape that many firms cannot even answer simple questions like: who is the most profitable client? Who is the largest client? Who is the largest supplier? Which business area is the most profitable?

The eyes of most leaders of knowhow organisations glaze over when they encounter debit and credit. Hardly any knowhow companies have an accounting system worth the name. But the accounting system is probably the easiest structure of all to create and it offers a great opportunity to give some formal substance to the ideas and principles of knowhow management we have been discussing.

The first step is to learn to look at costs and revenues in an unconventional way. Unfortunately very little research effort has been devoted to the accountancy problems of knowhow and service companies. This is virgin territory. Enlightened knowhow managers, aided by imaginative in-house accountants, have an opportunity to break new ground in this area. It is likely to be some years before the first useful **knowhow accounting systems** begin to emerge from the accountancy profession.

• How to measure success

Every business analyst will tell you that you cannot value a company and measure its success without looking at its **profitability and growth.**

Of course every knowhow company has an ordinary balance-sheet and profit and loss account. Of course every knowhow company must be profitable long-term, as measured by traditional financial yardsticks, in order to survive. And of course shareholders are interested primarily in the return on their capital.

But these 'key' financial indicators are of little use to the manager of the knowhow company because they give no clues as to the rate and direction of the development of the knowhow capital. The knowhow company manager desires above all else high **growth of the knowhow capital.** His relative competitive strength in the marketplace is determined solely by the level of his knowhow capital. As we shall see below the traditional 'key' financial indicators, as taught at business school, can sometimes give **dangerously misleading signals** to the managers of knowhow companies.

Profitability, or return on capital, **is misleading**. If it turns out to be the result of a failure to invest in **the maintenance and expansion of the knowhow capital** it may be a sign that something is going wrong. One should look askance at highly profitable knowhow companies. They may be milking their invisible balance-sheets.

The dilemma is most obvious in the publicly quoted knowhow companies. The problem for knowhow companies listed on the stock exchange is that their shareholders are more interested in the **development of the financial capital**, since it is their capital, than in the development of the knowhow capital. This can put executives under severe pressure. How do they explain to shareholders that high costs one year should be seen as an investment or that high profits the next may be dangerous?

High **volume growth rate** is not a good measure of success. It is at best a sign that the market accepts, for the time being, the company's problem-solving ability. At worst, high volume growth is merely a symptom of top management's futile **wish to build an empire**. In the long-term a knowhow company's most important success factor is its ability to persuade its clients that it is better at solving their problems than its competitors. The high growth rates of to-day's computer companies have much more to do with rapid market growth than with the quality of the companies engaged in the computer industry. And high market growth, by itself, is absolutely **no guarantee of long-term success**. This became abundantly clear in 1985 when many computer companies failed despite the computer market's 20% overall volume growth.

If traditional yardsticks are so misleading, what should be used instead? The best measure, of course, is the **increase in the company's market value** but that can only be established when it is sold or floated on the stockmarket.

• Client studies

A more difficult and much less precise approach to the measurement problem is to try to establish whether the knowhow capital is increasing or decreasing. As we have seen, such things are 'invisible' to the ordinary eye but quite a reasonable picture of changes in the knowhow capital level can be derived indirectly, through client opinion surveys. If the clients rate the company highly they are likely to say so when asked. The general trend of knowhow capital change can be tracked by regular surveys of client perceptions. Service companies have been using client studies for years; knowhow companies have yet to recognise their value.

• The case of Sales Consultants Ltd

The market for specialist education, seminars and conferences has been booming in Britain and Sweden for the past 10 years. An early player in this high growth market was a company we shall call Sales Consultants Ltd (SCL) which specialised in training courses for computer sales people. SCL was founded in 1970 by Dave, an ex-IBM salesman. After two difficult years he recruited a couple of former IBM colleagues and in 1975 SCL began to grow rapidly. Growth slackened subsequently but during 1977–80 turnover grew by 50% a year and the annual return on equity exceeded 100%.

The courses sold very well and were highly regarded. The personnel worked hard and enjoyed their jobs enormously. Dave had written the course books in 1970–71 and he and his colleagues had developed the training systems during the early years.

The change came gradually. The SCL sales team started to complain that the courses were too expensive and hard to sell and, as was only to be expected after 10 years of teaching the same courses, the enthusiasm of the instructors waned.

SCL still earned handsome profits, especially from its cash surplus which yielded interest income, and Dave was in good standing with his bank. But what could be done about the huge tax charge? Dave's accountant suggested a solution – invest the cash surplus in stocks to attract tax write-offs.

Dave started to import and sell books by foreign authors. The sales of the small publishing division grew rapidly. Dave was delighted when he secured the agency for a Japanese mini-calculator in 1979. The new businesses drained the cash surplus but Dave had no problem borrowing from his bank. Net interest became negative but that did not matter because it reduced tax.

Then one day catastrophe struck: the two most experienced teachers told Dave they wanted to leave and form their own companies. They liked Dave but they no longer found the job challenging.

The stock of books began to be a burden and new competitors put pressure on calculator margins. Dave, now past 50, lost his appetite for the business and in 1982 he sold it for a sum equivalent to less than one year's profit in the boom years. A year later its new parent went bust.

LESSONS TO BE LEARNED   Dave **failed to develop the core knowhow** of his organisation which was sales training. SCL earned abnormal profits during a period when its teachers were giving their utmost but instead of allowing them time off to develop and increase their knowhow – **investing in knowhow** – Dave put the surplus into stocks of books and in so doing changed the business idea. Catastrophe occurred when SCL's main assets, the two teachers, became fed up and decided to set up in competition on their own.

If Dave had instead allowed the teachers to reduce their output of courses and had encouraged them to develop their knowhow, or if he had recruited new, young teachers who could have then been trained by the two veterans, the visible profits would have fallen but SCL might not have found itself overrun by competitors. Then, because the tax charge would not have been such a problem, he would probably not have been tempted to invest in unproductive financial capital.

High apparent profitability in knowhow companies is not necessarily a sign of success. While it seemed to Dave that everything was going well he was actu-

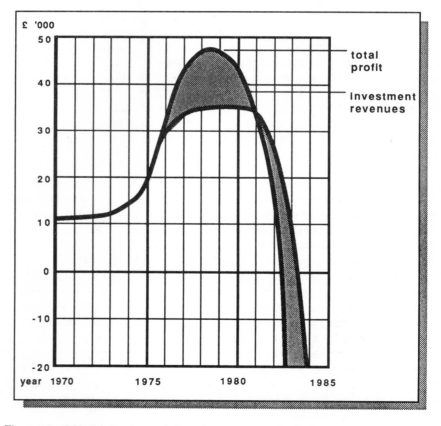

Figure 11   SCL failed to invest in knowhow, investing instead in other areas and thus changing the business idea.

ally digging SCL's grave. He had several of the attributes needed in a successful knowhow company manager but he allowed himself to be distracted by the misleading signals transmitted about his business by conventional, and thus inappropriate, accounting conventions.

• The invisible balance-sheet

Many knowhow companies seem to be very profitable indeed, typically generating returns on capital ranging from 20–40%, compared to average returns in traditional manufacturing of no more than 15%. However, these high percentage returns in knowhow companies are more apparent than real. They are the consequence of the failure of modern accountancy to accord a value to knowhow capital in the balance-sheet. While knowhow capital and changes in it remain hidden from sight on the 'invisible balance-sheet' it will be very difficult to know much about the real profitability of knowhow companies. All that can be said is that it will be extravagantly over-stated in the audited accounts.

This may be dangerous for investors. The problem with knowhow-rich companies is that their high profits are generated by **assets that are not only invisible but also highly mobile.** The other side of the coin is that even in industries with large, mature markets it is possible to find a few, small, very profitable companies which prosper because they are good innovators. But it should be remembered that an ability to innovate is a symptom of the existence of substantial, unrecorded knowhow assets.

Investors should always be mindful of how dependent knowhow companies are on a few key people. For a fuller discussion of knowhow company investment see Chapter Twelve (page 163).

• Surplus profits
Surplus profits are a real problem for knowhow companies for two reasons: the accounting systems give no indication about what constitutes a 'reasonable' profit level and tax systems throughout the Western world have yet to recognise that the companies of the information age are not typically builders of factories or producers of tangible goods.

Knowhow companies are lured into unproductive investments in property, stocks and finance mainly because the tax systems in most European countries provide **no allowances against the profits** of companies whose only assets are brains. A massive profit in a knowhow company one year might reflect a lack of investment or be a sign of an impending burn-out of personnel leading to equally massive losses the following year.

Anachronistic tax systems are among the most serious contemporary obstacles to the emergence of the information economy. The first country that sets out to adjust its tax system to the new reality is likely to benefit enormously. Such an exercise would involve the abandonment of a fiscal culture firmly rooted in the nineteenth century and based on the assumption that all companies are manufacturing companies.

The 15-year life of SCL illustrates the trap that lies in wait for knowhow companies which fail to **invest continuously in knowhow**. The profit boom SCL enjoyed after the start-up phase was the result of the experience Dave accumulated during his time at IBM and the heavy investment in knowhow during SCL's start-up phase. But the benefit only lasted a few years. The teachers performed magnificently during this period but their energies were soon exhausted. Instead of re-charging them with new challenges and new opportunities to develop their professional skills Dave continued to exploit his and their knowhow until his competitors caught up and began offering newer and better courses.

A major problem for the managers of knowhow companies is to work out **an 'optimum' profit level**, or rather its reciprocal – **an optimum investment level**. The 'experts' will be of no help in this endeavour while they and the tax man continue to regard expenditure on knowhow as a short-term, profit-reducing cost rather than a long-term, profit-increasing investment.

It is easy to forgive Dave his mistakes. He was not aware of the kind of company he had founded and was leading. It is much more difficult to understand the chief executives of knowhow companies who take pride in such utterly non-sensical figures as a 50% return on equity. A profitability of that order only indicates one thing: that financial capital is not crucial to success.

• Amstrad

The British consumer electronics company Amstrad has proved a very rewarding investment since its flotation on the stockmarket in 1980. Thanks to rapid profits growth and high apparent profitability, £100 invested in Amstrad at the time of the flotation was worth over £11,000 by May 1987. Amstrad had just launched a new range of IBM-compatible personal computers which were already selling like hot cakes.

Amstrad has never been a technological pioneer as have been less successful rivals like Sinclair Research and Acorn but it has been impressively innovative in other ways. Its trick has been to extract from pioneering products the key design and engineering features, to dispense with those components and features that are superfluous and to re-package the product and then produce it in ways and places (like South Korea) that permit aggressive pricing.

As founder Alan Sugar put it: 'We look at the competition, take it to bits and see if we can engineer something similar, better and cheaper. We identify the facilities that aren't useful and we ditch them to reduce costs.'

The formula has been remarkably successful. Aided by an equally remarkable quick-footedness which permits prompt exits from markets beginning to go sour, it has enabled Amstrad to grow strongly through difficult periods for the industry; so much so that in 1985 it bought out the loss-making Sinclair computer business for a paltry £5m.

The weakness of Amstrad is revealed by its name. It stands for Alan Michael Sugar TRADing and that is more or less what it is. Alan Sugar himself dominates the invisible balance-sheet. His end-1986 shareholding, amounting to 43% of the equity, was worth a cool £525m. That may even under-state his value to the company. If he is killed or incapacitated or if, for some reason or another, he loses his extraordinary 'feel' for the consumer electronics market, Amstrad will be in trouble.

'Key man' life insurance, often demanded by venture capitalists when investing in small, entrepreneurially-run companies, would offer investors little compensation for the loss of an asset as valuable as Alan Sugar's knowhow.

• Key indicators for knowhow management

The managers of a small knowhow company are generally well aware of how the day-to-day business is going. They do not need much written information. The bigger knowhow companies need more indirect ways to steer and control. The industrial companies have developed sophisticated steering systems using middle management and key financial indicators. Indicators such as profit margin, return on investment, return on equity and cash-flow are important in the management reporting of every large industrial company.

Financial analysts and investors use the same key indicators as company management but on a more superficial level.

The management of the big knowhow company and its investors need the financial key indicators too but above all they need **indicators which show the knowhow risk and track changes in the knowhow capital**.

We shall not attempt to provide a detailed accounting system for knowhow companies in this book. This is a task for the experts. We shall merely point to a few key indicators which we believe are essential to the proper monitoring of a knowhow business.

The management need to monitor:

1. The knowhow capital; its size, growth and quality.
2. The return on knowhow capital.
3. Efficiency and productivity.
4. Stability (knowhow risk).

• Knowhow capital

A rough definition of knowhow capital is **the total number of man years of professional experience**. This increases automatically each year. Of course not all professionals are as valuable as each other and neither is it the case that knowhow capital really increases by a year per head each year. However, as a general indicator, the man years count is quite sufficient. It gives a much more accurate picture of competitiveness than a simple professional head count.

The **quality of the knowhow** is also important and can be measured as **average knowhow capital per professional**. This is an indication of how skilled and experienced the professionals are. A better indication can be derived from regular, **systematic client research** (ideally conducted annually). The external analyst seldom sees these reports and must rely on more indirect indicators.

Apart from the conventional investment in hardware and machinery, the 'soft' **investments in knowhow** must be controlled. The first priority is to maintain the knowhow capital. Other investments in R&D must also be monitored. Total costs for R&D and education should be reported in absolute numbers as well as in percentage of turnover terms.

The R&D budget is a very important measure for knowhow companies. Though seldom formalised it is quite common these days to see R&D budgets stated explicitly in the annual accounts of small companies. R&D needs a separate budget because it gives management some control over the knowhow growth of the company.

It is not difficult to persuade a professional to increase his own knowhow, but it can sometimes be difficult to ensure that this kind of investment is always in the company's, as opposed to the professional's, best interests.

The process of drawing up the budget is more important than the budget itself. The management must win acceptance from the professionals that R&D is to be undertaken according to the plan. The budget process itself often helps to achieve this acceptance.

The education budget should cover costs associated with time spent inside the company by senior professionals **transferring their knowhow** to juniors and costs associated with external courses and travel. Again, it is the budget process itself which does most to concentrate the collective mind on the most appropriate areas for education.

Because the markets of most knowhow companies are rather esoteric and difficult to quantify, knowhow companies are seldom aware of their **market shares**. But this is very important information for assessing the company's competitive position so although the relevant data are hard to find they should at least be sought. Surprisingly good information can be found in databases, catalogues etc.

Average age is an important variable. It should be calculated each year and trends should be plotted. A rapidly growing average age is good because it shows knowhow capital is increasing but, as we have already seen, there is a danger of a 'spare tyre' developing which may need to be addressed by a change in the recruitment policy.

It is important to recognise when calculating the knowhow capital represented by the professionals in particular that there are **two kinds of experience**: general professional experience and company-specific experience. The significance of the latter is often under-estimated. Knowhow managers tend to assume that professional experience is all that matters.

Take the example of a knowhow company which recruits from another firm a professional with 11 years' experience following the departure of someone who has been with the company for all of the 10 years of his professional working life. The managers will tend to assume they have gained an extra man or woman year of knowhow.

But what has really happened, of course, is that general professional experience has increased by one man year while company-specific experience has fallen by ten man years.

Attributing a relatively high weight to company-specific experience is one way of allowing for some of the problems that can be encountered when recruiting experienced professionals who are set in ways that may not be readily accommodated by their new company.

- **Return on knowhow capital**
  A more realistic measure of a knowhow company's performance than return on equity is **profit as a percentage of revenues**. This does not change much as long as the company adheres to its business idea. A reasonable target might be 10–15% of revenues.

  Profitability ratios of more than 20% never last long. They fall because the company invests more in its invisible balance-sheet, thereby increasing costs or because, like SCL, it has invested too little in the past.

  Added value is a more reliable indicator of current capacity and future potential than profit. The yield of the knowhow capital is measured as the **total added value** (see below for a definition of added value) **divided by the total knowhow capital**. This is a key indicator and is equivalent to the conventional return on assets measure of industrial companies. Since knowhow capital increases each year the yield will drop unless the company can add more value at the same rate.

- **Efficiency and productivity**
  ADDED VALUE   Added value generated by a knowhow company is the most important measure of its productivity. There are many ways to calculate added value. The most common is **profit before net interest + salaries + social security costs + depreciation**.

  Since ordinary profit measures are inappropriate for knowhow companies, added value is the better yardstick for comparing knowhow companies in various industries. Using added value per employee, for example, we can compare the profitability of a law firm with that of an advertising agency.

  It is not humanly possible for people to produce extreme added value indefinitely, especially if they work in a team. The added value produced by teams tends to even out over time. This makes added value per employee an excellent comparative measure. Since salaries, which are a component of added value, are the most important costs in knowhow companies the added value per employee measure has the additional advantage of indicating whether an organisation is draining the profits through higher salaries.

  THE PROFIT PER CLIENT   Since many knowhow companies use time accounting it is relatively easy to calculate the profit per client or per customer. This is important information when it comes to deciding where to put the sales effort.

  ADMINISTRATIVE COSTS AS A PERCENTAGE OF REVENUE   Administrative support costs – the costs of administrative personnel, office space, telephones etc – as a percentage of revenue, show whether the cost burden of administration is rising or falling relative to revenue earning departments.

THE PRODUCTIVITY INDEX   The difficulty with measuring the productivity of a knowhow organisation lies in the equivocal nature of volume. Turnover in knowhow companies is not straightforward; it can seldom be stated with any certainty. There are ways round this problem however, if one is really determined to find out about a company's efficiency.

One way is to construct an index. The interesting object of measurement is not the absolute level of efficiency but rather the trend. **Is the organisation becoming more or less efficient**? To establish an index one begins by calculating the ratio between last year's sales and this year's. Let us suppose one gets the figure 110, indicating a growth of 10%.

Then one calculates the figure for the number of employees. If this is 110 too and there have been no price increases the productivity index for year 2 is: $110/110 = 1$ – no change has occurred in productivity. If, however, the price of services has been increased by an average of 4% it reduces the sales index which, in this example, would be 106. The productivity index for year 2 will thus be $106/110 = 0.96$ – productivity has decreased by roughly 4%. This indexing system can also be based on added value per employee and on many other variables.

One interesting variant of the productivity index is the use of knowhow capital instead of the number of employees. This involves calculating the total number of man and woman years of experience in all four personnel categories and then attributing weights to the different categories and perhaps also to each individual.

The resulting figure will change each year as a result of the passage of an extra year and of arrivals and departures.

- **Stability – the knowhow risk**
  Personnel turnover, the number of people who leave as a percentage of total employees, is an important indicator of knowhow risk. A high figure indicates dissatisfaction; a low turnover in a non-growth company suggests a lack of dynamism. The indicator may vary over time and between markets. It is thus important to track it so that trends can be analysed.

  Average age is also important. A high average suggests high stability (low risk) and low dynamism (low growth).

  Another important indicator of stability is the **age and experience mix** – the number of young and new employees in relation to the veterans. A high proportion of young and inexperienced professionals indicates relative instability. The indicator can be calculated as: number of veterans (over five years of employment) as a proportion of total professionals or number of recently employed (less than two years) in relation to total professionals.

SALARIES AS A PERCENTAGE OF ADDED VALUE   Salaries are by far **the largest part of the added value** in industry. The same usually applies in knowhow companies but there can be huge differences. In some knowhow companies the salary share is only a small fraction of the added value because each employee handles large amounts of capital. The salary share is a good indication of how sensitive the company is to surprises like the sudden breakaway of a group of employees to set up their own company.

The salary share is also **an important argument in pay negotiations.** If the employees are to have higher salaries if they produce more added value they must be prepared to accept lower salaries if they produce less added value.

SUMMARY

- **In measuring the development of knowhow capital** it is better to have **output-related information** than **input-related information.**
- There are no effective **knowhow accounting systems;** traditional yardsticks can give dangerously misleading signals.
- Volume growth is **no guarantee of long-term success** and **profitability may also be misleading.**
- The key is the **maintenance and expansion of the knowhow capital.**
- It is important to invest in the **core knowhow.**
- The main assets are **invisible** and **mobile;** high profits may thus be illusory.
- Present tax systems do not benefit the knowhow company.
- There is an **optimum profit level** and an **optimum investment level.**
- There are four key indicators for knowhow companies: **knowhow capital, return on knowhow capital, efficiency** and **stability.**
- **Added value and personnel** ratios are central to knowhow accounting.

6

• Structuring Knowhow

As we saw in Chapter Two the real power in a professional organisation lies not with the formal owners – the holders of the majority of the equity – but with those who have the knowhow. It is the **level of proficiency** which **is the measure of power,** not the extent of formal ownership.

This shift of power away from those who have and towards those who do challenges many of the presumptions and prejudices embedded in company law. Western legal systems are the products of an evolutionary process. One of the axioms that have guided the general direction of this development has been the **scarcity of finance** which has prevailed throughout the industrial age. In conditions of financial scarcity it was natural that corporate law should have learned to confer power on the owners of financial capital. Hence the modern obsession with the 'inalienable' property rights of shareholders and, more specifically, the deep distaste in some capital markets, particularly on the part of the big institutional investors, for restricted voting rights on certain classes of shares.

It is interesting to note the debate that has developed in Britain over the past couple of years about contested takeover bids. It has been argued that fund managers have become obsessed with short-term performance and are thus too willing to accept takeover offers, especially those with cash alternatives. This discourages managers who value their continued independence from taking the long-term view and so causes them to invest too little. Since this is obviously bad for the economy it has been suggested that some kind of protection from predators – such as restricted voting rights on shares held by outsiders – should be made available to companies which are being managed well.

This suggests that just as institutional investors expected to have victory in their grasp in their long fight against restricted voting rights, it may be snatched away from them. The sanctity of property rights, based on the assumption that financial capital is in short supply, is being challenged by those who feel **managerial knowhow has too little power.**

Legal structure

Financial capital is no longer scarce. On the contrary, it is very plentiful compared to the more precious resources of proficiency and knowhow. The knowhow company is thus confronted with a dilemma; anachronistic legal systems make it hard to devise **a corporate structure that takes into account the realities of the professional organisation**. A major reform of company law, reflecting the change in the relative scarcities of capital and ability, is needed.

In the meantime the legal structure of a professional organisation should, at the very least, incorporate the following features:

- IT MUST BE FLEXIBLE AND DYNAMIC.   It must be possible to change the structure from time to time, say every five years, without major upheavals.
- EMPLOYEES MUST BE OWNERS.   Some employee ownership is essential. If the employees are able enough – if their knowhow is sufficiently crucial to the company's success – they should be in a position to acquire a majority of the equity.
- TAKE ACCOUNT OF THE LIFE-CYCLE.   A person's relative propensity to consume or save varies according to his age and his attitude to ownership. The legal structure should reflect and accommodate the professional life-cycle.

• Ownership – power or investment?

The tax systems of most Western countries treat salaries and capital gains very differently. Generally speaking capital gains are taxed at a significantly lower rate than income.

This has led many knowhow companies to issue stock options. The tax differentials make it more profitable to distribute added value in this way rather than in salaries. The trend is also reflected in the rapid growth of management buy-outs in recent years, particularly the special case of the 'going private' buy-out where managers buy their publicly quoted company from its shareholders with the help of bank loans.

The peculiarities of the tax system also help to explain the upheavals in many knowhow areas, as professionals find it more profitable to work freelance in companies of their own rather than as normal employees. Setting up one's own company remains one of the very few legal ways of making a fortune through one's own efforts.

Ownership in knowhow companies should be seen as an attribute of power as well as the result of an investment act. But though the knowhow company should seek legal structures which entice potential employees in with the prospect of ownership, this should not be the only carrot. The modern appetite for employee-ownership often generates expectations of swift and substantial rewards which are quite unrealistic. Talented professionals cannot be expected to work for a pittance in return for the promise of too distant a reward.

And a knowhow company's founders must also learn to accept **the inevitability of dilution**. What has been described as the 'equity greedometer' – the very natural desire of founders to preserve if not to increase their equity stakes – will, if indulged too generously, make it harder to exploit the equity carrot in recruitment. New employees should not be prevented by the greedometer from becoming significant shareholders. In successful knowhow companies the net worth, the equity in the company, grows rapidly. It becomes increasingly expensive for new entrants to become equity partners. The older owners must therefore be prepared to sell their shares on very favourable terms if they wish to attract new partners. Similarly, voting power should be attached to the fact of partnership, not to the size of the individual's shareholding.

- **Differentiating power from investment**
One way to reduce the disruptive forces created by these kinds of tensions is to divide ownership into its two component parts:

  - ownership as an instrument of power
  - ownership as an investment

By a combination of shareholders' agreements and a customised corporate structure it is usually possible to give **new partners the same power as the more senior professionals** without requiring them to put up an equal amount of money.

However, clearly such generosity to new entrants can be taken too far. There is a real sense in which **profits** retained from previous years **belong to those who actually generated them**. One might regard them as salary 'discounts' or loans extended to the company by the founders during the difficult early years which should be repaid when the company becomes stronger. The increase in the value of founders' equity is a good way of repaying such debts.

The main point is that the knowhow company can and should construct 'packages' of ownership and remuneration which protect the interests of the older partners while giving new partners influence and the promise of capital growth.

But power in the professional organisation must not depend on what share one happens to own of retained profits and the equity. Such a hierarchy preserves a structure which might have been appropriate once upon a time but which will, if left unchanged, pose a serious threat to the company's long-term survival. A knowhow company that apportions influence according to possession of financial capital rather than possession of knowhow will have problems sooner or later. This applies just as much to internal as external ownership.

- ## Problems of employee ownership
Apart from the companies with a legal framework of employee ownership such as the unlimited liability partnership arrangements still required of UK law and

chartered accountancy firms (of which more later), most systems of ownership share some of the following characteristics:

- **Difficulties for new partners.** These arise when the capital grows. It becomes increasingly hard for new partners to enter the ownership group. Each new partner must, perforce, receive a smaller proportion of the larger cake which means that, whether they like it or not, the original owners remain the dominant force for a long time. This restricts the company's ability to exploit ownership to recruit and keep good people. Unless the original owners wish to encourage spin-outs (departures of groups of professionals to set up their own companies), which they may do as part of a federal development strategy, they should err on the side of generosity when it comes to giving equity to new partners.

- **Should everyone be a partner?** It is natural in start-up companies for everyone to be a shareholder, irrespective of his or her contribution. If the company grows so fast that all become millionaires then no-one begrudges the good fortune of the book-keeper or switchboard operator.

If – on the other hand – success is achieved more gradually and by dint of much greater effort, frictions may develop between the most skilled and industrious professionals and those who do not contribute as much. It is often hard not to bring everyone in generously at the start but the founders should be aware of the problems a wide mix of shareholders can create and should try to anticipate them.

- **No system will last more than five years.** The knowhow company is so dependent on its people that the founders should be prepared, at short notice, to revise and adapt agreements and profit-sharing arrangements to new circumstances, both internal and external.

- **A trial period is a must.** At the start of a company's life the period can be short, perhaps just one year. Later the period should be increased to three or even five years. The partner/shareholder is such a crucial player and carries so much responsibility that it is inappropriate to impose such demands on a new recruit. It takes a long time to integrate an individual with an organisation.

Such trial periods may seem irksome to ambitious new recruits who may decide they cannot afford to wait. This is a price that will have to be paid. In the long-run it is better to lose young talent than to adopt such liberal partnership admission procedures that the owning group becomes filled with people the founders hardly know and so cannot trust.

- **The need for an 'exit route'.** Share ownership is worthless if the shares cannot be sold. Sooner or later well-spread share ownership will provoke demands for a listing on the stock exchange or for a total sell-out to provide an 'exit route'. When the capital grows the internal market becomes less effective. No agreements or price clauses are valid when partners know they are sitting on millions they cannot realise. This must be understood from the outset and planned for accordingly.

Profit-sharing is an increasingly common way of remunerating key people. It has many of the advantages of share-owning without some of the disadvantages referred to above. Broad profit-sharing systems, incorporating practically everybody, are common among professional organisations.

Knowhow companies often try to tie their professionals in with contracts incorporating secrecy clauses and minimum employment periods.

But shares, high salaries and option schemes apart the all-important way to preserve knowhow in the professional organisation is to create an environment that encourages, motivates and challenges the professionals. At the end of the day high salaries and generous option schemes are no substitute for a creative and stimulating environment.

• The idea of partnership

The very different patterns of ownership that have evolved in the professions, notably law and accountancy, represent an interesting alternative to the limited liability joint stock company.

Law-makers have taken the view over the years that, generally speaking, professionals have to be responsible people. Their professional bodies are obliged to maintain high standards of training and to apply rigid codes of ethics, breaches of which can lead to the ejection of sinners from membership of the profession. To concentrate the minds of professionals on these requirements the law has deemed it prudent to withdraw the protection of limited liability. Every partner in a law firm is responsible to the limit of his own resources for his firm's actions.

Since it would be very unfair for past partners, who have resigned or retired, to be held liable for the mistakes of the existing partnership, lawyers and accountants have evolved corporate structures in which ownership is vested in the partnership as a collective rather than in the individual partners.

In these circumstances individual partners own a share of net revenues rather than a share of net worth and it is important to note that their ownership of these revenues is conditional on their membership of the partnership. In contrast to the legal position of shareholders in limited liability joint stock companies, the property rights of individuals are not inalienable in many professional firms.

An interesting example of how the legal environment guides the evolution of corporate structures is the effect on professional attitudes to unlimited liability of the huge damages the American courts in particular have been awarding in professional negligence and malpractice suits.

Many managing partners of British law and accountancy firms have been so horrified by the huge premiums being demanded by underwriters for professional liability insurance that they have begun actively to seek ways of incorporating themselves so that they can acquire the protection of limited liability.

• Circulating equity

The essence of partnership is the idea of circulating equity. Instead of defining the equity in, or ownership of, a company as a property in its own right that attaches to marketable securities such as ordinary shares, ownership becomes a conditional quality linked inextricably to the membership of a particular group. Those who leave the group lose the status of owner and those who join acquire it.

Circulating equity is ideal for knowhow companies. It goes a long way towards solving the problem of how to balance the ownership interests of veterans and recruits and it does so in a routine way which brooks no argument.

It is not surprising that some knowhow company managers have been tinkering with the joint stock, limited liability arrangement in attempts to combine its advantages with some of the more desirable features of partnership.

• Two case studies

• Helix

Helix Software Consultants (HSC) is a London-based computer consultancy specialising in the areas of finance and expert systems (the precursors of artificial intelligence). Its main shareholders are its directors, although the Industrial and Commercial Finance Corporation, part of Investors in Industry (owned by Britain's main clearing banks), has a minority stake.

Managing director John Berkin and his colleagues have been trying to develop what they call a 'commercial partnership' in which all directors are treated as partners.

HSC incorporates a number of subsidiary companies the managing directors of which are, by right, directors of HSC. All HSC directors are obliged to be shareholders, though this is facilitated financially by the holding company.

Similarly, the directors of each subsidiary have to be shareholders in that subsidiary. When they become managing directors they exchange these shareholdings for shareholdings in HSC. Parts of the former are then re-circulated to become available for the new directors of the subsidiaries. The new directors will normally come from the ranks of the 'associate directors', equivalent to the partner-candidate associates in law and accountancy firms.

Ownership is thus equivalent to partnership but there is no one-to-one correspondence between the level of ownership and the level of influence. Even with this sort of arrangement growth will tend to widen the gap between the shareholdings of the early and recent entrants. However, at HSC it will not widen the power gap because every partner/director, whether of the holding company or of a subsidiary, will have the same voting power as his or her fellow partners/directors.

HSC wants to become an organisation with great breadth but little depth. It believes the ownership structure it is developing should enable it to accumulate a large number of competent people and is convinced the more equal these people are the stronger the organisation will be.

- **Ardos**

  The customers of the Swedish management consultants Ardos AB perceive a medium-sized firm offering a fairly conventional product line, including specialisations in productivity, information technology and education. There is a distinctive philosophy called 'know-why' management which puts more emphasis on education than is common but there is nothing particularly unusual about the apparent 'modus operandi'.

  This impression is deceptive. In reality Ardos AB is an illusion. It has substance as a marketing vehicle and as a brand name, but the consultancy work is done by the members of the Ardos federation, acting as independent firms.

  Each member contributes 5% of its revenues to Ardos and when Ardos, acting as a marketing vehicle, finds business for a member it takes a 2% finder's fee. The money is not entirely lost because Ardos is owned by its member firms.

  The federation grows by a process resembling cell division. A new recruit joins one of the member firms on a salary enriched with a portion of that firm's equity and works as a junior consultant for a two-year probationary period.

  If the recruits turn out well and have an entrepreneurial turn of mind they can then spin out and become full federation members by swapping their stake in the member company for a stake in Ardos.

  The system provides some of the benefits of a large firm while avoiding many of the endemic tensions that make consultancy so prone to spin-out.

  The Ardos model is effectively a network of networks without a core. The absence of a core is a great advantage because it is the conflict between the core and the external network of each consultant – his or her intimacy with customers and other commercially significant contacts – that makes spinning out so attractive and so easy.

  The Ardos federation can grow without having to devote the management resources needed to create and maintain a strong culture. There is an Ardos spirit or philosophy but it is much more of a common, professional approach than a means of keeping the federation together.

- **Lessons to be learned**

  The examples of Helix and Ardos show that even within the limits of the limited liability joint stock company structure there is a significant and largely untapped **potential for corporate customising** to make the legal form of the organisation suit the needs of the knowhow company.

  It is hard to over-estimate the importance of a knowhow company's accounting and legal structures. They give **shape and substance to organisations** that are peculiarly lacking in such qualities and, through the influence they exert on recruitment, profit-sharing and the distribution of power, they have a profound effect on the pattern of the company's development. The knowhow companies of to-day tend to neglect long-term structures, believing such things to be trivial compared to the need to expand the business. In so doing they often set in motion tension-generating mechanisms that could tear the organisation apart a few years later.

SUMMARY

- In a professional organisation it is **the level of proficiency which is the measure of power,** not the ownership of equity.
- Corporate structures must be devised which are **flexible and dynamic, employees must be owners** and founder members must acknowledge **the inevitability of dilution.**
- It is useful to **differentiate power from investment** so that new partners have **the same power as the more senior professionals.**
- The **idea of partnership** has much to commend it; it incorporates the concept of **circulating equity** which fits with the knowhow company's need to spread ownership.
- The legal and accounting systems give **shape and substance** to knowhow companies.

7

• Leadership

Leaders of professional organisations do not fit the stereotype of 'the manager'. They may not be prolific decision-takers and their diaries are unlikely to be bursting with appointments. They may not even have their own offices but may prefer to sit instead with their fellow professionals.

• The leader as patriarch

During the early stages of industrial evolution, despotic owners of the local iron-works would declare when distributing gifts at Christmas time that 'our most important assets are our loyal and skilled employees'.

Though ritual acknowledgements of the 'efforts and loyalty' of the workforce are still to be found in the modern chairman's annual statement, the owners have been largely replaced by 'scientific' managers, mass-produced by the business schools, whose first sight of the factory is when they are appointed to run it. To them the patriarchal style is an anachronism, wholly inappropriate in the modern age.

But the managers of knowhow companies can learn a thing or two from the old ironworks proprietors.

They were **intimately involved in the life of the local community**. They presided at the retirement ceremonies of long-serving employees, they made speeches at works weddings and awarded medals for distinguished service. Their ideas and attitudes reflected their times. These are largely unacceptable to-day but we can still learn from their style.

It was the product of life-long companionship and involvement with everyone in the village. The owners knew their workers by name as their fathers and grandfathers had done before them. To ensure the availability of apprentices they supported large families and provided medical care to maintain the health of the workforce. They were anxious to discourage the most competent workers from joining competitors. They gave land to some specialists, needed only part of the year, to encourage them to stay (an early version of the modern 'golden hand-cuffs'). Another, less enlightened way of keeping the best workers was to encourage them to become indebted to the company store.

The fame of the most skilled smiths spread far and wide. It was not unusual for an ironworks owner to pay off the debts of a skilled smith to induce him to move – an early version of the modern 'golden hello' or of the transfer fee system in professional football.

• The leader as creator of the environment

Leaders are low-key players with **few overt symbols of power**; no flowers or secretaries and probably only one phone. They will have the same equipment as the other professionals although perhaps, because they have been there the longest, they may have claimed a desk near a window. To a visitor the leader may not be immediately apparent.

When pointed out he or she may be engaged in earnest conversation or be working on apparently trivial tasks such as helping the office boy look after a visitor. She could be praising one of the professionals for a good piece of work, briefing herself about the illness of a colleague's husband or laughing at a story one of the older employees is telling for the fifth time.

He or she will spend a large part of the day with new recruits, showing them around, explaining practical details and introducing them to everybody. The leader may be very interested in the physical characteristics of the office; how people are grouped together, who is sitting with whom and where groups are situated in relation to each other. If the leader is a man he may show an unmasculine interest in colours.

If all this suggests a weak person the impression is mistaken. This particular leader has a very clear, goal-oriented day. He creates environments. In this case he is creating an internal environment. Leadership in professional organisations has a great deal to do with creating environments, establishing frame-works, delineating boundaries, goading the professionals to ever greater efforts and **transferring culture and knowhow to new employees**.

• The leader as tutor

The leader of the professional organisation also tries to stretch people by exposing them to challenging opportunities. For example, the leader:

- always takes someone with him to visit a client
- allows someone else to present to the client
- tests various combinations of professionals in project teams
- gives new professionals their own projects
- sends an old professional on a trip to the US
- supports a business project initiated by the least skilled of the professionals
- supports co-operation with another company, although the profits seem a long way off

- assigns young, able professionals to tough negotiations
- puts the new, charming male graduate in the same room as the company's lonely female professional
- re-shuffles an effective top management team

Able people wish to control their own development, exploit their own ideas, take their own decisions and be confronted by challenges. Leadership in professional organisations is thus not so much a matter of decision-taking but more of creating frameworks, structures, cultures and environments.

The leader does not lead the work in the traditional way by telling others what to do but **creates opportunities for employees** to find their own way. The professional organisation is full of highly educated and creative people who wish for nothing more than a chance to prove themselves. The leader's task is to give them the opportunity to demonstrate their ability to colleagues and outsiders.

It takes a very human leader, with integrity and a high level of knowhow, to be accepted in a professional organisation.

And it is equally important for managerial and professional activities to be combined in some way, whether in one person or in two or more, despite the often conflicting nature of the two roles.

• The leader as the guarantor of continuity

Professionals are usually bursting with ideas and creativity and often act spontaneously. They always seem to be one step ahead of the organisation and on the point of leaving. They are constantly seeking new knowhow, new experiences and new contacts. Wilfulness in the skilled professional is natural and must not be suppressed, otherwise creativity will suffer.

Leaders must try to **complement and channel the intellectual energy** of the professionals. They are responsible for inspiring creativity and for maintaining continuity. They must steer a course between the shoals of ideology and the whirlpools of unbridled enthusiasms, always keeping in their minds and in the minds of others **a clear sense of direction**.

Professionals are always dreaming up impractical business ideas. The leader must moderate them gently, without disillusioning the dreamer. A sure way of killing wild ideas is to ask the dreamers to implement them. It will take them a couple of days to lose interest – or dream up others.

• The leader as a symbol of security

Professional organisations lack visible security symbols like large buildings, factories and tangible products. The leader must therefore try to create a substitute for the productive process by undertaking other tasks which yield security, like taking care of personal problems and uncongenial clients, filling in gaps or ensuring that the services work when professionals pay their rare visits to the office.

This is a common role for good leaders in all organisations. It is crucial in the professional organisation.

Professionals can be unhappy souls, often working alone and away from the office on long-term assignments. **They need a fixed point of reference**. The leader must provide it because no-one else can. A trivial problem, like someone 'tidying up' a professional's desk when she's away, can trigger an alarming explosion of frustrated anger on her return.

• The leader as coach

He is standing on the touch-line watching the game with great intensity. Were it not for his highly emotional state he might be mistaken for an ordinary enthusiast or supporter.

Occasionally he shouts to the players or curses under his breath when the game goes the wrong way. At half-time he encourages, comforts and cajoles the team, helps them with refreshments or finds a doctor for an injured player.

He is the coach – one of the most popular role models in modern management literature. The coach is not an active player which is why the job can often be frustrating. When the match has begun there is very little the coach can do except support the players.

His most important tasks are undertaken off the field. He is the chief strategist, the recruitment officer and the selector – the one who decides who is to play and who is to watch with him on the touch-line. The Swedish soccer coach, Laban Arnesson, **ranks recruitment as the single most important task**. He must find not only technically proficient players but also individuals who fit into the team. The coach is always an ex-player but seldom an ex-star. He needs wisdom and the capacity to tolerate a high level of stress.

The present vogue for the coach as a managerial role model reflects the increasing number of knowhow organisations. The world of sport contains many clues for modern business management. Some of the key characteristics of the leader as coach are sympathy, empathy and a supportive rather than a despotic way with people.

The coach formulates strategy, defines the arena for the game and selects the players but takes no active part in the actual delivery of the service.

• The leader as manager

As companies grow, organically and by acquisition, the role of the leader begins to focus more on the strategic issues such as acquisitions, major diversifications and matters to do with the balance of the company in its marketplace and knowhow area. But success during this phase remains very dependent on the qualities we have considered above. The strategic role is an addition to, rather than a replacement of, the role models we have already discussed.

- **The case of Oxford Instruments**

Oxford Instruments is one of Britain's most conspicuously successful professional organisations. However, for the best part of a decade after its formation by Martin Wood in 1959 it had all the fragility of a young, under-managed knowhow company.

During its development into a quoted technology company with a market value of £210m by the spring of 1987 it underwent three generations of leadership.

Like many technology-driven companies Oxford Instruments (OI) is a spin-out from a university, in this case Oxford University's Clarendon laboratory. Martin Wood was working at the Clarendon as an engineer, alongside the eminent physicist Rex Richards (now Sir Rex and one of OI's non-executive directors). Richards became very interested in the use of high powered magnets in spectroscopy.

Wood, in response to ever increasing demands from Richards for more powerful magnetic fields, began to make magnets exploiting the phenomenon of 'superconductivity' (the disappearance of the electrical resistance of some materials at very low temperatures) identified by the Dutch physicist Heike Kamerlingh-Onnes in 1908.

Wood became adept at applying three basic technologies: high-field magnetism, the high-vacuum technology needed to achieve ultra-low temperatures and cryogenics (the technology of low temperatures). He established a world lead in the design and manufacture of superconducting magnets. Soon scientists from all over the world were beating a path to the Clarendon's door.

Wood formed Oxford Instruments to satisfy the demand. The company prospered but by 1969 Wood felt it was getting too large for him to manage on his own and that if it was to survive it would have to become less dependent on magnets.

He hired Barrie Marson from a larger company, Kent Instruments, to assume some of the managerial load and to implement a change in the business idea. Marson's brief was to acquire and develop new products and businesses which he did very successfully. Several of the new businesses failed to match the criteria Marson had established and were sold off, usually to their managements. Oxford Medical Systems and Oxford Analytical Instruments survive as the two main results of his diversification programme. Marson became chief executive and Wood was appointed non-executive chairman.

In the late 1970s a dramatic change occurred in OI's marketplace with the successful application of a phenomenon known as Nuclear Magnetic Resonance to medical diagnostics. It was a major improvement on the hitherto dominant technology of X-ray scanning. The technique became known as Magnetic Resonance Imaging. It was immediately apparent to the manufacturers of MRI machines that OI was the only company in the world with the design, development and manufacturing knowhow needed to supply superconducting MRI scanning magnets in the volume the market required.

OI made a quantum jump in size. As MRI scanners swept all before them in medical diagnostics profits soared from less than £1.3m before tax in 1981 to £20m for the year to March 1987. Others, including some of its main customers, tried to compete in magnet making but OI maintained its technological and cost leads and in 1987 still claimed over 80% of the world market for superconducting MRI magnets.

The company's academic culture, the exploitation of which was a feature of the Wood/Marson managerial knowhow, persisted during most of the Marson era while the new businesses were developed. The explosion in the MRI market and the flotation of OI on the stockmarket in October 1981 required a change of emphasis.

In 1983 a new managerial era was heralded by the arrival of Dr Peter Williams, formerly deputy managing director of VG Instruments. Within a year he was appointed group managing director and in August 1985 he became chief executive. Marson stepped down to become non-executive chairman in place of Martin Wood, the founder.

Williams set about the task of redefining the company's culture. He introduced a more coherent management structure and hired a new finance director. He also managed to re-focus the group's objectives onto profit without losing key scientific professionals. In 1986 Williams was declared *Guardian* Young Businessman of the Year.

A potentially much larger market than MRI magnets awaits OI in the form of compact, low-cost synchrotrons for use in research and, more importantly, in the manufacture of the next generation of Very Large Scale Integration (VLSI) microchips. Most experts believe a technique known as X-ray lithography will be a key element in the production of VLSI chips. OI has developed a 'mini-synchrotron' which looks set to become much the cheapest X-ray source available.

Looking further ahead it is not wholly inconceivable that within a decade or so OI will be making magnets for awesome weapons such as the 'rail gun' or the 'free electron laser' that scientists are investigating as possible ballistic missile killers in America's 'Star Wars' programme.

- **Lessons to be learned**
The story of Oxford Instruments is very much the story of the wisdom of Martin Wood. He was the typical entrepreneur of the 'I didn't mean to go into business' variety. What marked him out was **an awareness of his limitations**. The appointment of Marson was wise but wiser still was Wood's readiness to give Marson a free hand. **Having found the right man he trusted him** and in so doing established a precedent Marson was obliged to follow when it was his turn to hand over the reins.

OI was conceived and born within Oxford University. Its culture for most of its life has been uncompromisingly academic. The technology, OI's core knowhow, was everything. The business idea was, if not an afterthought, at least no more than a context for the development of the core knowhow.

Though the culture has changed, OI's core knowhow remains fundamental to its business idea. This has not been fully understood by many City analysts who question OI's long-term growth prospects on the grounds that it is a one-product company which will run into serious problems when the market for MRI scanners starts to decline.

OI's core knowhow is NOT the design and manufacture of MRI magnets but rather the mastery of the product and process technologies associated with high-field magnetism, high-vacuum technology and cryogenics. The main application of this knowhow at present just happens to be MRI magnets. To-morrow it may be synchrotrons or free electron lasers.

• The leader as knowhow tycoon

Occasionally knowhow organisations break out of their natural environment and begin to assume some of the characteristics of traditional companies. Encouraged by the contemporary 'internationalisation' of business, their leaders embark on acquisition-led development strategies which force them to become more and more remote from the day-to-day professional operations. In this role they are knowhow tycoons, indistinguishable from the tycoons of traditional industries.

• The case of Saatchi & Saatchi

'From a rented office in Soho to World Number One in under 16 years' was how one commentator described the achievement of the brothers Maurice and Charles Saatchi after Saatchi & Saatchi bought US agency Ted Bates in May 1986.

The $450m Bates deal, subsequently billed as the group's last major purchase in the advertising field, was the culmination of a 10-year buying spree involving nigh on 30 acquisitions. In recent years many of the deals have not been in advertising at all but in related business services such as public relations, management consultancy, marketing and market research.

There is no doubt the Saatchi brothers have revolutionised the advertising industry, or perhaps a better way of putting it might be that they have **industrialised** the advertising profession, over the past one-and-a-half decades.

Their first significant achievement was to overcome the City's perception of advertising firms as 'arty' companies, all glitter and no substance. It was a necessary task if, following the flotation of Saatchi & Saatchi in 1976, they were to have any chance of successfully pursuing their chosen, acquisition-led development strategy. The City had its reservations – 'my biggest problem was overcoming the fact they had no underlying assets' was how one fund manager put it – but in the end it was persuaded. Thanks almost entirely to the Saatchis the City and Wall Street have come to see advertising as an industry with prodigious growth potential, that can be levered further by acquisitions, and is thus an extremely promising area for investment.

The other great achievement was to evolve during the same period the management knowhow needed to contain the powerful centrifugal forces endemic in the profession. There were no blue-prints. The Saatchis were boldly going where no agency had gone before. They had to invent group management skills that preserved the internal spirit of creativity on which successful advertising depends and at the same time deliver to their new-found friends in the City the financial results – in terms of growth, profitability, earnings per share and dividends – needed to sustain the share price.

It was a masterly sleight of hand. Insiders continued to see the growing collection of agencies as a stimulating family of creative professional teams, while investors were persuaded that here was a dynamic group of companies that could be judged alongside the best manufacturing groups in the land.

So convinced did the City become that in April 1986 it quite happily paid over £400m for a 47% share of the company. A month later most of that money was spent on New York agency Ted Bates Worldwide. The deal followed swiftly on the heels of a three-way American merger of BBDO International, Doyle Dane Bernbach and Needham Harper Worldwide and robbed that grouping of its briefly held title of the world's largest.

The Ted Bates merger has confronted the group's prodigious management knowhow with its stiffest test to date. The jury is still out at the time of writing in summer 1987 on whether it will be up to the job. We have our doubts (see Chapter Fourteen, page 197).

There were bound to be problems. The Saatchis knew Ted Bates was likely to lose the $100m a year Colgate-Palmolive account because Saatchi & Saatchi worked for its main competitor, Procter & Gamble. Colgate-Palmolive pulled out in June 1986. Other account losses in the ensuing months, not all connected with conflicts of interest between Saatchi & Saatchi and Ted Bates but almost all connected with conflicts of interest of some kind, included McDonald's (UK), RJR Nabisco (US), Warner-Lambert (US), United Biscuits (UK), ABC Entertainments (US), part of Procter & Gamble (US), Rowntree Mackintosh (UK), Wendy's International (US), part of Procter & Gamble (UK) and *The Independent* newspaper (UK).

The group was picking up new business at the same time and by the end of 1986 the net loss was tiny in relation to the enlarged group's total annual billings of $7.5bn. But loss there was. The merger had had a negative effect on growth.

At the same time internal tensions began to become apparent. Even before the Bates merger Saatchi & Saatchi had not been immune from the knowhow leakage endemic in the industry. It had lost Tim Bell, one of the most admired professionals in the business, and finance director Martin Sorrell who had been the chief architect of the group's acquisition programme. Sorrell's new company WPP was later to acquire Saatchi & Saatchi's arch-rival J. Walter Thompson.

Post-Bates the leakage grew worse. In September 1986 Robert Jacoby, chairman and chief executive of Ted Bates and formerly a significant shareholder in the US agency, left after disagreements with his new British masters over senior management appointments.

By October rumours were rife that the Saatchis were planning a major restructuring of the group that might rob Ted Bates of its identity. The managers of the Bates operation in Paris produced a press advertisement picturing themselves as pregnant men (following Saatchi's famous Health Education posters of the 1970s) with a copyline that read: 'Nous sommes baisé' – 'we've been screwed'.

Chris Woollams, the 36-year-old whizz kid appointed by Jacoby a year earlier to run the Bates operation in London, was equally outspoken. In an interview with *Marketing Week* he described his role amid all the rumour and speculation as '. . . management by Sellotape. All I can do is patch things up until I know exactly what is going on'. He said business was suffering as a result of the uncertainty and suggested 'it would have been nice to have been given some guidelines about what to tell clients'.

A fellow director expressed concern in the same article about a spate of resignations: 'Some people are already off and many others are talking about it. There isn't a lot you can do to convince them to stay when you're as much in the dark as they are.'

In the end Ted Bates was not integrated with the Saatchi & Saatchi master company but Woollams left anyway. He had been besieged by offers from rival agencies and had no need to put up with that kind of 'mushroom management' (keep 'em in the dark and throw dirt over them from time to time).

J. Walter Thompson, still independent at that stage, threw itself gleefully into the fray claiming in newspaper advertisements that it had replaced Saatchi & Saatchi as the UK's top agency. Saatchi responded in kind, spending £40,000 denying its loss of leadership and likening the JWT attack to 'being savaged by a dead sheep' – a famous barb aimed some years previously at Tory Chancellor Sir Geoffrey Howe by Labour's veteran in-fighter Denis Healey.

But JWT's leader Jeremy Bullmore struck a chord with many professionals when he claimed his agency was 'getting business on merit, not with a chequebook' and reminded Saatchi & Saatchi that advertising was about 'selling, not buying'.

Signs that the departure of Woollams had failed to resolve the unrest at Ted Bates came in January 1987 with the loss to a rival firm of the assistant chief executive and the departures of the joint creative directors to help set up a new agency.

The following month a Saatchi & Saatchi main board director resigned to join rival agency Abbott Mead Vickers and three directors of the Saatchi subsidiary Sales Promotion Agency left to set up on their own, taking business with them.

It is easy to over-estimate the significance of these spin-outs and defections. Saatchi & Saatchi is a very large group of agencies and such knowhow leakage is by no means unknown elsewhere in the industry. Saatchi & Saatchi itself was pinching senior figures from other agencies at the same time.

Even so, it is hard to escape the impression that the Ted Bates merger, the 'coup de triomphe' of this extraordinary company's bid for world leadership, has also tested the limits of the acquisition-led development strategy in advertising. It heralded a time of increasing unrest in the group and approached the point where conflicts of interest were seriously limiting the scope for further organic growth.

The business idea of the Saatchi brothers seems to have changed twice since they started out in 1970. They began with the intention of forming a first-rate creative agency, moved on, as their managerial knowhow grew, to the acquisition-led strategy and then, emboldened by their global reach, they widened their functional horizons to embrace the whole gamut of business services, including management consultancy, marketing and market research as well as advertising.

It is clear that the core knowhow of Saatchi & Saatchi has precious little to do with advertising creativity and almost everything to do with management. The brothers have become knowhow tycoons. By grafting onto knowhow businesses a style of management that is recognisably 'sound', 'disciplined', 'tight' and otherwise redolent of the traditional virtues they have won the access to capital markets they needed to lever their knowhow.

But a price had to be paid for this **industrialisation** of the knowhow business of advertising. The all-important culture was diluted by growth and polluted by acquisitions; the managerial problems increased exponentially; the Saatchi brothers themselves became remote, almost legendary figures, seldom seen by the 'shop-floor' professionals. The leadership became alienated from the day-to-day operations.

It remains to be seen whether the knowhow tycoon will survive as an important role model in knowhow areas. If it does the likelihood is that it will be confined to those businesses with a high potential for industrialisation.

• The leader as despot

A role model still evident in many knowhow areas like journalism is the **despotic leader** – those who 'kick arse' and generally make life hard for their professionals. This kind of leader seems **certain to become extinct** in the coming years for the simple reason that no good professional will want to work for such people. The quickest way for a knowhow company to go bust in the information society is to be led by a despot who gets tough with the staff.

SUMMARY
• Leadership styles can be classified in terms of their adherence to different **role models**.
• The leader is **creator of the work environment**.
• The leader may be a **tutor**, creating **opportunities for employees**.
• The leader is also the **guarantor of continuity and a symbol of security**, responsible for channelling the **intellectual energy** of the professionals while maintaining a **clear sense of direction**.
• A popular leadership role model these days is **the coach**, one of whose most important tasks is **recruitment**.
• The leader may also be **manager** or knowhow tycoon.
• The old role model of **the leader as despot** is inappropriate for knowhow companies.

8

• The Ten Success Factors of Knowhow Management

Most professional organisations have some common features or '**success factors**' as we call them. We have met a few of them already in previous chapters. In this chapter we shall identify 10 success factors and look at how a knowhow company, through **knowhow management**, can use them in its task of turning itself into a professional organisation.

First, let us enumerate the success factors:

1. **Day-to-day leadership.**
2. **Quality and quality-control.**
3. **Respect for knowhow.**
4. **Combination of professional and managerial knowhow.**
5. **A strong, well-defined culture.**
6. **Focus on core knowhow.**
7. **Knowhow preservation.**
8. **Developing the people.**
9. **Changing key people.**
10. **Stable structures.**

• Factor 1: day-to-day leadership

The role of the leader is never easy, least of all in a knowhow company. Leaders are constantly torn between the demands of administrative and managerial responsibilities and the need to keep their hands in professionally so that they retain the respect of and maintain their authority over the other professionals. How they reconcile this tension depends on what kind of human being they are, who the others in the management group are, their relationships and the history of the company. Traditional organisational charts, of the kind depicted in management textbooks, are worse than useless. The best structure varies from company to company and from time to time within the same company; it has much more to do with personal chemistry and the accidents of the company's development than with the application of allegedly 'ideal' structures.

There is a vast difference between leading a team of professionals and managing subordinates. The leader of the professional team is almost always an old hand – an experienced professional whose role is to be 'primus inter pares'. He or she is respected, and therefore can lead, because of professional knowledge and an ability to inspire the team. It is impossible to lead professionals without being a professional yourself.

Professional leaders must win their spurs. It is not sufficient to be 'appointed' by top management. A new leader must earn the fealty of the professional barons to be able to operate effectively. The professional barony has great power. It will destroy an unacceptable leader without compunction.

One of the leader's main tasks is to develop a style and, with it, to create an environment, capable of accommodating a wide variety of personality types. It is an unfortunate fact of life for managers that some of the best and most able people are also the most difficult to handle. This is particularly true of professionals in knowhow companies.

Remember the leadership problems associated with the flawed 'superpro' Knot we encountered in Chapter Four. It is the same for the circus manager who must sweet-talk the stubborn tightrope-walker; for the film director who must extract the brilliance while digesting the profanity of the temperamental star and for the partners of a law firm who must accommodate their egocentric but extremely talented young solicitor. Knowhow organisations are full of Knots. Their leaders have to deal constantly with the flawed genius.

Great gifts come in untidy packages but great gifts are what enable knowhow companies to excel in their marketplace. If managers choose the quiet life and deliberately avoid hiring 'knotty' superpros their companies will die a quick death.

As we have seen the most respected leader of a knowhow organisation is almost always the professional leader who has developed an ability to inspire other professionals to greater efforts.

But many knowhow companies have two leaders. One will be responsible for the service functions of the company such as accounting, administration and marketing. Though this position is often called chief executive or managing director it may be relatively powerless.

The influence of this kind of leader depends entirely on **the extent to which he or she is accepted by the rest of the organisation**. If the person is not appointed or at least approved by the professionals he or she will soon be reduced to the status of some sort of head clerk.

And it is not sufficient to be approved initially. The managing director must also take part in the daily grind; he must be seen to be **involved in the 'production'** associated with the business idea. If he fails to involve himself in this way his title will become worth little more than the business card it is printed on. This is rarely appreciated in knowhow organisations, especially in the public sector.

Power of the initiative

It is obvious that in any organisation the leader must have and must take the initiative. This is particularly important in the professional organisation.

Professionals are naturally inclined to be eager about new ideas, brilliant solutions or exciting possibilities. The initiative in such discussions confers an advantage because it acts as the yardstick for other proposals. The leader who never comes up with original ideas will soon lose the leadership. The result will be a powerless organisation in which the leader is reduced to the status of a servant.

Leaders must have the power, though they should use it sparingly, to dominate meetings with intellectual arguments and the strength of their convictions. They cannot rely on the trappings of authority or on the superior information they have by virtue of their position. Their power must be 'real' in the sense that it is given to them by those they lead. Since they are powerless to order people to follow them they must have the power to persuade them to do so.

In the professional organisation **information is an instrument of power**. We are not concerned here with written information but rather informal, spontaneous, often subtle eddies of discontent and gratification that constantly circulate within an organisation and for the reception of which leaders must establish their own, **informal monitoring systems**. This 'feel' is essential because it is impossible to lead a professional organisation from the outside. A typical complaint of the leader of a consultancy firm would be: 'I took a fortnight's holiday in the autumn and found I needed almost two weeks to regain my grip when I returned'.

This is why the leaders of knowhow organisations who start with separate offices, secretaries and executive wash-rooms may soon find they have no organisations to lead.

• Factor 2: quality and quality control

Quality is a fashionable but frequently misused word. No serious management strategy includes amongst its objectives the deliberate production of poor quality. Everyone wants to be proud of their production and to be praised for its quality. This is important in knowhow companies – so important that the successful company may go to **extreme lengths to maintain quality**.

The problem with quality as an objective is not the objective itself but the follow-up and control which are the real keys to quality improvement. Successful knowhow companies have **uncompromising quality control systems** but are constantly struggling with the problem of **how to measure quality**. The quality of the advice consultants give can only be measured in terms of the consequent success of their clients. But how do you measure the quality of an audit – by how heavily the accounts are qualified?

Individual consultants, auditors or solicitors are not qualified to assess and control the quality of their own work. The professional organisation often appoints an internal person responsible for quality control; sometimes a senior consultant or another, self-appointed professional.

Other companies have **internal discussions** where they pick up and criticise each other. As we have seen, **periodic client surveys** are also useful tools for quality measurement.

• Factor 3: respect for knowhow

The professional organisation has an almost fascist attitude to knowhow. It ranks people internally according to their professional knowhow and it is knowhow which determines the power a person has to accomplish anything within the organisation.

The professional organisation devotes a great deal of time and effort to **internal education** and does not neglect the administrative staff. There are often formal systems for education, like in-house schools or 'universities'.

The management also finds **resources for in-house R&D** within the relevant areas of knowhow and may occasionally allow a professional paid study leave to write a book, for example (See Chapter Nine, page 116).

• Factor 4: combination of professional and managerial knowhow

A basic thesis of this book is that it takes two distinct skills to develop a knowhow company into a true professional organisation: the professional and the managerial. The challenge is to find the right balance between the two. Much the most common and frequently fatal weakness of knowhow companies is that their professional skills are not matched by their managerial abilities. Professional organisations have, by definition, learned to combine these two skills into a new skill that we call **knowhow management**.

• Factor 5: a strong, well-defined culture

Managers of professional organisations are jealous of their own culture. They support and nourish it. Knowhow companies wishing to develop into professional organisations must **start by defining their culture**. They must ask themselves questions like: 'Who are we? What do we want? What is our core knowhow? Which are our distinguishing features?'

Corporate culture as a concept and management tool has become fashionable in the 1980s but is still too new to have had much real effect on ordinary management. So far only the managers of professional knowhow organisations have realised the importance of culture. Some have become positively evangelical about what makes a successful culture. Doubtless the area will soon be thronging with 'culture consultants'.

This book contains no nostrums for succesful corporate cultures. The problem with a strong culture is that what has been successful in one era can be catastrophic in another. The culture is created in the success era – the first growth stage of a knowhow company. Afterwards it frequently **lingers on far longer than is healthy.**

Many of the problems of modern railway systems can be traced to the fact that they are burdened with a culture left over from the late nineteenth century. The architecture of the mainline stations still proclaims it.

The great advantage of culture as a management tool is that it **can be used as a frame-work**, like the Ten Commandments: this is how we do it, this is what we are not allowed to do, this is the way we do things around here. The existence of a strong, well-defined culture allows top management to give the entrepreneurs a free rein, knowing their basic allegiance to the culture will keep them from straying too far from the straight and narrow.

Ingmar Kampard, legendary founder of the furniture warehouse company Ikea and one of Sweden's super-entrepreneurs, is very conscious of the importance of culture in the management of his worldwide empire. His successor Anders Moberg is only 37 but has worked for Ikea all his life and was born in Almhult, Ingmar Kampard's own home town. This fact weighed heavily at the time Kampard chose his successor. He knew Moberg would be unlikely to change Ikea's basic philosophy and culture.

• Factor 6: focus on core knowhow

The professional conglomerate is an impossibility. There is no management in the world which can maintain quality – let alone improve it – in an organisation with many different knowhow areas. This was one of the reasons for the disinvestment wave which began to sweep through most Western economies at the end of the 1970s. **Narrowing the focus onto the core knowhow** where the company has clear competitive advantages became a success factor for many of the old, tired conglomerates of the 1960s.

The problem with focus is that its object, the core knowhow, must first be identified correctly. Ironically this is one area where knowhow companies might need the help of a management consultant. If asked outright some professionals would find it hard to articulate just what it is that they and their colleagues can do better than anyone else.

• Factor 7: knowhow preservation

Since accumulated knowhow is the professional organisation's most important asset and since this knowhow is possessed by individuals, it is important for the long-term survival of the company that these very mobile assets do not decide to leave. Successful knowhow companies have developed various ways of **keeping key people** of which ownership is one of the most important. (See Chapter Six.)

Most modern knowhow companies have some form of **employee ownership**, either direct in the form of shares or indirect in the form of options or convertible loans. Most knowhow companies also run **profit-sharing** schemes.

• Factor 8: developing the people

Because there is only one asset worth anything – the people – the only way to develop a knowhow company is to develop the people. One might even say that the management of the professional organisation boils down to a single activity; recruiting and developing people. (See Chapter Six.)

• Factor 9: changing key people

The professional organisation has, by definition, accomplished the most difficult task of all. It has managed to change the key people without endangering the whole organisation. Because people are crucial for both production and business ideas, knowhow companies are extremely sensitive to leadership changes.

• Change leaders

The problems associated with a change of leader extend way beyond the implications of losing one of the most valuable employees. The leader carries the business idea. A change of leader may even involve changing the business idea itself.

A change of leader **will often be seen as a threat**. So much of the organisation of the company rests on the leader that others may find it hard to imagine how the company can survive without him or her. Leaders tend to build organisations around them that trust them and depend to a large extent on their personal relationships with their colleagues.

When the leader passes the baton on, important informal channels of communication between the leader and other employees are broken. They are important to the leader but they are equally important to the employees who have, thereby, had direct access to the top. However skilled the professionals, managers or administrative staff are, they all have a need for security. The leader is an essential part of the security system in a professional organisation. Apart from anything else the leader is often the personification of the business idea. He or she will have created or accumulated an enormous amount of important knowhow about how to do, what to do and who to do it with, will have often had direct responsibility for the production process or been the key contact with important clients. A change of leader always puts the flow of revenues at risk because clients will very often (rightly or wrongly) detect a consequent deterioration in quality.

The leader has also made mistakes. Mistakes have two important characteristics: they cost money and the same person seldom makes them twice. When the company changes leaders this crucial knowhow disappears. Old mistakes may return to haunt the company. This may cause costs to rise at the same time as revenues fall. What was once a good business may suddenly become a bad one.

How should the professional organisation handle this process? There seem to be two key components of the successful changeover: the leader must **become dispensable** and the rest of the organisation must learn that a leadership **change is an opportunity rather than a threat.**

- **Making oneself dispensable**

Of all the many stages of development the leader undergoes in a professional organisation the most difficult and arguably the most important is the last one – the stage at which he succeeds in making the company independent of him. 'One must go to work with the attitude that this is the last day' was how one successful leader put it.

By this he meant that if he died the organisation would manage anyway. Ingmar Kampard of Ikea has understood this better than most. He has often been ridiculed for 'preparing for his own death' for ten years. Martin Wood of Oxford Instruments is another business founder who recognised the need to develop a new leader in good time and who gave his chosen successor the room and the authority he needed to establish himself. (See Chapter Seven.)

It is extremely hard for leaders deliberately to prepare for their own withdrawal. In many ways they will have **built the organisations in their own images** – as monuments to their ability and vision. When they leave and their companies fall apart they may be tempted to see such disaster as evidence of their own strength rather than their failure. This is a foolish notion but a human one, nonetheless. The rest of the organisation must try to find ways to prevent the leader from committing this kind of corporate suicide.

The fact that established leaders are always part of the top management makes the change even more delicate. Each organisation must seek its own solutions to the problem of indispensability and should have that problem very much in mind when recruiting potential leaders.

- **Change – an opportunity**

Most leaders find **organisational inertia** and reluctance to change one of their major challenges. Knowhow companies are no exception. They are not burdened by masses of financial capital which makes change in a manufacturing company such a complex and difficult process. However, the human problems are often greater and can be very serious.

In the professional organisation change is seen as an opportunity rather than a threat. The replacement of an entrepreneur/leader in a professional organisation is one of the greatest changes and thus one of the greatest opportunities. It creates opportunities for younger potential leaders and entrepreneurs. They get a chance to test their mettle. The new leader will have the opportunity to develop the business further by adding to it new ideas and new activities. As we have seen all business ideas go through a life-cycle, sometimes short, sometimes long. The leader is intimate with the business idea and lives with it more intensively than anyone else – so intensively that the business idea tends to follow the life-cycle of the entrepreneur. But what good is a 60-year-old business idea? Periodic changes of leadership protect the company from atrophy and stagnation; they are essential for the survival of the business.

- **Changing professionals**

  Much of what has been said about changing the leader is, of course, also true of changing the senior professionals. They too must be constantly trying to make themselves dispensable so that opportunities become available for the younger professionals.

  The ability to survive is, to a large extent, equivalent to an ability to transfer knowhow from the old to the young – from the more to the less experienced. The sudden departure of a key professional, before any of his knowhow has been transferred to others, creates severe problems. It is even worse, of course, when the professional resigns after a row. In that case it is certain that some of the company's revenue stream will be lost. The defector will either take clients with him or see to it that they experience such a serious deterioration of quality that they switch subsequently.

  Leaders and key professionals are the repositories of a large portion of the company's knowhow capital. Top managers must work out ways of 'cloning' this knowhow in others so that the organisation can change leaders and professionals without courting disaster.

- ## Factor 10: stable structures

  Knowhow companies only appear to be devoid of structure and substance. In reality, what they lack in the concrete substance associated with manufacturing companies, they more than make up for in intangible brain substance.

  But this substance needs to be embedded in structures to give the professional organisation coherence and stability. The corporate culture, invisible on the surface but very strong internally, is part of a professional organisation's informal structure. The informal ways of creating structures are so personal and individual – so specific to the particular company – that we shall not attempt to describe them here. We concentrate instead on the more formal structures.

  As we have seen there are two kinds of formal structure in the professional organisation; the accounting system and the legal structure.

SUMMARY

- There are 10 success factors for a professional organisation.
- **Day-to-day leadership:** a leader must earn respect and become involved in everyday 'production' while retaining the **power of the initiative**.
- **Quality control:** quality in a knowhow company can be increased by quality controllers and **informal discussions** and can be measured and monitored by **client surveys**.
- **Respect for knowhow: education** and **inhouse R&D** are key factors here.
- **Combination of professional and managerial knowhow.**
- **A strong, well-defined culture:** can be used as a **framework** within which the entrepreneur has freedom to operate.
- **Focus on core knowhow:** diversification is often at the expense of quality.
- **Knowhow preservation: employee ownership** and **profit-sharing** are ways of keeping key people.
- **Developing the people.**
- **Changing key people:** leaders must make themselves dispensable. Change should be an opportunity, not a threat.
- **Stable structures:** the formal structures of the professional organisation are the **accounting system** and the **legal structure**.

9

From Knowhow Company to Professional Organisation

In previous chapters we have met the knowhow company, introduced ourselves to the categories of people who work in it and we have described its initial objective – to become what we call a professional organisation. We have also equipped ourselves with a tool-box for knowhow management in the form of our ten success factors. We shall now try to map out a route towards achieving the objective of becoming a professional organisation.

Life-cycle dynamics and the age pyramid

It is no coincidence that in new industries, like electronics and computers, and in rapidly growing markets, like financial services and stockbroking, the average age of professionals is very low. It is also quite natural that the older, more mature industries like accountancy and computer services should be staffed by relatively old professionals. **Growing organisations recruit young people**. Stagnating organisations try to cut the head-count and in so doing they inevitably increase the average age of their employees by one year each year. They begin to lose the vigour of youth.

The ability of a knowhow company to survive long-term depends in part on how well the top management **manipulates the age structure** of the company. This is particularly important when it comes to recruitment. If left to itself the process of ageing changes a company. Management must keep in mind the age requirements of the industry in which they operate and should plan ahead at least five years to meet them.

Each year adds another year of experience and increases the organisation's knowhow level. At the same time the passage of each year ages a company and, in the absence of rejuvenating recruitment, causes it to become less adaptable.

The exhaustion of professional creativity

The leader of a well-known advertising agency was once asked at a seminar where all the 40 plus advertising people were. He thought for a moment and then said, in a surprised voice: 'I don't know!'

The exhaustion of professional creativity in early middle-age is not confined to advertising. The life-expectancy of journalists is said to be lower than that of miners and there is hardly a money broker to be found over the age of 30. The reasons are not hard to find. The lot of the professional is not an easy one. The demands on creativity are incessant and stressful confrontations with clients and the public are daily occurrences. The peak pressure years are the 30s. Few professionals emerge from that decade with stamina levels half as high as those with which they entered it. A frightening proportion end their lives as alcoholics or bitter, lonely burn-outs.

Even when professionals approach retirement peacefully, without trauma and tragedy, their ageing has a profound effect on the development of the knowhow company. One need only compare the loose, untidy, frenetic culture of the young computer company with the well-structured, sober atmosphere of an accountancy firm to understand the influence the age pyramid has on the organisation's business idea.

The 'problem matrix' to which knowhow companies of all kinds address themselves is in a state of constant evolution. While the problem-solving abilities of professionals improve as they grow older the problems they are called upon to solve change. Managers of knowhow companies must recognise that there is **a trade-off between a familiarity with yesterday's problems and an appetite for today's.** If they fail to mix in their knowhow capital cocktail the right proportions of mature wisdom and youthful vigour their business idea will become out-dated.

- **The 'spare tyre effect'**
Managers should always remember that left untended the age structure is certain to become distorted. **The spare tyre effect** is an attribute of the life-cycle of organisations. It is formed mainly by recruitment during the growth phase. When the company is young and growing the leaders tend to recruit people of their own age; 25-year-olds recruit 25-year-olds. When the 25-year-olds become 35-year-olds they usually find good reasons to recruit 35-year-olds. The 25-year-olds, after all, are so very inexperienced . . .

In this way a spare tyre develops round the company's midriff, consisting of professionals of the same age and outlook who try to maintain their positions and status.

- ## The life-cycle of the professionals
Successful professional organisations are very conscious of the long-term implications of the age pyramid and try hard to develop ways of accommodating the professional life-cycle. The most sophisticated of these systems usually involve some kind of **career path** giving the professionals scope for personal development. The large consultancy firms like Arthur Andersen, Price Waterhouse,

Arthur D. Little and McKinsey all have career systems of this kind. The McKinsey version is called '**up or out**'. It sounds harsh but it guarantees a professional starting a career with McKinsey a personal development path of progressively more challenging work. Those who find this too demanding will probably be better off outside the firm anyway.

Other knowhow companies have developed more informal career paths, of the kind pictured below.

• The ideal life-cycle

In this theoretical ideal professionals are recruited as young graduates and begin their careers as 'juniors', usually acting as assistants to senior consultants.

After a few years they become more independent and will eventually be elected 'partners'. Most consultancy firms have some form of partnership system. In certain professions such as law and accountancy the partnership arrangement

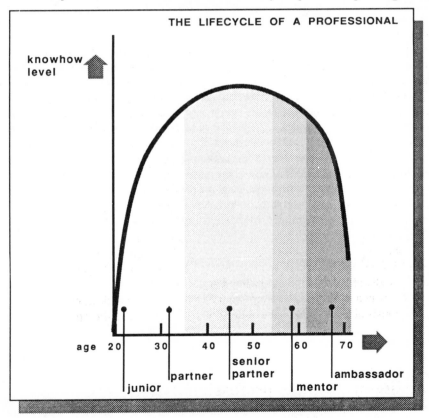

Figure 12   Professionals increase their knowhow as they get older and may develop into mentors. The ambassador has left the company and cannot maintain his or her professional knowhow level but may prove very valuable as a link to the external network.

is required by law. It is hard, though no longer impossible, in an accountancy firm to become a partner without having a formal status in the profession.

After election the partner can look forward to a long, productive and lucrative career. There is more challenging work to be done, more complex problems to solve and there is the new experience of becoming the leader and mentor of a team of 'juniors'.

The older partners tend to become more involved with the company itself. This is a very difficult stage. There is **no guarantee that a skilled professional will turn out to be a good manager of people**. Indeed the two skills often tend to conflict with each other. An important measure of a knowhow company's fitness to survive is its ability to develop good leaders. And if it is to survive long-term the professional organisation must develop enough competent 'seniors' to discharge the responsibilities of top management.

In this way a few seniors are guaranteed **a second career as managers, leaders or 'mentors'**. The mentors, usually the best of the older professionals, are important. They have been around a long time – perhaps since the very beginning. Though not necessarily the best consultants or even the best team leaders, they have high status and command the confidence and respect of the younger professionals. The mentors will sometimes be the policymakers or **cultural gurus**. They are the link between the organisation's past and present; the ones who explain 'why we do things the way we do round here'.

They can also act as foils to the enthusiasms of the young, eager professionals and can be their confidants when they have personal problems. Few people have that rare mix of qualities, a high level of professional ability, long experience and empathy, that add up to 'mentor'.

When senior partners retire or find other careers they may become '**ambassadors**' for the company or elder statesmen. They can be links in the external network, door-openers and public relations people. They seldom have a formal status in the company but with their many valuable contacts both inside and outside the organisation they can be important assets.

• The components of the personnel idea

We noted in the previous chapter that the personnel idea is extremely important to the market position of the knowhow company. Let us look at it in more detail.

The personnel idea has four components:

- arrival (the recruitment idea)
- personnel development
- personnel motivation
- departure

• The recruitment idea – a strategic weapon

We have a vacancy. Whom should we recruit? Shall we hire youth or experience; an engineer or an accountant; a team-orientated professional or a potential leader? Top managers often struggle with these questions. They are wrong to do so because they are the wrong questions.

The recruitment idea is top management's most important strategic weapon because it is the most powerful long-term instrument for changing the company's position in the market, altering its knowhow level or adapting its business idea. Through the deliberate recruitment of a certain type of person the manager can, even if he does nothing else, bring about profound changes in the organisation.

If hiring is merely a matter of filling vacancies there is no recruitment idea. Like for like replacement is a recipe for stagnation. The recruitment need, whether created by retirement, resignation or the exigencies of growth, is an opportunity to adapt the organisation to its constantly changing environment. It should, on no account, be wasted.

Conscious and structured thinking about the concept of the recruitment idea is an essential element in strategic planning but growth is not the only consideration. Strategy in its widest sense has as much to do with consolidating and preserving what has already been achieved as it has to do with the conquest of new markets.

A few examples will illustrate the point:

RECRUITING YOUNG PEOPLE   Recruiting only young people tends to conserve and strengthen the company's existing culture. This may seem an odd assertion. Are not the young the well-springs of dynamism and change? They certainly can be if given their head but they are also impressionable. They learn fast and are easily indoctrinated. Eventually – when they acquire influence – they can become powerful advocates of the existing culture.

RECRUITING MANY PEOPLE   Recruiting a large number of people at once is an infallible way of creating a climate of change. But such a stratagem can be dangerous, especially if the new group lacks a positive attitude to the company at the outset as can be the case after a hostile takeover or when there are clear differences of opinion about where the company should be going.

RECRUITING SKILLED PEOPLE   One very effective way of changing the business idea quickly is to recruit experienced, skilled and well-known professionals. These new professionals bring with them new business, new clients, new networks and new ideas. But there are dangers here too if the high-powered recruits are unable to accept their new company's culture or if their arrival is perceived as a threat by existing professionals.

RECRUITING NICE PEOPLE   Recruiting nice people who are liked by all existing employees is a recipe for conservatism. Nice people create no conflicts but neither do they come up with new ideas. If their 'likeability' is their only asset, long-term quality will be compromised. Young, inexperienced executives sometimes fall into the trap of hiring too many of their friends. This can often create a community of 'yes' people lacking the inspirational spark needed in a professional climate. On the other hand, the recruitment of friends can, when change is already in the air, help to smooth the way and minimise the stress personnel conflicts impose on leaders and top management.

RECRUITING A TEAM   Sometimes, when one knowhow company merges with another, a new team enters the organisation with different ideals and aspirations. The new team members, because they know each other, will tend to stick together. Conflicts between the cultures are unavoidable, even when the two groups are all members of the same profession. It is surprising how frequently the managers of knowhow companies are caught unawares by the storms of controversy and conflict that blow up following mergers. Perhaps it is because they rely too much on the 'synergy' rationale for mergers – the way the businesses 'fit' in terms of markets and skills – not realising that compared to personal chemistry, synergy in knowhow company mergers is of minor importance.

RECRUITING FOR BALANCE IN SEX   Changing the balance between men and women can often improve the climate in a company. Few knowhow companies are dominated by women – Steve (Stephanie) Shirley's F International computer systems company is a notable exception – so the new women should be professionals or potential leaders if the existing male dominance is not to be strengthened.

RECRUITING FOR BALANCE IN AGE   An important aspect of recruitment is the age structure. Most knowhow companies have an unbalanced age structure – the 'spare tyre' legacy of their growth period. The recruitment idea must recognise that stability requires a good age mix. If the leaders and professionals are too young the company will be unsettled and its fortunes will fluctuate. If they are too old the company will decline and die.

The **recruitment idea** consists of two parts: **what kind of people do we want** (age, education, culture) and **how shall we find them?**

● Consultancies

One can tell a great deal about a company or firm from the sort of people it recruits and the way it recruits them.

Consultancies who mainly recruit young people have usually developed a comprehensive box of tools with which they try to turn young men and women into effective consultants within a few months. Procedures and techniques take the place of experience. It is like the McDonald's 'industrialised' model of the service company (see Chapter One, page 19). Research, development and education have high priorities. There is also a strong, collegiate kind of culture and a readily digestible philosophy. The personnel idea, indistinguishable in this case from the business idea itself, is to develop a homogenised consultancy style that can be sold by young 'clones' all equipped with the same tool-box.

The US consultancy Bain & Co, some of whose characteristics came to light during the Guinness scandal in Britain in 1986, is a good example of the type.

The 'big two' international consultancy firms, Boston Consulting Group (BCG) and McKinsey, have pursued very similar recruitment policies but sharply contrasting growth strategies. The story of their struggle for market leadership in strategic consultancy illustrates the importance of the recruitment idea.

McKinsey, the large, well-established consultancy firm which had been market leader almost since its foundation in 1921, was suddenly challenged in the first half of the 1970s by BCG, founded by Bruce Henderson a few years earlier.

BCG's success was based on product innovation of such brilliance that it changed the consultancy ball-game. Generalising from his pioneering study of the 'experience curve' at the end of the 1960s, Henderson forged a new set of tools for strategic consultancy based on portfolio analysis. 'The Boston matrix', with its 'dogs', 'cash-cows', 'wild cats' and 'stars', had a tremendous impact on the top executives of large companies struggling with the legacies of decades of unplanned, incoherent development.

BCG grew like Topsy. Within a few years it was employing more than 300 consultants. By offering 50-100% higher salaries than its competitors BCG succeeded in recruiting the best young brains from Harvard and other prestigious universities. Its competitors even had to pay students to induce them to attend a first interview. BCG's talent scouts employed such aggressive recruitment methods that at one stage they were banned from the Harvard campus.

The simplicity and power of the BCG matrix attracted a great deal of attention which further fuelled demand for the firm's services. This too was new. Previously consultancy firms, following McKinsey's traditional style, had adopted a low-key, almost secretive approach. BCG, in its bid for market share, raised the profile of consultancy and introduced the idea of 'the consultant as hero'.

But McKinsey responded vigorously to the challenge. It improved its methods of presentation and launched matrices of its own. At the same time it raised its public profile by encouraging its senior partners to speak at seminars and write books. Several of the management best-sellers of the early 1980s – *In Search of Excellence* is the best known example – were written by McKinsey consultants.

In the meantime BCG began to encounter difficulties. Their young, inexperienced, 'cloned' consultants often lacked the authority needed to deal on equal terms with top executives of large, international companies. BCG's credibility was called into question. Its smart alec kids were simply not plausible purveyors of managerial wisdom. Growth slowed.

• Lessons to be learned

The recruitment idea must be tailored to fit the knowhow company's market and ambitions. Strategic consultancy, almost by definition, involves interaction with clients at the top level. Notwithstanding its early success, BCG's experience shows that taking people straight from college and training them up is a laborious way of growing. It takes years for the young graduate to acquire enough authority to deal with top management.

McKinsey's growth has been much slower than BCG's, seldom exceeding 10% a year, but it has also been much steadier. Throughout the BCG-inspired revolution in consultancy during the 1970s McKinsey managed to retain its quality image.

But the story of the BCG/McKinsey struggle also shows that recruitment of young people and investment in innovative analytical tools – the substitution of technique for experience – offers considerable scope for growth. Marketing is freed from its dependence on individuals. The system itself can be sold. Consultancy firms which recruit older, more experienced professionals can seldom grow so large so quickly. Their skills are more catholic and thus their styles are less coherent and therefore less marketable.

• Personnel development

We encountered the four personnel categories in the last chapter. We shall now look at each of them in turn in the context of personnel development.

DEVELOPING MANAGERS   Why are there so very few skilled managers in knowhow companies? One reason is that the role of manager in a knowhow company is often a lonely one. The professionals are the core of the personnel. **The administration and marketing departments are normally quite small**.

Management in the knowhow company is seldom challenging enough to attract able and ambitious executives. The chief accountant in a knowhow company is under little pressure to develop his or her own professional skills (although, as we have seen, new knowhow capital accounting techniques are urgently needed).

Leadership in a knowhow company with 100 or so professionals is **a more complicated business** than leadership in an industrial company of the same size. This is because the complexity of the business lies along the professional axis. The managers, isolated from the inner professional circle, have to content themselves with the relatively humdrum, knowing the glory and the top jobs will invariably go to the professionals.

The attitudes of the professionals merely corroborate the manager's feelings of inferiority. Generally speaking the professionals are contemptuous of and uninterested in the problems and achievements of the managers. In some knowhow areas this fastidiousness about all things commercial is manifest in price cartels and codes of ethics which, amongst other things, proscribe 'touting for business' (a pejorative term for marketing). Such systems retain many of the qualities of craft guilds. These days their main purpose seems to be to limit competition. One important side-effect is seriously to **inhibit the development of managerial skills**.

So if a manager wishes to develop his professional skills he is likely to leave. This drains the company of precious managerial knowhow. Leaders and top management should try hard to prevent such departures by providing managers with the opportunities and challenges they need to **develop their own careers**. Clearly these arrangements will have to be very different from those designed to motivate the professionals.

Managers are interested in expanding the company because this is normally their best chance to grow and develop themselves. A larger company means larger problems – more people to manage, for example. At worst, managers just build empires. At best they become powerful allies of the leadership in its efforts to develop the business.

DEVELOPING THE CLERICAL STAFF   While it is natural to send professionals and (to a certain extent) managers on various courses and to give them new, challenging problems to work with, the clerical staff are not so easily stimulated. A gulf tends to develop between them and the other employees. They see others having fun and making progress in their careers and they feel left behind, **imprisoned in boring jobs** which appear to have no potential to develop into something more interesting or more rewarding.

One of the most successful professionals of the financial market once said, before he had developed into a leader, that 'information is not something you are given. It is something you have to get.' This is true for all personnel categories in a knowhow company except the clerical staff.

The clerical staff are always complaining about bad communications. 'No one tells us anything!' they cry in frustration when, without warning, a new professional arrives in the office one morning and asks them where he should sit. The professionals keep aloof and the managers forget the clerical staff do not receive the same information as themselves and the professionals as a matter of course. The clerical staff, or the 'front office' as we call them, are always **on the periphery of the information flow** because they take no part in the coffee break discussions of the professionals or in top management committee meetings.

One way of counteracting this alienation is to **educate the clerical staff** about the business idea and about the profession that drives it. They should be allowed into meetings from time to time though they may not be able to participate. It is important that they understand the business idea. If they do not any information they do receive will be wasted because they will have no way of judging its significance.

Hospital book-keepers should be allowed into the surgery. Advertising staff on magazines and newspapers should be allowed to attend editorial meetings. The secretaries of solicitors should take part in important court cases.

The clerical staff must also be given opportunities to **develop their own skills**. This is desirable in any company; in knowhow companies it is essential otherwise the clerical staff will be a constant undercurrent of discontent within the organisation which will **pollute the culture**. Surprisingly little grumbling is needed to turn a generally positive feeling into a negative one throughout the organisation. In the end it is bound to affect revenues.

One of the most common causes of the failure of a knowhow company to develop into a professional organisation is the failure of the leader to learn to develop the managers and clerical staff.

The focus on knowhow makes this need obvious. The knowhow company depends for its success and development on all its knowhow capital, not just that portion of it associated with the professionals. But though the need is obvious once the focus is on knowhow the means to develop the clerks and managers are seldom readily at hand. Imagination is needed and a willingness to seek inspiration and help from outside.

It is important to see the good salesman or the efficient book-keeper as **a**

professional within his or her profession. All that has been said so far in this book about developing the professionals is just as valid for these 'pros' – even though their knowhow is not part of the business idea itself.

All knowhow companies have extensive networks. These should be used to give **alternative careers** and new experiences to the clerical staff. It is possible, for example, for two companies to switch chief accountants with each other, or secretaries or receptionists. One might allow a young clerk to go on secondment for a few months to another company in a similar industry or with a client or supplier.

After all, the professionals often get such opportunities; why not the rest of the staff too?

DEVELOPING THE PROFESSIONALS Chief executives of professional organisations must be **flexible** about the careers and remuneration of their professionals – sometimes much more flexible than European labour market traditions permit.

Consider the following:

- A computer company allows one of its professionals to work with a partner company in another country because his wife wants to live abroad for a year.
- A publishing company gives one of its journalists leave to work freelance for other magazines and live in New York for a couple of years with a 'return ticket'.
- A media company allows one of its managers to work for a competitor part-time because she sees a challenge there.
- An accountancy firm sends one of its junior assistants on a two-year secondment to a manufacturing company to give him some experience of the shop-floor.
- A consultancy firm establishes an office abroad to indulge one of its senior consultants.
- Another consultancy firm recruits the managing director of its client – in exchange for one of its own consultants.

These unusual careers were devised by enlightened knowhow companies to give their professionals far wider scope for personal development than has traditionally been possible. Such bold initiatives require a massive personal commitment by top management and an empathy with the needs of the individual so far unknown in traditional industries.

DEVELOPING NEW LEADERS The leader is the head of business in a knowhow company and normally the chief executive. To a large extent leaders ARE the business idea and they frequently act as the 'champions' of individual projects. Moreover, they are normally the prime movers in the development of existing and new business ideas.

They need a high level of professional knowhow and the management ability to lead a team of people. There will always be **a paucity of potential leaders** in any organisation. It is important to identify them early and give them as much scope as possible for development.

Potential leaders should be encouraged to cut their teeth as champions of small, interesting projects where their mistakes will cause little damage. It is useful to keep in reserve a few minor business ideas for this purpose. This is important, especially if the potential leader is a professional rather than a manager. On a diet of exclusively professional work, the crown princes and princesses will be starved of the managerial experience they need to lead an organisation.

However, these leader training runs should be intermittent and brief. The potential leader's main task is to **establish his or her professional credentials** so that he or she is accepted as leader, when the time comes, by the other professionals.

This acceptance is so crucial that it is probably wise to recruit primarily professionals when seeking potential leaders. Future leaders should not be allowed to champion small projects until they have reached a minimum and relatively high professional standard.

THE STATE   The public sector is full of knowhow organisations, many of them run alongside more general service organisations. One of the themes of modern, democratic government is cost reduction in public service. Since the Conservative Party came to power in Britain in 1979 central government costs have been cut by 10% by dint of a series of swingeing economy drives.

But it is remarkable how often the focus of cost-cutting is on out-of-pocket costs like magazine subscriptions and travel rather than on the 'fat' that has accumulated over the years in the internal bureaucracy.

The state also tries to save costs by maintaining tight control over public sector salaries. Socialist governments are often ideologically committed to reducing differentials between the lowest and highest paid civil servants. The result is that though the public sector often pays competitive salaries in the lower brackets, it is inclined to underpay the top jobs very substantially. It is also at a disadvantage to the private sector when it comes to providing senior professionals with creative or unusual careers. The inevitable result of this wholesale violation of the rules of knowhow management, with the best of intentions of course, is that the quality of people in the public sector is declining fast, especially in areas like law, accountancy, computer services and education, where the state has to compete for talent with a more generous and enlightened private sector.

THE PROFESSOR   In universities the title of professor is the highest accolade of all, awarded only to those who have demonstrated exceptional professionalism in research and teaching. But when professors are 'promoted' further to dean of faculty or vice-chancellor they become involved in administrative tasks like managing clerical personnel, answering letters, drawing up budgets etc. Soon, very little time is left for research and teaching.

THE CIVIL SERVANT   In most public offices there are teams of officials who prepare policies and problems before the decision-making stage. The most skilled and ambitious officials are promoted to become heads of departments or sections. They become involved in administrative tasks like managing clerical personnel, answering letters, drawing up budgets etc. All too often the state exchanges skilled and knowledgeable officials for unskilled and inefficient chief clerks.

The career system in the civil service and other state organisations has the remarkable feature of **forcing the most skilled professionals to abandon their profession**. Of course some professionals like administration but they are rare. For most the chores of seniority are the price they pay for advancement.

This unhappy state of affairs has come about because the state has **confused the role of the professional leader with that of the manager**.

In the public sector a higher status attaches to being a departmental manager with many subordinates than to being a skilled professional. Salary and status are linked to age and responsibility. This is also true of the private corporate sector where the Chief Executive Officers (CEOs) of large companies with many employees have higher salaries, and thus higher status, than the managers of smaller companies.

This class system is quite inappropriate for the knowhow company. As we have seen the professionals are the most valuable productive resources and revenue earners. Most organisations in the public sector are knowhow organisations and should follow, rather than flout as they do, the rules of knowhow company management. **The best professionals should earn more than the managers**. And it is of course quite wrong to force skilled professionals to take on administrative tasks just so that they can be paid more.

It is not surprising that public sector organisations find it hard to compete for good people with the private sector when professionals are so systematically promoted to their level of incompetence.

- **Personnel motivation**

Hiring good people is just the start. Ability changes over time and according to the situation. All large professional organisations have their own **feed-back systems** to monitor these changes. The larger the organisation the more elaborate such systems tend to be. Executives are required to complete detailed reports on the performance of each employee and very often departmental managers have to discuss, in open committee, the progress of each member of their team. The results of monitoring are collected centrally for use in career planning.

In some countries, like Sweden, there is a tendency to look down on this kind of feedback system. It smacks too much of old-fashioned feudalism. But there is nothing controversial about performance assessment and feedback in the world of the professional. It is readily accepted that some tennis players are better than others and that some consultants are better at solving a certain type of problem than others. How can one judge one's relative skills without some kind of feedback? Though there are few professional fields in which ability differentials are as clear as in professional tennis, feedback remains an essential stimulus for self-improvement.

THE IMPORTANCE OF THE SUCCESS SPIRAL **Positive feedback loops** are also important for the organisation as a whole. Success breeds success. We all want to work for a successful organisation. It gives us a feeling of being successful ourselves. Success feeds on itself, creating spirals that motivate professionals to ever greater effort and achievement. This creates a stimulating working environment, word of which spreads throughout the industry. The company becomes more attractive to other professionals which makes it easier to hire good people. The increased professional quality thereby acquired further enhances the company's achievements in the marketplace causing the spiral to wind up another cycle.

The dynamics of the success spiral, once it begins, are so valuable to professional organisations that managers try to do everything in their power to keep the momentum going. Bragging shamelessly in recruitment advertising about the quality of existing employees is common practice. Modesty has no place in the modern knowhow company. Lights are seldom allowed to remain under bushels for long.

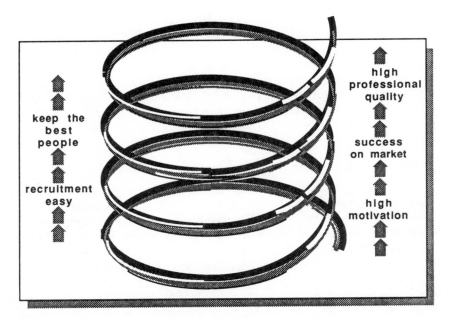

Figure 13   The success spiral is all important to the knowhow company. Highly motivated people produce success in the marketplace. This makes recruitment easier, bringing in even higher quality which in turn increases motivation.

The importance of success spirals is also evident in bought-out or spun-out companies. There is often a feeling of great achievement in reaching the starting grid as an independent company and there is a determination to do better than the former employer. This **'freedom factor'** can be exploited by management to inspire the professionals to new heights of effort and achievement.

Because planning is an uncertain art the skillful manager will take pains to **re-define the measure of success** at regular intervals so that the employees always feel they are achieving it. But though it is important to define the measure of success, it does not matter much what yardstick is used, just so long as it measures something real. Volume growth and profitability are conventional measures of a company's performance but they have the weakness of being merely symptoms of success in the marketplace. A better yardstick, though much more difficult to measure, is the growth in the professional knowhow.

• Personnel departures

The departure of an experienced professional is always a blow to a knowhow company because **part of the accumulated knowhow is lost**. But it need not be lost completely. When people leave it is either because they feel there is no suitable development path for them or because of personal chemistry.

However if the leaver remains an ambassador for his old company, something valuable is salvaged. Ambassadors can be very useful. Many professional organisations set up 'alumni clubs' for ex-employees to help them find better jobs or even start their own businesses. Ex-employees who do well outside the organisation help recruitment. They are **advertisements for the organisation's quality**. And applying the principle that behind every problem there lurks an opportunity, a resignation can often **stimulate creativity** and sometimes even **initiate a new success spiral**.

Sometimes a departure can inspire a fundamental re-assessment of the business idea which leads to the conclusion that the best thing to do is close down the company and start again.

• The living knowhow

• Knowhow development

Most successful knowhow companies have their own knowhow development programmes, similar to research & development programmes in traditional companies. This is common, for example, among large accountancy firms and computer companies. The professionals are encouraged to spend time preparing internal reports or management books or to engage in research. The recent flood of management books stems from this kind of programme in consultancy firms. The books, having served the purpose of stimulating the author and improving his or her understanding of a particular knowhow area, can be used to raise the company's public profile.

It will be **impossible** in the future for any knowhow company **to survive**

without R&D. It is not hard to encourage professionals to do research; the problem for management is how to monitor it and make sure it turns out to be useful for the company as well as for the individual.

- **Knowhow transfer**
The more senior professionals have an enormous amount of knowhow, most of which lies latent. Managers must find ways of transferring this untapped wealth to the more junior members of the organisation. Successful knowhow companies have their own **education programmes** for this purpose, sometimes even their own universities, and they are avid buyers of external education. But that is not enough.

It is hard to formalise knowhow transfer systems. Some say the most valuable knowhow of all comes from one's own mistakes. This is why successful knowhow companies use **training on the job** as the main method of knowhow transfer. The senior professionals in accountancy, law and consultancy firms always have a team of youngsters to do the donkeywork. The seniors are the motivators and quality controllers and at the end of the day they present the results and take all the credit, or so it often seems to the frustrated juniors.

Accountancy and law firms are more or less obliged to work this way, witness the 'pupil' system at the British bar, but in other industries this kind of **professional 'shadowing'** by new recruits is rare. It seems to be difficult to find in the same person both professional competence and an ability to transfer knowhow effectively.

Indeed in some industries there is even a professional prejudice against knowhow transfer. Who knows, one of those youngsters might learn enough to take over the professional's job? Ironically this attitude is common in those very organisations, such as the universities, where knowhow transfer is the business idea. Nowhere are the worst excesses of professional jealousy and egoism more evident than in the competition for professorial chairs. The same jealousies exist in most professions. Try asking a journalist for his contacts book.

- **The experience curve – knowhow leakage**
The success of Bruce Henderson, founder of the Boston Consulting Group, was based on his skillful exploitation of a concept known as 'the experience curve.' He drew general conclusions about the transfer of knowhow and experience from his studies of computer manufacturing companies. He discovered that the marginal cost of making computers declined as volume increased, not just because of the traditional economies of scale in marketing and buying, but also because as people became familiar with the production process they learned how to improve it.

Knowhow companies have similar experience-curves of both the positive and negative kinds. **A negatively sloping learning curve is a sign of knowhow leakage**. There is leakage to clients with every assignment, to other professionals at seminars and to competitors when they poach staff.

Professionals also love writing books and articles. Because of the plethora of professionals eager to share their knowledge with the world at large for the sake of their name on the front page of a book, traditional authors of technical and management literature have a tough time these days.

For society as a whole knowhow leakage is a good thing. It means that one can always learn something new in the information society. The alert and trained analyst can find titbits of knowhow everywhere. This is why all knowhow areas are developing so rapidly to-day. Knowhow spreads (leaks) quickly in the information society.

However carefully the knowhow is protected, it will become public knowledge sooner or later. It cannot be kept from prying eyes even by locking it in a safe and giving only one person the combination – like the recipe for Coca-Cola. If the knowhow is valuable it will be copied and sometimes, as with Pepsi-Cola, the copy may conquer the original.

It is in the nature of the knowhow company to share its knowledge. The client learns from the consultant and in so doing erodes the consultant's competitive advantage.

Knowhow leakage cannot be staunched, it can only be replaced. New knowhow must be created constantly if the knowhow company is to maintain its lead and thus its competitive advantage.

Companies which fail to focus on their core knowhow will be ambushed. Their carefully nurtured competitive position may, at any time, be abruptly neu-

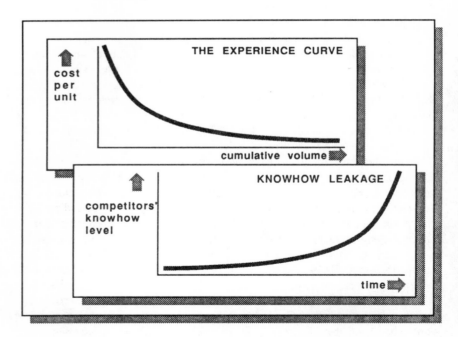

Figure 14 As volume increases unit costs fall, but this also increases the risk of knowhow leakage as competitors become familiar with your knowhow.

tralised by other companies catching up or by technological developments that turn an edge into a liability. In the information society knowledge flows freely. A knowhow company that stands still is doomed.

Technological change in knowhow areas is rapid and has been accelerating during the past 20 years. Take the case of the calculator. The first electric calculating machines appeared in the early 1970s. They were large, clumsy and expensive. A few years later the second generation arrived. They were smaller, lighter and better engineered. Then came the first electronic calculators. By the beginning of the 1980s the product life-cycle was down to about six months. Today calculators are as thin as credit cards and cheap enough to be given away as company presents.

In such circumstances it takes very sophisticated knowhow in knowhow development to maintain a competitive advantage.

Even in areas where product life-cycles can be measured in years it is obvious that the information society reduces quite dramatically the time it takes for knowhow to spread. A knowhow lead is as ephemeral as a fashion. It needs constant renewal if it is not to be lost.

It is hard to over-estimate the significance of this **change in the rate of change**. In the agrarian societies of the sixteenth to eighteenth centuries it could take more than 100 years for a new technology to disseminate. Inventors had little contact with the outside world. Knowhow was transmitted mainly by word of mouth. It was not until the beginning of the twentieth century that knowhow transmission began to speed up. A striking symptom of the change was the sudden eruption of patent offices all over the world. The idea of 'intellectual property', needing protection from predatory competitors, had been born.

It is important to focus on knowhow for another reason too. Some changes are so dramatic that they can invalidate the business idea. Early warnings of such developments are essential for survival.

- **Computer service bureaux**
The computer service market is a good example of how a knowhow area can change and develop. At the beginning of the computer age 20 years ago the computer service bureau had its heyday. The new electronic brains were clumsy and expensive. Even the simplest routines had to be handled by experts. It was natural that the bureaux should evolve into companies servicing the needs of several clients, using large, powerful machines operated by specialists.

Then computer prices began to tumble at a dizzying and accelerating speed. At the same time advances in software technology made the machines much easier to use. The bureaux selling merely computer power encountered serious problems. Their knowhow was being incorporated into the hardware. Machines that had seemed dauntingly complex and temperamental to their clients became accessible and much more reliable.

Sweden's largest computer bureau, Datema, recorded losses for three consecutive years and was bought out in 1985. Before then many of the best programmers had left to start their own companies. While struggling desperately for survival, Datema had spawned a new generation of Swedish computer companies.

SUMMARY

• A knowhow company's **age structure** must be watched carefully because of **the exhaustion of professional creativity** and the need to balance the ability to solve old and new problems.

• Professionals need a **career path** progressing towards **leader or mentor** roles.

• There are **four components of the personnel idea.**

1 **The recruitment idea.** This is an important strategic weapon; the type and number of new employees will help determine the direction of the company's development.

2 **Personnel development.** Managers must be made to feel as important as the professionals. Clerical staff must be educated, encouraged and involved. Professionals should be recognised and rewarded as such and not be bogged down by administrative tasks.

3 **Personnel motivation.** Feedback and performance assessment are important tools in monitoring and encouraging employees' progress. Success breeds success.

4 **Personnel departures.** These should be viewed in a positive way: the leaver may become an ambassador for the company and an advertisement for its quality.

• The dynamic nature of knowhow requires **R&D, education** and **knowhow transfer.**

• **Knowhow leakage** is inevitable so knowhow must be constantly replaced.

10

- # Making a Business out of Knowhow – the business idea

- ## The case of Cergus

The information company Argus was operating successfully in the areas of economic information, financial analysis and publishing. The staff consisted mostly of journalists and financial analysts. In the summer of 1980 two of the professionals became interested in a new business idea – professional consulting in the financial information area.

They put a proposal to their colleagues which was discussed and finally approved. The following autumn the entrepreneurs founded an Argus subsidiary which they called Cergus.

They took with them a third professional from Argus and recruited another from outside. All four were experienced journalists, trained in financial analysis. They found a small office, stole some of Argus's toilet paper and a couple of typewriters, had some trouble with their telephones but were well ahead of budget within a month. They were fully occupied from day one preparing financing proposals, annual reports and brochures for their clients. They worked hard. During the first year they sold their services for about SKr600,000 (approximately £60,000) a head.

The business prospered for two years but the founders soon realised their knowhow was not being rewarded at its full value. The Swedish securities industry was booming; capital markets were undergoing a transition and droves of new companies were coming to market. Stock exchange turnover leaped from £2bn in 1981 to £7.5bn in 1983.

Between 1980 and 1986 no less than 160 new companies joined the Stockholm market, doubling the number of quoted companies in Sweden. The timing of the Cergus project was perfect. The new public companies needed help with their annual reports and prospectuses and were avid buyers of advice on mergers and financial strategy. Cergus had just the kind of knowhow the boom market wanted.

But the Cergus quartet found it hard to increase billings above £100,000 a head per year. The big money was being earned by the banks and the brokers who had the underwriting capacity. The reward for their 'risk' was a fee on each share sold to the public. Though Cergus would prepare the whole prospectus for a flotation they would receive only a small fraction of the fees earned by the underwriting banks.

The founders concluded that their original business idea of 'consulting' was not the most profitable long-term way to exploit their knowhow. They decided their skills would be much more profitably employed if they were selling broker-age and merchant banking services. For this they needed capital. Argus lacked the necessary resources to finance such a development and its leaders also felt that combining journalism with merchant banking posed ethical problems.

However, since the Cergus team were determined Argus gave them leave to seek backing from a wealthy third party who would take a majority stake in the company. Argus was to retain a symbolic minority holding.

Cergus soon found a new partner who was already active in the capital mar-kets but had no experience in the stock market. A new merchant bank was formed in the autumn of 1982. There were a number of start-up problems. Many new people had to be recruited and no-one in Cergus or the new parent had any experience in stockbroking or in how to manage the back-office of a merchant bank. In addition, the four founders themselves, though they relished the challenge of merchant banking, disliked the idea of being brokers.

The youngest disliked it so much he left and another soon followed. The two original entrepreneurs found themselves with a large number of newly recruited people, half analysts and brokers and half back-office staff.

The new parent appointed a representative to manage day-to-day operations but he knew nothing about the stock market. His lack of appropriate pro-fessional knowhow soon made his position impossible and he withdrew. The two founders were left to solve the managerial problems themselves.

The booming stock market buoyed up the brokerage operation but the profit in the first year was low. The parent company became concerned but had no idea how to handle the situation. It was, in any case, heavily pre-occupied with making other acquisitions and so had little spare management capacity.

The Cergus management team – by now increased to five – considered their strategy. They found pure broking as a long-term business idea uninteresting but thought their considerable skills in financial analysis could become the basis for a portfolio management and investment banking business. Without inform-ing their parent they recruited more financial analysts.

In its second full year as a broking firm Cergus earned SKr50m (£5m), well in line with the market average. The profits came mostly from the brokerage busi-ness but portfolio management was showing good progress too. By now the company was employing 60 people, considerably more than its original parent Argus, and profit per employee had risen to the £90,000 a year level.

However, the managers of Cergus feared that this profit level would not be sustainable in the long-term since it was largely the result of booming market conditions. New entrants into the stockbroking market, several of American and European origin, were putting pressure on margins. The managers felt Cergus needed a strong, international partner.

The parent company managers disagreed. They believed the future was bright in brokerage and were wary about bringing in another partner who would dilute their interest and might pull Cergus away from them. They were doing very nicely out of Cergus. Its rapid profits growth had increased their own profits by 50% in the previous year.

The disagreement festered and in the autumn of 1984 developed into open conflict. A large institution acquired 50% of the parent in an agreed takeover. The Cergus management had been kept in the dark during the merger negotiations and when the staff and managers found out they objected strongly to the new arrangements. The 35 professionals were particularly angry and demoralised.

During a stormy week in the autumn of 1984 the two founder members were fired. They went straight to a competitor and during the following month another 25 professionals, some three-quarters of the revenue producing team, left. Most of them went to join the founders despite the generous golden handcuffs proffered by the new owner.

Cergus had previously estimated its market value at about £35m, equivalent to £600,000 per employee or £1m per professional. When the news broke the parent group's market value slumped by £10m in one day. That implied a value for Cergus of £15m. Its value had more than halved within a month.

- **Lessons to be learned**

The story of Cergus contains a number of clues about how to value knowhow companies, how to make money out of them and about how *not* to manage them.

1. THE START-UP PHASE   The start-up of Cergus was typical for a knowhow company. Money was no problem because all the capital they needed was in the heads of the founders. The start-up phase was easy because the network and the clients were already there. This is a common feature of spin-outs; the entrepreneurs are invariably well established in their market before they go into business. These contacts put flesh on the bones of the business idea and make the project viable.

The original parent Argus made the first strategic move by **letting the subsidiary leave the premises**. After that the connection between the companies was merely the sum of the relationships between the people. The decision to let Cergus go was deliberate. There was a feeling that physical separation was necessary because of inherent conflicts of interest, but it meant that in flying the nest **Cergus became isolated from the Argus culture**. After that it was just a question of time before it began developing its own strategy. This led to the next phase – the change of business idea.

2. THE NEW BUSINESS IDEA   Cergus was very successful right from the start and was quite profitable when it changed its business idea.

Creative consultancy is demanding, high pressure work and is well paid but a single consultant can only create **a limited amount of added value** if clients are charged on an hourly basis. The market itself imposes limitations on the price per hour or the 'billing rate' as it is sometimes called. Clients will simply refuse to buy the service if they are charged £1,000 an hour, for instance, even if it could be shown that such fees were a fair reflection of the value actually added by the work. Cergus, in common with every other consultancy, was unable to charge the actual value of its services. By comparison, the fees charged by the banks and brokerage firms were enormous.

It was thus natural to look for a way of exploiting the knowhow other than through straightforward consultancy. The solution Cergus chose was to **link its knowhow to financial capital**, thereby giving it 'leverage'.

At this time the value of the company was roughly £100,000 per professional – about £400,000 in total if anyone had been foolish enough to acquire it. A small consultancy firm with little need for financial capital has no need of external owners who can only contribute money.

But with their knowhow tied to a good, capital-intensive business idea the Cergus consultants were worth a lot more and they knew it.

3. ARGUS' STRATEGIC DILEMMA   The management team at Argus was faced with a strategic dilemma. Professional ethics and the lack of financial resources made it impossible for Argus to fund the start-up of a brokerage firm.

But there was no way back for the Cergus consultants. They were eager to exploit the potential they saw on the booming stock market and anyway the relationship with Argus had become attenuated after the years of isolation.

Argus therefore decided to allow their colleagues in Cergus to **develop their own strategy**. If they had not done so there would almost certainly have been a row. Instead the two companies could now maintain a professional relationship and act as **each other's ambassadors** in their respective markets.

Argus acted like a true professional organisation. It preferred to preserve the relationship in a **'federation'** instead of trying to keep the subsidiary within the formal framework of a conventional group. A normal industrial company would regard the Argus decision as pure folly, especially in view of the very high profitability Cergus was to achieve with its new business idea.

4. THE NEW PARTNER   The new majority owner of Cergus was invited in by the Cergus management. They had a high regard for the company despite its lack of experience of the stock market. It is important to note, however, that **its only contribution was financial**.

When the new parent's management representative failed to win the respect of the Cergus professionals and thus the power to manage effectively, the parent made a serious strategic error: it withdrew and thereafter hardly involved itself at all in the activities of its new subsidiary. By not assisting the

Cergus management during the difficult early years it lost an excellent opportunity to show it had considerably more than money to contribute.

5. THE PROBLEMS OF TRANSITION   The assets of Cergus grew extremely fast. The number of professionals increased to over 30 in a three-year period and the number of non-professional staff increased even more. This caused many managerial problems for the founders who were used to managing small teams of professionals as 'first among equals'. A large number of new professionals and back-office staff were confused by the unusually laid-back management style. This added to the difficulties during the company's first year as a brokerage firm.

The new parent was concerned but lacked both the professional knowhow and the management insight to handle the situation. It chose to keep its head down and its fingers crossed.

6. A NEW STRATEGIC DILEMMA   The managers of the new Cergus saw financial analysis as the key to successful portfolio management whereas their parent wanted to stay with stockbroking which a raging 'bull' market was making so profitable. When this basic disagreement broke out into open conflict the parent reacted like an industrial company and put its own interests first. It was another **major strategic mistake to ignore the views of the professionals**.

The key people in Cergus acted as professionals are prone to do when they feel angry or threatened – they left, much to the surprise of the parent which merely indicated just how out of touch with Cergus it had become.

The departures halved the value of Cergus. This brings us dramatically to a question that is one of the themes of this book: to what extent can the holders of a majority of a knowhow company's equity be deemed to be the organisation's true owners?

• Making a business out of knowhow

The Cergus case shows very clearly where the value of a knowhow company lies and the importance of **choosing the right business idea**. The market value of an individual with specific knowhow varies immensely depending on the business that is made of it. In the Cergus case the consultants had a market value of £100,000 whereas with another business idea they had a market value of about £1m a head.

It is thus very **important to distinguish between the business idea and the knowhow it exploits**.

An experienced financial analyst, a creative cartoonist and a gifted computer programmer all possess substantial and potentially valuable knowhow, but if they cannot organise themselves to work with other people and if they are unable to acquire and keep clients, their professional knowhow is worthless to anyone except themselves. The eventual **profitability** of a given knowhow **is** determined by the extent to which it is combined, within the context of a sound business idea, with managerial ability.

A professional can choose various ways to approach a client. Cergus had roughly the same customers before and after the switch of business idea but was able to charge them considerably more because of the extra services a brokerage firm could offer.

• A limit to added value per individual

• Maradona Inc.

Human beings have a limited ability to generate added value. It varies between individuals and professional areas and with age. The career of the Argentinian soccer player Diego Maradona illustrates the point. In his first year as a professional in 1979, when he was 18, he earned $250,000. Seven years later the 25-year-old superstar led Argentina to World Cup victory and was being hailed as the greatest soccer player in the world. In 1986 he earned $3m. By then Maradona was being accorded another kind of value too, equivalent to the capitalised sum of his ability to generate added value for his club. In 1985 he moved from the Spanish club Barcelona to the Italian club Napoli for a transfer fee of $7.75m. The following year he returned to Spain, moving to Real Madrid for a transfer fee of $11m. He had become a one-man institution, moving from club to club and contract to contract for ever higher salaries and ever higher transfer fees. His retirement, it seemed, would not be long delayed.

The professional career of the Swedish tennis player Björn Borg lasted about 10 years. His added value – his prize-money less the direct costs of his organisation – increased rapidly to several million pounds a year but fell equally rapidly thereafter. Borg retired from professional tennis at the age of 26 but by then he had amassed enough wealth to last him the rest of his life. Pop stars and other professional athletes have similar added value life cycles (see Figure 15).

At the other extreme there are statesmen like Henry Kissinger. Their added value (salaries, consultancy fees etc. less direct costs) have a very slowly rising curve. They become more valuable as they grow older.

Ordinary people like us **have intermediate curves** (see Figure 15). The particular shape depends on the market, the business idea and the individual. However, the average added value per individual working in teams tends to be very similar. This means the overall differences between knowhow companies in the same market are rather small.

• Converting knowhow into business ideas

As we have seen the ability of a single human being to make a business out of his or her knowhow is strictly limited. Only by **multiplying the knowhow or by connecting it to financial capital** can an individual get real leverage and high added value. When a company links its knowhow in this way, through its business idea, to other resources such as finance, its profit potential may become substantial enough to attract the interest of investors.

1. MULTIPLICATION Not much financial capital is needed to multiply knowhow by doing the same thing over and over again. Typical examples from the information industries are the production of multi-client studies (supplying the same research to several clients) and selling computer software packages. Before the personal computer entered our homes nobody thought it was possible to sell a word processing software package for under £5,000 and still make a profit. Today the PC versions of the most popular word processing programs sell for less than £100. Mass-production, combined with the very low marginal costs of making extra copies of the software, have forced prices down. The most popular programs sell in their millions. Other examples of knowhow multiplication and the exploitation of rapidly declining marginal costs (high operational gearing) include newsletters and specialist magazines.

The process of knowhow multiplication may involve the recruitment of less educated and so less expensive personnel like distribution staff, order entry book-keepers or the sub-contracting of support functions to typesetting and printing firms. This leaves the professionals free to concentrate on exploiting their knowhow – to become 'knowhow multipliers'. They manage to increase

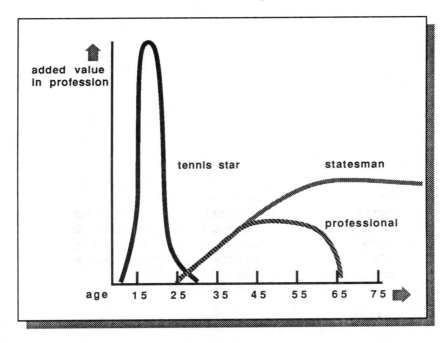

Figure 15   The ability to add value varies between professionals and according to age, usually coming to an end at retirement. Some, like the tennis star, peak early. Others, like the statesman, increase their added value steadily, throughout their lives

their ability to create added value by systematising their knowhow in such a way that it can be multiplied by less educated people.

The problem consultancy firms have with multiplication is that it can only be taken so far. In the end the product has to be delivered by a consultant, irrespective of how many support staff and researchers there are back in the office. The **operational gearing** of a consultancy firm – the extent to which a particular cost base can support an increase in revenues – is much less, for example, than for a specialist publishing firm which can, in theory, double its circulation without increasing the number of professionals.

The UK consultancy firm Butler Cox & Partners, which specialises in the area of information technology (IT), has devised a way of winning a little operational gearing through a development of the multi-client study idea. It has formed the Butler Cox Foundation which companies interested in the firm's knowhow pay a large annual fee to be members of. In return they receive several detailed studies of particular IT areas each year, have the right to attend high-powered seminars and go on study tours, to Japan for example. The Foundation also acts as a marketing agency for the mainstream consultancy business. Its operational gearing is much better than that of the consultancy business although it is clearly very dependent on the knowhow of the mainstream business.

- **Connecting knowhow with financial capital**
  This is the other way to increase the added value of a knowhow company. Typical business ideas of this kind are merchant banking, venture capital, property development and portfolio management.

  A knowhow company with the business idea of 'consulting' needs very little financial capital so outsiders have no reason and no opportunity to invest in it. An 'ordinary' advertising agency, computer consultancy firm or law firm is thus able to produce only limited added value per employee. Unless the employees are allowed to consume practically all the added value themselves they are unlikely to take kindly to the existence of an outside investor. As we have seen external shareholders who only contribute financial capital lead a dangerous life even in capital-intensive knowhow companies, though here, of course, the justification for their existence is more obvious to the ever sceptical professional.

  A particular knowhow can be the inspiration of various business ideas. **Each business idea relates to a specific customer need**; it may vary from newsletters to property management. A team of people with knowhow in building and property might become publishers of a newsletter or a magazine, they might become consultants or they might seek the finance needed to set up a fund management company. All these ideas are valid for those with knowhow about buildings and property.

- **Centrum Invest**
  Centrum Invest was started in 1969 by two people who knew a lot about shopping centres. They worked as consultants for 10 years, helping clients to

develop shopping centres in Scandinavian cities. Their knowhow consisted of expertise in retailing, project planning and architecture. They made good money during their consultancy years but achieved a fairly average added value.

In 1981 they realised that for every £100,000 they made their clients were making millions so they formed an investment company to take equity stakes in the projects they were working on. Several institutions backed them but they retained a significant stake in the investment company. They had leveraged their knowhow with financial capital.

Venture capital works in a similar way. The essential components here are knowhow about entrepreneurs and an ability to evaluate business ideas and strategies. It is difficult to leverage this knowhow without financial capital. However, it is clear that **financial capital plays a minor role** in the successful venture capital firms. This may explain why the European venture capital industry has got off to such an unsteady start.

In too many cases investors have identified venture capital as an interesting 'business idea', founded a company and hired management. They have not realised the key to success in venture capital is knowhow. Venture capital firms have to be managed and monitored like knowhow companies, not like the mortgage departments of banks.

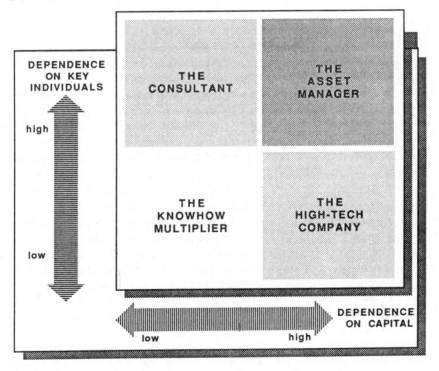

Figure 16   Knowhow companies are either dependent on individuals or on capital. This dependence creates four different business ideas.

• Four generic business ideas

The four business ideas in the diagram above represent general ways of making a business out of knowhow. The professionals may elect to remain pure consultants, they may try to multiply their knowhow or they may choose to link it to financial capital.

• 'The consultant'

This idea requires 'pure' knowhow. Such companies tend to put a high value on professional standards and ethics although not all of them succeed all the time. The revenue-generating ability of a consultancy is always limited to what the team of individuals can produce in terms of added value per hour.

Strategic management consultancies like McKinsey, Boston Consulting Group and Bain & Co. are good examples of the type. Law and accountancy firms are actually imprisoned in this business idea because they are prevented by law from moving to the right of the grid above.

• 'The knowhow multiplier'

The knowhow multiplier multiplies the knowhow of a few key people into systems and routines which can be handled by less educated people and by computers. Accountancy firms are typical examples. The owners are a few people with the core knowhow who act as 'knowhow multipliers'. They add the value of the work of less educated staff to the value of the company they own, leveraging their own knowhow. The staff are seldom shareholders.

The knowhow multiplier has succeeded in embedding some of the knowhow he or she is exploiting into the infrastructure of the organisation – into systems, procedures, routines and the like. This makes such companies much less vulnerable to spin-outs and resignations than the consultancy firm. On the other hand the services these companies provide, despite their high knowhow content, are more subject to price competition so, as a rule, margins tend to be lower.

• 'The asset manager'

The combination of financial capital with knowhow is a rich source of profitable business ideas. In the beginning it was a combination of the inventor and the capitalist which forged the industrial society and created some of the large multinational companies that survive to this day such as Alfa-Laval and ASEA in Sweden or Pilkingtons and Rolls-Royce in the UK. These partnerships were the driving force behind the tremendous growth of Western economies this century.

However, they produced goods made by machines operated by poorly educated workers. To-day's inventors create information and services which can be supplied only by highly educated and knowledgeable people. Finance remains important but these days it is the people with the knowhow who determine the profitability of the financial capital, not the other way around. Financial capital enjoys high profitability when enriched with knowhow or, to put it another way, knowhow is powerfully leveraged when combined with financial capital.

Merchant banks, venture capitalists and other asset managers are examples of this kind of mutually beneficial combination. Capital intensive knowhow companies are very different from their consultancy cousins. As the Figure 17 below shows the pure consultancy firm has a very low total capital – £50,000 per employee at the most. Many consultancy firms and advertising agencies have less than £30,000 of capital per employee.

Those who work in capital intensive knowhow companies are often in charge of enormous resources. In Sweden the big investment companies are at the top with a capital of £10-30m per employee. They seldom have more than 10 employees.

Construction and property companies are next with an average capital per employee of £1-5m each while finance and leasing companies reach about £2m per employee.

In contrast some manufacturing companies have capital per employee levels of £50-100,000. The process and chemical industries are a little higher at £200,000 per employee but no manufacturing company is as capital intensive as the knowhow companies which manage capital in the form of cash, real estate or other assets.

There is a **close correlation between capital intensity and** one of the most important knowhow company performance measures – **added value per employee** (AVPE). Leasing and building companies achieve AVPEs in excess of £100,000 and investment companies can reach over £500,000.

It is not surprising that those who work in these industries are well paid. Money management knowhow is a very valuable commodity when linked to money. Salaries of $300,000 are commonplace on Wall Street, New York's central financial thoroughfare. In the City of London and in Stockholm's financial area market values are around £100,000 and £50,000 a year per head respectively.

These salaries reflect the quantity of capital such people move at high speed between the world's money markets. But handsome though their pay seems to outsiders it pales into insignificance compared to the value they add to the capital of their employers. They get 10-20% of the value added. It is no wonder their loyalties are tested when they know that booming markets make them worth many times their weight in gold to their employers.

But despite the high value of portfolio managers, capital owners have much **greater power in fund management companies than they do in consultancy firms**.

Consultancy organisations have **a fundamental fragility**. They fall apart overnight if key people leave. Financial capital stays on the balance sheet after a 'walk-out'. It might be difficult to find equally good people but a walk-out seldom endangers the whole company. In the case of Cergus, for example, only a quarter of the professionals remained after the conflict but the company, represented by the financial capital, remained more or less intact. The parent could recruit new people and start all over again. Cergus lost much of its value but the company still survives without its founders.

- **'The high-tech company'**
  The high-tech company combines investments in equipment, mainly computers, with investments in routines, systems and software with which it provides goods and services for its customers and clients. It tries to multiply knowhow by incorporating it into products which will sell in large numbers.

INTER INNOVATION   The Swedish company Inter Innovation, now world leader in the design, development and manufacture of systems for counting and sorting bank notes, was set up in 1973 as a licence broker. Its founder, Leif Lundblad, was interested in the idea of transferring knowhow between Sweden and other nations.

Lundblad was also an inventor. He developed and patented a system for sort-

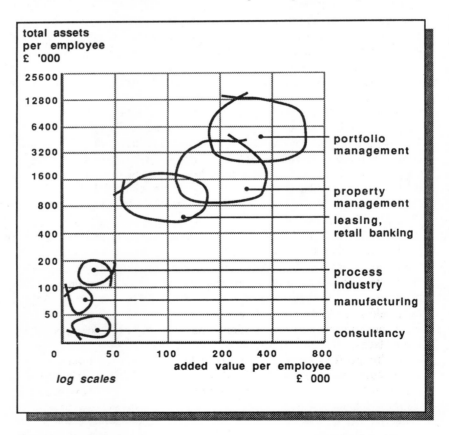

Figure 17   The amount of added value per employee is closely linked to capital intensity and the business idea.

ing bank notes. Initially it was only a small side line and Inter Innovation merely sold systems, sub-contracting the actual manufacturing to outsiders.

After a couple of years, however, it became essential to control the manufacturing so Lundblad acquired one of his suppliers and started his own production line.

The growth of Inter Innovation, where the inventor built a company around a unique and proprietary technology, is a classic case of entrepreneurial development.

• A business idea a day

The leader of a manufacturing company visiting a professional knowhow organisation is in for a few surprises. One of the first things that will strike him is that the company is positively **buzzing with new business ideas**. The place seems saturated with them. All professionals worth their salt should be able to come up with at least one business idea a day each (though here, as elsewhere, quantity has little to do with quality). The fertility of the professional mind is very loosely bridled by considerations of practicality. For managers it is often hard to distinguish the good idea from a passing whim. The acid tests are whether the idea is based on the company's existing knowhow and whether there is a market for it.

The typical 'agency' knowhow company is bursting with fine notions and fantasies that never develop into business ideas. The typical 'factory' service company, a fast food restaurant chain or a retail bank for example, normally suffers from a dire shortage of new business ideas. It manages well enough in its existing marketplace but its leaders tend to regard the problems of adaptation to a new business idea or market as being, for all practical purposes, insurmountable.

The 'factory' has become successful because it has managed to industrialise the supply of its service by dint of heavy investment in equipment and the recruitment and training of a special kind of personnel. McDonald's is a case in point. The company will find it very hard to develop new business ideas out of its present one. It has built expensive, special-purpose kitchens and committed itself and its cost structure to the recruitment of relatively uneducated employees.

McDonald's, notwithstanding its enormous success, seems stuck fast in its niche. It could run into serious problems in the future if the world's appetite for 'fast food' fades.

Only the professional organisation has both new ideas and the power to turn them into viable businesses. In this endeavour it invariably employs what we shall call an **entrepreneurial business development system**.

SUMMARY

- There are limits to the **added value** that can be created by a professional.
- They can be raised when knowhow is **multiplied** or **linked to financial capital.**
- It is important to **choose the right business idea** and to **distinguish between the business idea and the knowhow it exploits.**
- The profitability of a given knowhow is determined by its **combination with a good business idea and managerial expertise.**
- Each business idea is **related to a specific customer need.**
- Even in capital-intensive knowhow companies **financial capital plays a relatively minor role.**
- There are four generic business ideas: **the consultant; the knowhow multiplier; the asset manager; the high-tech company.**
- There is a **close correlation between capital intensity and value added per employee.**
- Suppliers of financial capital **have more power in fund management companies than consultancy firms.**
- Only professional organisations have **new ideas** *and* **the ability to turn them into viable businesses**.

11

• Making a Business out of Knowhow – expansion and growth

• Grow or die

Companies must grow or die. Expansion and development are as necessary for a knowhow company as they are for any other. Without them organisations stagnate, become brittle and break. It is **the methodology of growth and development that is different** for knowhow companies. The distinguishing feature of development in such companies is that **it *must* be based on the organisation's knowhow**.

It is not enough to have a knowhow edge in one particular area. It is also necessary for this knowhow to be in demand – for there to be customers willing to pay for it. For this to be the case the knowhow must be unique or at least readily distinguishable from that of the company's competitors.

First, **the company's knowhow must be defined**.

It consists of two elements: the **professional knowhow** which carries the business idea and the **managerial knowhow** which is accumulated while the organisation is being run successfully in a particular marketplace. These two elements can be seen as the products of the dual expertise requirement we encountered in Chapter Four.

Successful development in knowhow companies is usually the result of a combination of these two elements; that is to say it is **entrepreneurial** – it consists of a series of marriages between new business ideas and the managerial ability needed to implement them.

• Entrepreneurial business development

The prime responsibility for business development in the professional organisation lies with the leader. No new business idea can succeed without his or her intimate involvement. Indeed new business development is so dependent on the key people that it is often easy to trace each of a professional organisation's businesses back to the individual who first had the idea and then implemented it.

Many professional organisations have only one leader. An important part of his or her job is to look at all the ideas, which the organisation generates, to distinguish those that are mere professional day-dreams from those with real promise and then to arrange for their implementation by appointing '**project champions**'.

A distinctive feature of business development in knowhow companies is that it is **wholly dependent on the ability of a few individuals**. These people must work on their projects themselves. They must immerse themselves in them utterly, doing everything in the early stages – researching, preparing proposals, writing reports, consulting with colleagues, negotiating for R&D resources and collecting together the knowhow that is to be exploited. Typical entrepreneurs relish the role of 'project champion'. It becomes a part of themselves. They will often wander around the office in a dream, like a pregnant woman totally pre-occupied with her baby. After a while the project becomes so large the champion needs the assistance of others. This is the birth; the point at which the project emerges from the womb to become a business in its own right.

- ## State supported development companies
During the late 1970s and early 1980s national governments throughout Europe, notably in France, the UK, Sweden, Norway, West Germany and Italy, began to inject millions of pounds into development organisations in attempts to revive industrial activity, and more specifically employment, in their depressed regions.

An 'experienced' managing director was appointed to lead each agency supported by a few assistants and secretaries. Today very few of these organisations survive and most of the money has been lost. It is the same all over Europe. Most of the development agencies have incurred heavy losses and have had to be wound up.

Why have these programmes failed? Some blame the incompetence of the politicians but that is not a sufficient explanation. Many large multinational groups experienced the same problems when trying to start small companies in the new, high-tech industries. Oil giant Exxon's ill-fated venture into office equipment a few years ago is just one example of big business' inability to nurture small businesses in knowhow areas. Another is the failure of the attempt by the French, state-owned motor giant Renault to wrest leadership of Grand Prix motor racing from a highly innovative group of small, UK companies including Williams, McLaren, Brabham and Lotus.

The most important lesson to be learned from such failures is that business development **cannot be administered from the outside** through the injection of money by special purpose development organisations. This is true of all businesses but is particularly true of knowhow companies.

The leader of a knowhow company cannot simply give a senior professional money and tell him or her to go away and dream up a new business idea. Business development in the professional organisation and the ideas that inspire it are the **spontaneous results of a creative environment** which not only permits but actually encourages people to test themselves in projects of their own. The environment must encourage risk-taking, emphasise results-orientation and inculcate quality-consciousness and a sensitivity to the needs of clients. If the management succeeds in creating such an environment business development will occur automatically.

- **The prime mover**
Professional organisations depend for their business development on individuals – **entrepreneurial leaders** – who wish and are able to exploit their own knowhow and that of other professionals.

   The professional organisation is incapable of starting a new venture, however tempting it might be and no matter how close to the core knowhow, if it lacks an entrepreneur. If it has an entrepreneur starting a new business is easy. It is simply a matter of appointing a project champion, giving him or her a budget, agreeing a framework within the existing culture and telling the entrepreneur to get on with it.

   Entrepreneurial business development begins with **the development of entrepreneurs, not businesses**. This is one of the reasons why the pan-European experiment with regional development agencies and the Exxon and Renault ventures referred to earlier went so badly wrong. Viable new businesses, on which the creation of lasting jobs depends, cannot be conjured out of thin air by managers appointed by the owners of capital, whether from the public or private sector, and instructed to throw money around. These days money is a relatively plentiful commodity. The main constraint on the development of new businesses is **a dire shortage of entrepreneurs** enthused with sound and imaginative ideas.

• The case of publishing

Why do publishing company managers assume the only way to develop their businesses is to launch or acquire new titles?

   The question seems trivial and the answer obvious. It is the result of the conventional wisdom within the industry. Such companies have acquired a certain managerial knowhow about how to publish newspapers and magazines, find interesting authors or reach readers in a mass market. They expand their business by exploiting this knowhow. This might be called **managerial business development**.

   But another publishing company, with a knowhow-orientated business idea, might adopt a very different approach to the development of its business. It might decide instead to build the business **on the professional as opposed to the managerial knowhow** within the organisation. Thus, a company publishing books or magazines about sailing may try to develop this knowhow into new businesses like building yachts or running sail-training courses. A company publishing cookery books might decide to open a restaurant or sell gourmet holidays.

It happens. The two British companies which publish *The Economist* magazine and the *Jane's* defence titles both offer specialist consultancy services based on their knowhow.

The specialist publishing company will often have a unique vantage point within its industry because of the broad spread of its interests and, more specifically, its total overview of technical development. This valuable, generalised knowhow is locked up in the heads of a few of the company's senior journalists. With proper management it can be developed into consulting, venture capital or new companies formed to exploit new technologies. But entrepreneurs are needed for this kind of business development and most publishing companies lack entrepreneurs. Without them it can be dangerous to adopt this kind of business development based on professional rather than managerial knowhow.

The new media – videotex, cable TV, satellites, computer networks and databases – offer publishing companies a cornucopia of new opportunities to exploit their professional knowhow in media other than the printed word. Some publishing companies have responded to these possibilities in one way or another, by venturing into databases and videotex for example. So far – largely because of a chronic lack of the entrepreneurial resource – the results of such diversifications have been indifferent.

• Two knowhow company start-ups

• Venture Capital Report

Lucius Cary was educated at Eton and Trinity College, Oxford where he read Engineering Science and Economics. After serving a year's apprenticeship at the UK Atomic Energy Authority's research centre at Harwell he borrowed some money and went to Harvard Business School.

He returned in 1971, armed with an MBA, and joined Hanson Trust, the successful conglomerate which has subsequently become one of Britain's largest companies. Cary was sent to Gloucester to help look after Hanson's agricultural division but after a few months he became disenchanted with his work as a roving consultant. As he put it: 'I had never intended to be a consultant, knowing that by temperament I was a doer rather than an adviser, and the expectation when I joined Hanson had been that I would be given responsibility and be judged on results'.

It did not work out that way. Bored and frustrated Cary determined, in the spring of 1972, to start his own business. The trouble was he had no business idea. In the end he decided, 'more or less on impulse', to try to open a chain of American-style hamburger restaurants. He admits he knew nothing about catering but he had seen how well the Great American Disaster hamburger restaurant had done in London (its rival the Great American Success was a disaster) and had observed there was nothing like it in the provinces.

Working in the evenings he wrote a 26-page business plan entitled 'Proposal to establish a chain of fast food bars'. He approached the only two UK venture capital organisations prepared to invest in small, high-risk businesses – ICFC (now part of Investors in Industry or '3is') and the Small Business Capital Fund (now Development Capital Ltd.) but was turned down by both.

Advertisements in the *Financial Times* and the *Daily Telegraph* plus other contacts elicited, after numerous setbacks and disappointments, the £26,000 of start-up finance needed. 'Cary's' restaurant opened in Bristol in March 1973. After a hesitant start it made a small profit in year two and by 1976 there was enough cash to open a second restaurant. This was instantly successful and a third opened the following year.

In 1978 Cary sold two of the restaurants and went into publishing. He had developed a completely different business idea involving the exploitation of the knowhow he had accumulated during his search for start-up finance.

He reasoned that if there had been a simple way for him to present the bones of his restaurant business proposal to 200 or so 'people of the right sort', investing institutions and wealthy individuals, instead of having to rely on the 30 or so respondents to his advertisements, he would have been able to raise the money he needed more easily and more quickly.

So Cary founded the monthly *Venture Capital Report* to provide, as he put it, 'a marketplace in which people seeking risk capital and other resources for their business could present their propositions in some detail to several hundred potential investors, each of whom would be able to provide money, and many of whom would also be able to provide other resources'.

VCR now has about 900 subscribers, paying £180 a year each. Companies featured in the report are charged a nominal £100 cost-recovery fee and if they succeed in raising money as a result of appearing in the report they pay a percentage commission to VCR on a sliding scale beginning at 4% of the first £10,000 raised and reducing to 1% on sums over £30,000.

The company also sells over 1,000 copies each year of its £25 annual 'Guide' to venture capital.

In recent years Cary has found another, much more profitable use for his knowhow. His long experience in venture capital has convinced him that despite the great strides the UK venture capital industry has made in the 1980s there remains a serious financing gap at the bottom end of the market. Entrepreneurs and inventors with a new product idea find it very hard to raise the money needed, (typically £20,000), to finance the building of a prototype. The sum is too small for established funds to bother with and generally speaking such projects are too risky for all but the very well-heeled private investor.

So Cary has leveraged his knowhow by connecting it with financial capital. He has raised two specialist funds, Seed Corn Capital Ltd. which began with £200,000 to invest and, more recently, Seed Investments Ltd. to which one of Britain's largest venture capital firms, APA, has subscribed £250,000. APA's leader, Ronald Cohen, acknowledges the venture capital industry's neglect of the small start-up and recognises how well equipped Cary is to run such a fund.

Cary and Cohen both realise that the size of the initial financing requirement has very little to do with the ultimate value of the investment. Cary is fond of citing the example of ARD, the US firm that contributed £25,000 to the start-up of Digital Equipment Corporation and whose investment later became worth more than £200m.

From Cary's point of view fund management dovetails very neatly into VCR. The publishing side, though much less profitable, generates the 'deal flow' for the funds.

The structures of the two funds provide an interesting indication of how the relationship between knowhow, represented in this case by Cary, and financial capital, represented by the subscribers to the funds, is changing. Cary received a 10% 'carried interest' (that means he gets 10% of the capital gains without having to invest) in the first fund set up in 1983 but won a 20% carried interest in the APA-backed fund set up three years later. In venture capital, at any rate, the bargaining power of the professional seems to have doubled in three years (see Chapter Fourteen for a fuller discussion of changes in bargaining power).

- **Venture News**

If Sweden has an equivalent of Lucius Cary he is 34-year-old Lars Lindgren. He has been on the move for most of his life and has always been interested in information and in starting new projects. When still at university he got a part time job as a public relations manager for the quoted Swedish development company, Hexagon. He learned to handle networks of both the computer and personal kinds and picked up knowhow about producing reports, press releases and newsletters.

His entrepreneurial qualities began to blossom during the venture capital boom in Sweden in 1982-3 (the British venture capital boom had begun a few years earlier). Venture capital appealed to Lars Lindgren. There was a pioneering feeling to it, a flexibility, and an emphasis on human contacts that suited his inclinations and aptitudes. He wanted to be involved and felt that with his background some sort of information activity would be most appropriate. While pondering how to start he made contact with Venture Economics of the US, an information company that had built a database containing information about US venture capital suppliers and all the companies they had invested in. Venture Economics also publishes newsletters covering recent investments and statistics about the venture capital industry culled from its databases. Perhaps, Lindgren suggested, this could be something for Sweden. Venture Economics, which had just started up in the UK, advised him against it. Founder Stan Pratt said the Swedish market was too small.

But Lindgren was not to be deterred so easily. During 1984 he collected together as much information as he could about the Swedish venture capital market and in the autumn of that year he left Hexagon to start his own company, Venture News. The first year was spent collecting addresses and phone numbers, making contacts and building a simple database containing all the companies Swedish venture capital firms had already invested in. In the process he learned to handle a personal computer.

The first year's revenues were about £40,000 in the form of subscriptions to his newsletters and access fees to his data and files of clippings from news-papers and magazines about venture capital all over Sweden. Stan Pratt was impressed. He appointed Lindgren the agent of Venture Economics in Scan-dinavia with the rights to sell the US database.

The following year Lindgren began to build a similar Swedish database on his computer, started constructing a pan-Scandinavian network of partners and set up a Venture Capital Club where venture capitalists meet for lunch once a month.

In 1987 Lindgren's entrepreneurial spirit alighted on another enthusiasm. He bought a TVR, a specialist British sportscar, and was so impressed by it that he requested and was granted the agency rights to sell the TVR range in Scan-dinavia.

• Lessons to be learned

Venture Capital Report and Venture News are good examples of what knowhow-orientated business development is all about.

An entrepreneur finds an unexploited knowhow area, collects as much infor-mation about it as possible, establishes a network of contacts, finds tools to process the information, constructs a vehicle or vehicles for selling it and goes ahead. It matters little, for the purposes of our argument, whether Lucius Cary's nine-year old VCR and Lindgren's much younger Venture News con-tinue to prosper, though we personally hope they will. What is interesting about the examples is the light they shed on the methodology of knowhow company formation and development in the information society.

Let us try to summarise the characteristics of the knowhow company that shape the **methodology** of its development:

LITTLE NEED FOR FINANCIAL CAPITAL   The need for financial capital in new knowhow companies is normally very low, consisting of little more than money for a small computer and a living wage for the first year. The entrepreneur may supplement revenues by consulting in the beginning but if the business idea proves viable he or she will normally, after the initial period, concentrate wholly on developing it.

LOW BARRIERS TO ENTRY   It is easy to start a knowhow company if you have the knowhow but though the need for financial capital is normally fairly low, ideas are very easy to steal. The entrepreneur must therefore find ways of protecting his niche from competitors. It is rarely possible to patent abstract business ideas of this kind so effective defences are more likely to be found in agreements with suppliers or clients about exclusive rights, or something unique like a database, rare personal knowhow or ability or an unusually large and valuable personal network. Taken together these defences can prove just as strong as patents and may last much longer.

INTERNATIONALISATION   The business ideas of Cary and Lindgren are similar; the supply of information and related services about venture capital. Neither of the business ideas are restricted to the UK or Scandinavian markets. It is theoretically possible either to export knowhow about UK and Swedish venture capital abroad (not a large market) or to start similar operations in neighbouring countries. Venture Economics of the US has already begun to 'internationalise' its service and thus to export its knowhow. Cary and Lindgren have similar opportunities. There are always numerous possibilities for business development in knowhow companies. Ideas are seldom the limitation.

HUMAN NETWORK   New knowhow companies characteristically try to reach agreements and form friendly relationships with customers, suppliers and other companies in similar industries. This is a way of reducing risk, of course, but it also helps to expand the network through which flows the information that is the knowhow company's raw material. Cary's relationship with APA is a good illustration of an interactive network. APA began as a customer of Venture Capital Report and has now become a joint venture partner. Cary has leveraged his knowhow by winning access to APA-raised capital and APA has leveraged its capital by gaining access to Cary-accumulated knowhow.

LOW LEVEL OF MANAGERIAL KNOWHOW   A knowhow company is rarely started by an entrepreneur with a high level of managerial knowhow. More often than not the companies are set up by professionals who see a chance to develop into entrepreneurs. The first years of the young company will be riddled with mistakes resulting from its lack of managerial knowhow. It makes no difference whether the company consists of chartered accountants or advertising copy-writers; they invariably fall into most of the traps that lie in wait for inexperienced managers.

DUAL EXPERTISE   The most important task in the start-up phase is to master both the professional and the managerial skills. The former can be more or less taken for granted; it is lack of the latter that makes the early years so risky. A study by statisticians at Britain's Department of Trade and Industry based on VAT returns has shown that the first three years of a young company's life are by far and away the most risky. Corporate mortality rates drop dramatically thereafter. In this respect knowhow companies are no different from any other kind of company although it is probably true that they are more at risk from managerial mistakes than most and, because they should not be great cash consumers in the early stages, less at risk from the classic cash flow crisis. Most start-ups in knowhow areas consist of groups of skilled professionals who break away from existing organisations and begin with virtually no managerial skills.

• Turn-Key Data

In the summer of 1979 two young men, fresh from college, decided to form a computer company, Turn-Key Data (TKD). Their business idea was to import peripheral hardware for the booming market in personal computers and to sell software and training. The start-up was very successful. Within two years sales had exceeded £500,000 and there were still only five employees. When TKD was introduced onto the new Over-The-Counter share market in Stockholm in 1983 it had 11 employees and sales were running at the rate of £1.3m a year.

The company raised £400,000 of new equity to finance the creation of a chain of computer stores all over the country. The budget was forecasting sales growth of 300% a year. A year later TKD went bankrupt. There was no shortage of bidders for the remains but all but one, which went bankrupt itself two years later, lost interest when the deficiency in the liquidated balance sheet emerged at £1.8m.

- **Lessons to be learned**
  The post-mortem showed the young company had no professional management accounting system. The managers simply did not know how bad the situation was until they ran out of cash. And they and their investors appeared not to have realised that it is virtually impossible to quadruple turnover every year even in a high growth market. Clearly the company had been sadly **lacking in managerial knowhow**.

  It is arguable that it also **lacked adequate professional knowhow**. TKD's managers and the financial analysts who supported them believed Turn-Key Data to be a 'computer company'. In reality it was much more like a run-of-the-mill retailing chain where the important knowhow included the art of monitoring stock turnover, point of sales ability and pricing skills. If the managers had hired an old TV salesman they might have avoided some of the basic mistakes.

- # Knowhow export
  'Service exports' has become a popular concept for European politicians in recent years. The companies of the 'post-industrial society' must export their products, it is argued, in the same way as traditional companies have always done. But **it is impossible to export services** in any volume. The service is typically sold at or near the place where it is produced. How can you export hospital services or haircuts? As soon as the hospital is moved abroad the service is moved abroad also; the only income an exporter can earn is through dividends. Little increase in employment can be expected from this kind of 'export'.

  But though it is impossible to export services **it *is* possible to export knowhow**. The hospital in question can export its knowhow about treatments and medication by transferring that knowhow from its own people to people in the other country and it can export managerial knowhow too, about hospital administration for example.

  As in any other export business knowhow exporters must have a clear idea of the uniqueness of their products – their knowhow in this case – and they must be confident there are markets for them abroad. They must be clear too about precisely what kind of knowhow they are exporting. Is it professional knowhow? Is it managerial knowhow? Or is it a mixture of both? These distinctions are vital. Soaps and cars work in the same way wherever they are sold but there is no point in trying to export British legal knowhow to France.

- **Service Management Group**
  The consultancy firm SMG, set up in 1980 by Richard Normann, formerly of the Swedish consultancy firm SIAR, is an example of a successful knowhow exporter. Normann left SIAR after leading a major project, financed by large service groups, to invent and develop a new way of managing service companies.

  The project was so successful that Normann decided to form his own company to exploit the knowhow he had developed. To-day he heads a successful business employing more than 60 consultants in six countries, working for clients in the service industries. This knowhow, developed in Sweden, proved eminently exportable because there was nothing like it anywhere else in the world.

• Growth = expansion of the knowhow capital

One of the greatest errors the leader of a knowhow company can make is to accept the methods, objectives and yardsticks of the conventional industrial company.

While it may be quite acceptable for the industrial company to strive to maximise the growth of financial assets, to apply the same objective to a knowhow company would be to court disaster. For the knowhow company it is the expansion of the knowhow capital which is the measure of growth.

Knowhow capital growth normally involves growth in the number of professionals but the company's clients are not interested in whether it is the biggest in the world in terms of numbers of people or turnover. Clients do appreciate, however, a company that can show it has more knowhow than its competitors. The contemporary focus on growth of turnover or capital as evidence of success is **a left-over from the industrial age**. For members of the knowhow society volume measured in that way has no meaning. Whether an organisation is large or small is likewise a matter of indifference to the professionals. All they care about is whether the work and their colleagues are interesting and stimulating and whether their clients appreciate them.

A knowhow company that can grow organically is demonstrably successful and there can be no doubt about the soundness of its business idea. In contrast, a knowhow company that grows only through mergers and acquisitions **cannot demonstrate the soundness of its core business idea**. The acquisition-led strategy may be acceptable in mature industries but in mature industries knowhow companies are thin on the ground.

However, managements who wish to grow faster than organic growth permits can do so successfully as long as they do not neglect their core knowhow and the rules of knowhow management. A healthy core business combined with a careful acquisition strategy may prove the quickest and safest way of expanding a knowhow company.

• Barclays Bank buys knowhow

The most dramatic sign of the current 'convergence' of the service-orientated banking industry with the knowhow-orientated securities industry came in October 1986 when the so-called 'Big Bang' brought an end to the City's commission-fixing cartel in stockbroking.

It all began in 1976 when the scope of British restrictive practices law was extended to the service sector. Three years later the rule book of the Stock Exchange, which gave force to the cartel's fixed commissions, was referred by the Office of Fair Trading to the Restrictive Practices Court.

The case never came to court. In 1983 the re-elected Conservative government said it would instruct the OFT to withdraw the case if the Stock Exchange promised to phase-out its fixed commissions structure by the end of 1986.

This apparently simple change was to revolutionise the City. It made the old 'single capacity' system – the separation of stockbroking from stockjobbing – impractical. Dual capacity, requiring massive injections of capital into stockbroking, became inevitable especially if London was to survive as one of the world's major financial centres in the increasingly competitive world markets.

Barclays Bank, one of Britain's 'big four' clearing banks, was determined to become a major player in the 'converged' financial services industry. It was widely believed the future lay in huge financial services supermarkets. Barclays had the banking knowhow but not the securities knowhow. Its great opportunity, or so it seemed, and the opportunity of groups like it, was that it had the capital the securities industry so desperately needed.

Barclays, in common with other banks, decided to give effect to the integration of the two industries by buying securities knowhow. In March 1984, two-and-a-half years before 'Big Bang' was due, it announced it had agreed to buy, when Stock Exchange rules permitted, London's top jobber Wedd Durlacher Mordaunt with 55 partners and 400 staff and leading broker de Zoete & Bevan with 39 partners and 380 staff. A nice touch was that Barclays chairman Sir Timothy Bevan was related to the Bevans who had joined with the de Zoetes in 1970.

Since Wedds and de Zoetes were both private partnerships there was no requirement to reveal the prices Barclays would pay for the two firms. However unofficial estimates, never denied by Barclays, suggested the figures were in the region of £100m for Wedds and £50m for de Zoetes indicating about £1.8m per Wedd partner and £1.3m per de Zoete partner. In retrospect it is hard to see quite what Barclays believed it was buying with these not inconsiderable sums. If it was knowhow capital then the bank was in for a rude shock.

In September 1984, 37-year-old gilts jobber and Wedds partner John Hutchinson left because of what he called 'a difference of philosophy over the way to proceed'. It was an unsettling development not helped by Wedd's decision to withhold the Christmas bonus that year. There were rumblings in the ranks especially from the so-called 'marzipan' boys – professionals just below partnership level who were missing out on the £1.8m a head bonanza. Wedds tried to defuse the situation by quickly making 12 new partners.

At the same time the strains of integration were beginning to show on the other side. It was estimated within the bank that there were more people at de Zoetes earning over £30,000 a year than in the whole of the Barclays UK operation.

Early in February the mobility of the professional knowhow Barclays believed it had 'bought' became more evident. Hugh Hughes, the Wedds partner in charge of European dealing, left and was followed almost immediately by six other members of the team, five of whom followed Hughes to rival firm Savory Milln. The 'team' raid had arrived and a Wedds spokesman expressed himself as being 'none too pleased'.

Less than a month later three more Wedds 'marzipan' boys left to join Schroders. In a desperate attempt to staunch the haemorrhage Wedds asked the Stock Exchange for special permission to appoint another 40 partners, making 105 in all.

That brought the average price Barclays had agreed to pay per partner to around the £1m mark and things began to settle down a little. The lull was short-lived. In July 1985 Wedds was rocked to its foundations ('wherever they are?' Barclays must have been asking itself) when six partners and three 'marzipan' boys left. Eight of them joined Kleinwort Benson from whom Barclays de Zoete Wedd (BZW), as the Barclays securities operation had been christened, had recently poached its chief executive, Sir Martin Jacomb. Two of the Kleinwort defectors were senior partners and members of the nine-man management team. One of them, Charles Hue-Williams, had been expected to become Wedds' next leader. The Kleinwort eight were believed to have moved for a transfer fee of £1m and for salaries totalling more than £2m. One Sunday newspaper estimated the raid had reduced Wedds' value by a third.

A week later yet another Wedds partner left and in October Wedds staff were told there would be no interim bonus because soaring costs – largely associated with the huge salaries Wedds had had to pay to make good its horrendous staff losses – had reduced profits to practically nothing.

In September Barclays announced the structure of BZW and revealed that former Wedd and de Zoete partners would retain 20% of the shares. A number of senior executives at the bank, already smarting from the huge salaries their new colleagues at BZW were receiving, turned a deeper shade of green.

In November the de Zoetes senior partner James Titcomb announced his retirement. It was not unexpected and seemed a minor loss compared to the mass desertions from Wedds. A month later the balance was redressed somewhat when nine senior analysts and salesmen and one member of the support staff left de Zoetes to join rival jobbers, Smith Brothers.

Back at Barclays strains of another kind were beginning to show. Just after

Christmas the Banking Insurance and Finance Union (BIFU) said it would take the bank to an industrial tribunal because of a failure to consult with BIFU during the planning of BZW's structure, implemented in June 1986. BIFU was annoyed about a clause in BZW's contract of employment which stipulated no union recognition or representation.

March saw the departure of de Zoete's banking analyst Tom Bennett to Morgan Grenfell and in June it was announced that following a weekend of tough bargaining in the Channel Islands the formal birth of BZW would be celebrated with goodwill payments to salesmen and analysts of up to £200,000 and nearly 200 company cars. The 'marzipan' boys, their bargaining power enhanced by the defections, had flexed their muscles to good effect.

'Big Bang' in October came as something of a relief to the battered BZW though it must be said it had suffered no worse than many of the other big players who had bought securities firms. They were as bemused as Barclays by the rapacious greed and gross disloyalty of their new employees.

More trouble surfaced early in the new year when de Zoete & Bevan's banking analysts issued a circular advising clients to sell shares in Barclays. The report predicted Barclays earnings growth would be the lowest of the 'big four' banks in 1987 and said: 'There is something wrong with Barclays. The performance of the stock in recent years and the present rating are evidence'.

Barclays chairman Sir Timothy Bevan, who had family links with de Zoete & Bevan, was reported to be furious. There was talk within the group of instructing BZW not to comment on Barclays in future but in the end wiser counsels prevailed. A Barclays spokesman, with a curious choice of words, said 'it would be inelegant to stop BZW analysts commenting on a major stock in a major segment of the market'. The professionals had demonstrated their power. No considerations of parentage were going to stop them from discharging their professional duty as they saw it.

It remains to be seen how BZW finally settles down within the Barclays group. Some say the trials and tribulations of the past few years, since the deals with Wedds and de Zoetes were struck in 1984, have had more to do with the upheavals of 'Big Bang', the shift to a new trading system and the progressive internationalisation of the British securities industry, than with any fundamental flaw in the concept of the financial services supermarket.

● **American lawyers – big is not beautiful**
If profits are equal to beauty in business, then large size appears to have little going for it, at least in the US law business. In 1985 the magazine *The American Lawyer* published an analysis of the country's top 50 law firms. As the table below shows there was a conspicuous lack of correlation between profitability and size. On the contrary, it looks very much as if a statistically significant **negative** correlation between profitability and size might have been established with a larger sample of, say, 250 firms.

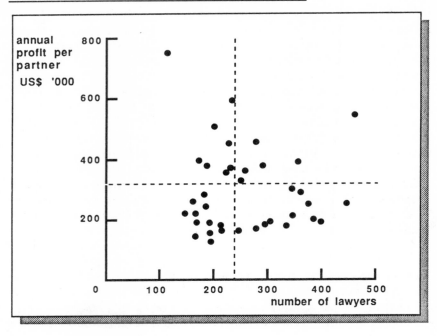

Figure 18   Big is not beautiful for law firms.

- **Swedish advertising industry**
  The Swedish advertising industry is highly fragmented. The largest agency had only 174 employees in 1985 and generated revenues, in the form of commissions and fees, of only SKr80m (about £8m). Fragmentation is a natural quality of the advertising industry because the phenomenon of the spin-out or break-away – the departure of a group of professionals to set up on their own – is endemic. As soon as an agency reaches a certain size, the centrifugal forces seem to go critical and it breaks up or divides into smaller units.

  Five years ago Sweden's largest and apparently most successful agency was Anderson and Lembke. It was a spurious and ephemeral pre-eminence. Today, following a series of major upheavals, Anderson and Lembke consists of a number of independent agencies spread throughout four countries.

  The main reason for the instability of large agencies is that creative people clearly prefer to work in small teams. It has proved very difficult in Sweden to organise and manage large agencies. And there has been little commercial pressure on Swedish agencies to grow large. Clients have been concerned much more with the quality of the service they receive than with the size of the agencies supplying it.

But as we have seen the trend elsewhere has been very different. The age of the giant agency has arrived with a bang in Britain and America, although whether it will last long is far from clear (see Chapter Fourteen, pages 198-9). The theory behind the giant agency strategy is that large, multinational companies demand services which only large, international agencies can offer. This has been the main inspiration of the prodigious growth of Britain's Saatchi & Saatchi, now the world's largest advertising agency, over the past few years. (See Chapter Seven, pages 94-7).

Why has the Swedish advertising market not evolved in the same way? After all, many of the larger agencies are now parts of international groups. It is not as if the local industry has been insulated from international trends.

There are many possible explanations, such as the small home market, language differences and the difficulties associated with the export of knowhow. Another reason might be that **Swedish advertising agencies are badly managed.** Very few achieve profit margins (net margin before tax as a percentage of turnover) of more than 10% and employees claim an unusually large proportion of the added value, close to 80% on average, in their salaries.

The debt :equity ratio of Sweden's top 15 agencies averages 6.5. These figures suggest the managers of the Swedish advertising agencies have signally failed to build organisations strong enough to act as platforms for business development and acquisition-led growth.

• The three strategies for growth

Knowhow companies can choose between three basic strategies for growth:

1. **organic growth**
2. **merger and acquisition**
3. **combining financial capital with knowhow**

We will look at each of these strategies, one at a time below.

• Organic growth

Organic growth is **the most natural expansion strategy** for knowhow companies. It occurs because the business idea is so strong and the knowhow level so high that more and more customers demand the same services. Knowhow companies growing organically recruit more professionals, thereby increasing their productive capacity within the same business idea. They **advance along the professional axis**.

The main draw-back of organic growth is **the problem of control**, particularly quality control. The new professionals, often working in various offices dotted throughout the world, require new control systems and middle management. Both of these additions **increase the complexity of the organisation and tend to undermine professional standards**.

Organic **expansion is constrained both by the ability to recruit** new professionals of good quality and by the ability to manage more complex organisations. Since the supply of professionals is limited, professional organisations tend to rely heavily on internal education, training and the recruitment of young people who can be developed internally.

The problems of complexity and the availability of the right professionals impose limits on the potential of organic growth. It thus seems **hard to grow at more than 10% a year by volume** if you rely purely on organic growth, even when the market is growing at a much faster rate – witness the McKinsey-Boston Consulting Group case discussed in Chapter Nine.

Organic growth is probably **the safest expansion method** for knowhow companies. The trouble is that for ambitious managers 10% a year volume growth is paltry. The ability to build organisations and expand the organisation rapidly is the stuff of managerial knowhow. Most **managers and entrepreneurs cherish dreams of empire**. Their role models are the tycoons lionised in the financial press. The managers have to believe it is possible to achieve their ambitions within a reasonable time. This requires growth rates well in excess of the 10% a year that organic growth permits and which only doubles the size of the organisation in seven years.

Knowhow companies which grow organically tend to be **biassed towards professionalism rather than entrepreneurialism**. To the managers of

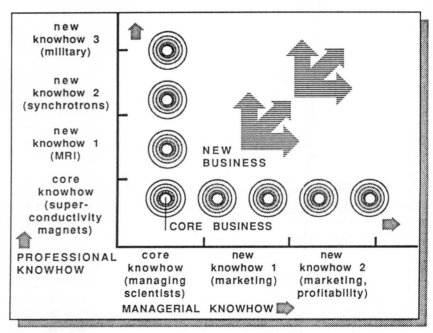

Figure 19   The expansion of Oxford Instruments, moving into new professional and managerial knowhow areas is a good example of the growth of a knowhow company.

such companies volume growth is not an end in itself but a means to the real goals of knowhow growth and professional development and fulfilment. Organic growth is still the most common expansion strategy in traditionally professional industries such as the law, accountancy and consultancy although lately there have been signs of an out-break of empire building in some of these areas.

• Growth by merger and acquisition

The revival of capital markets in the 1980s, combined with the re-emergence of the entrepreneur and the generally more positive attitude towards management, has bred a new kind of knowhow company manager – **the professional chief executive**. That he or she is often indistinguishable in style and methodology from the chief executives of traditional industrial companies is only natural – there are no other readily visible role models. It is only natural too that in adopting the style of industry leaders knowhow company chief executives should also assume their attitudes and appetites – particularly their appetite for **maximum growth of market value**.

These knowhow tycoons are invading knowhow company boardrooms and engineering a spate of mergers and acquisitions. We met the best known exponent of the mergers and acquisitions strategy, Saatchi & Saatchi, the world's largest advertising agency, in Chapter Seven.

• Merger mania

The widely publicised merger mania in Western economies during the mid-1980s was inspired largely by the financial advisers to the big industrial companies. Surprisingly few of the predator groups justified their activities in terms of industrial 'synergy'. Instead financial arguments, like 'it is in the interests of shareholders', dominated the rhetoric.

Many deals are the products of the imperialist visions of entrepreneurs with financial skills, such as Lord Hanson or Robert Maxwell, who manage their mergers. 'Managed mergers', which are difficult to justify industrially, are usually carried out over the heads of the companies involved and often against the wishes of the employees.

But they are part of capitalism. Financial capital must be allowed to find its most profitable use in the free market. The stock exchanges of the world are the marketplaces where financial capital, deployed by financial advisers and investors, tries to maximise its profitability.

• Mergers don't work

The problem with mergers is not that they are morally wrong but that they do not work. It has been estimated that almost two-thirds of all mergers fail (*Business Week*, June 1985) and that about one-third fail because of poor, post-merger integration (*Journal of Business Strategy*, summer 1986). Numerous problems emerge after deals are closed and the new management take charge of day-to-day operations. A third of acquisitions are subsequently sold.

The post-merger problems of industrial companies pale into insignificance beside the difficulties associated with the knowhow company merger.

Following the trail blazed so successfully (until 1986, at least) by Saatchi & Saatchi, other advertising agencies have acquired the acquisitive habit. The rationale is logical enough at first sight. In this era of 'global marketing' the big international companies need big, international agencies with representatives all over the world. If an agency wants to compete for the Unilever or ICI account it must, it is argued, have a presence in every territory in which the latter operate.

These new 'professional' agency executives are trying to substitute the knowhow conglomerate for the 'creative' shop which was the high flier of the 1970s. They offer a solution to every problem in every country from advertising to strategic management consultancy.

Growth is achieved by fusing together a number of small, previously independent agencies into a single, large organisation. The independents become subsidiaries run by professional executives and made subject to tight financial controls. The financial control systems developed and employed by Saatchi & Saatchi are often billed as one of the secrets of the group's prodigious success.

It is likely that the urge to merge in the agency industry will turn out badly. The mergers are handled by managers who are, for the most part, totally ignorant of the basics of knowhow management. **There is no such thing as a neutral merger**. One party always has ascendancy over the other. Since merging knowhow companies is tantamount to merging people the question such a growth strategy begs is to what extent is it possible to 'acquire' human beings?

- **Merger problems of knowhow companies**
  The main problem with knowhow company mergers lies in the **importance of culture** to the knowhow company, the effect that a cultural disturbance has on morale and the negative impact a low morale can have on a knowhow company's results.

  As the Saatchi & Saatchi case shows the aftermaths of knowhow company mergers can swiftly become battlegrounds on which opposing camps of professionals wrangle about conflicting business ideas and about what constitutes the enlarged company's core knowhow. Because the knowhow is so intimately connected with revenues, mergers inevitably lead to lower profits initially.

  Let us look at mergers and acquisitions using some of the 10 success factors discussed in Chapter Eight.

DAY TO DAY LEADERSHIP Company management is removed from day-to-day operations and becomes 'corporate management'. All growing companies encounter this problem, of course, but it is particularly serious with knowhow companies because mergers tend to dilute and distort the various business ideas and almost always alienate the professionals from their new 'owners'.

QUALITY AND QUALITY CONTROL Quality and quality control is made more difficult if the merging companies operate in different knowhow areas. The corporate managers find it hard to understand, let alone reconcile the professional demands and ethics of other knowhow areas. Some of the professionals are always alienated and leave even when the merger appears to 'work'. At the very least this reduces quality immediately after a merger.

Clashes between cultures and concepts are unavoidable even when the merging companies share professional ethics and the basic knowhow.

The quality of work tends to be eroded further by the inevitable shift in focus from professional knowhow to the managerial and entrepreneurial aspects of the business.

COMBINATION OF PROFESSIONAL AND MANAGERIAL KNOWHOW A key success factor in the knowhow company is what we call 'knowhow management' – the ability to combine and reconcile the entrepreneurial/managerial skills with the professional skills. Both types of skill must co-exist in a balanced way within a professional organisation. The traditional knowhow companies tend to lack the managerial skills. Merger mania is not a solution to the problem but rather a symptom of another problem – that the balance has tipped the other way and allowed managers to gain a strong foothold in many knowhow areas.

Too strong, perhaps, since very few professionals prefer to work in large organisations. On the contrary, most fear big bureaucracies because of the suffocating effect they have on creativity. Professionals prefer to maintain a few, high quality contacts with colleagues in a wide variety of other organisations. Their networks are not confined to particular organisational structures. The coming together of large numbers of professionals within one organisational framework is not, of itself, an encouragement to change established patterns which have proved rewarding in the past.

A STRONG, WELL-DEFINED CULTURE What happens to the culture? Cultural conflicts are among the greatest obstacles to the successful implementation of mergers. Cultures are the creatures of people and thus always different. Conflicts invariably arise between people and between cultures even with 'successful' mergers.

It is hard to change a culture without changing the people. The characteristics and qualities of the new subsidiary tend to be defended with the same zeal that threatened minorities exhibit all over the world.

FOCUS ON CORE KNOWHOW The all-important focus of the knowhow company is diffused by mergers, even if the acquired company is in the same knowhow area. If it is in a different knowhow area, the immediate result will be that the 'acquired' professionals perceive on the part of their new managers a more cursory attitude towards what was previously acknowledged as the core knowhow of the company. The professionals begin to question their role and status and this causes the quality of their work to deteriorate.

KNOWHOW PRESERVATION   A 'walk-out' by a number of the professionals is the inevitable result of any merger. Their knowhow walks out with them, very often accompanied by a number of clients. The scale of the walk-outs varies, of course. At worst they can threaten the whole company, as happened with the UK public relations firm Good Relations in 1986 when the departure of key professional Maureen Smith caused enormous problems and led ultimately to the sale of the company.

DEVELOPING THE PEOPLE   The ability to develop employees is not affected directly by mergers. It may even be enhanced. The professionals in the new company will have a wider variety of possible careers and professional synergies may result which further improve career paths.

CHANGING KEY PEOPLE   And the task of replacing key people may be made easier by a merger simply because there are more key people.

STABLE STRUCTURES   The structures of the merging parties will be in disarray after a merger. The acquired company may have to move from their premises. Old agreements may be questioned and the accounting systems will be changed. Established networks are inevitably disturbed by walk-outs and walk-ins.

A merger cleans up a lot of the dust that has settled in the organisations but also interferes with the professional peace of mind, causing the quality and quantity of output to decline. Thus the immediate effect of a merger is normally to reduce the overall effectiveness of the organisation.

It can be seen that the net effect of applying our 10 success factor tests is rather discouraging for the idea of the acquisitive knowhow company. Most factors speak against mergers between knowhow companies. That does not mean that successful mergers are impossible but it does mean that management skills of a very high order are required if an acquisitive strategy in the knowhow area is to stand any chance of long-term success.

- **Accountancy in Sweden**
  During a brief period at the beginning of the 1980s merger mania swept through Swedish accountancy like a forest fire. Accountancy is a growth industry all over the world and Sweden is no exception. The number of chartered accountants has doubled in five years and the growth continues.

  There are two reasons for the rapid expansion: a new law in Sweden now requires a chartered auditor for most limited companies and demand for specialist knowhow in areas like taxation and data processing has increased dramatically. The smaller auditing firms could not cope with the increased demand in these areas so firms began to acquire each other at a considerable pace. By 1985 the 10 largest firms employed about 75% of chartered accountants in Sweden. They now typically employ 800–1,000 people and operate 50–70 offices throughout Sweden.

The chartered accountancy firm is a typical knowhow company. The professionals – the accountants – have a highly specialised professional knowhow which they use in tackling problems which are very difficult to industrialise.

The professionals were quite disturbed by the merger mania. Every quality-conscious accountancy firm develops its own systems, methods, forms, definitions and rules about what is 'right' or 'wrong' both internally and as regards clients.

The culture – 'the way we do things around here' – is an essential part of the business idea. It is inevitable when two knowhow companies merge that the two business ideas and the two groups of professionals who subscribe to them will come into conflict. **Each firm fights for its own systems**. In one celebrated case the confrontation between business ideas ended in a fist fight. The losing accountant, nursing a bruised jaw, left the newly-merged company and started his own firm taking two colleagues with him.

Mergers cause **enormous managerial problems** too. Many of the top management teams of the merged firms found that though their competence had been quite adequate for the needs of the smaller organisations they came from, it was simply not sufficient to cope with the new problems associated with increased size and the conflicts between cultures and business ideas. In a sense the leaders of newly-merged firms have to start all over again. They have a new and often highly sceptical professional constituency to win over.

The merger of accountancy firms, and of every other knowhow company for that matter, represents a special case of the classic dual expertise dilemma discussed in Chapter Four. **The professional and the managerial problems must be taken care of simultaneously**.

All the big accountancy firms in Sweden are now suffering from this 'morning after' syndrome. Several have had to call in management consultants to assist them. This must have been galling for them because large accountancy firms the world over now regard management consultancy as a natural area for their own expansion.

• Combining capital and knowhow

The combination of financial capital and knowhow is the third of the growth strategies to be covered.

It has been the classic, capitalist model for growth since the beginnings of financial capitalism.

The inventor with his invention (=knowhow) was supported by risk-taking financiers (=capital) to exploit the invention on the market. Most large, modern European and American companies were born at the beginning of this century as the fruit of a mating of the business/managerial ability of the financier with the professionalism of the inventor.

The principle of growth is the same today as it was a hundred years ago; a combination of knowhow and capital generates growth by boosting the profitability of capital.

In most respects there seems little to distinguish these hundred-year-old combinations of inventor/financier from today's combinations of capital and knowhow. The difference, and it is huge, is that the inventions of the twenty-first century are not things but ideas – not products but services.

The difference is crucial because services are produced by able people (professionals) in knowhow companies whereas the products of the early twentieth century were produced by expensive machines tended by unfortunate, ignorant workers. Wallenberg and Rockefeller had a much easier task than their modern counterparts because they were more educated than their employees and their financial capital was in short supply.

The capitalists of to-day are as educated as their potential employees but they have no more knowhow, especially not in the areas where the knowhow companies of to-day and to-morrow tend to emerge. And they constantly find themselves in tough competition with other capitalists with equally abundant financial resources. It is not financial capital that is scarce to-day – it is knowhow capital.

However, even if financial capital is a less important factor these days, there are in each knowhow area business ideas which rely on financial capital for their success. It is also common that the same knowhow yields a variety of business ideas some of which need financial capital for their fulfilment while others do not.

And it remains true in the information society that the highest value added per employee and the highest growth are to be found in business ideas incorporating a combination of knowhow and financial capital.

The difficulty, as the Cergus case shows (see Chapter Ten), is to find the proper balance between the representatives of capital and the representatives of knowhow. The interface between the two and the personal chemistry are the keys to success or failure. A lack of understanding between the two areas is usually fatal.

It is much more difficult now for the two parties to establish a good working relationship than it was at the beginning of the century. In those days it was enough for the inventor and financier to be on speaking terms. The workers and the rest of the staff had to do as they were told. The managers and the capitalists of twenty-first century knowhow companies must win over much larger groups to succeed with their business idea. Failure results in the defection of professionals. It is a little like the science-fiction vision of an industrial society in which machines, apparently bolted firmly to the floor, suddenly come alive and go on the rampage. The only role of the financier in these businesses is to contribute money. Success and failure are balanced on a knife edge. An excellent business idea may fail simply because the professionals and the financier don't get on.

• The three phases of growth

The combination of financial capital and knowhow is a classic but far from easy growth strategy. Expansion of this kind causes profound changes in an organisation which, in their turn, inevitably cause frictions. If managers are unaware of these problems of transition or turn out to be incapable of handling them they may run a previously successful company into deep trouble.

The most difficult transition is the switch from the business idea of 'consulting' to other ideas involving either new personnel or more capital. The typical growth pattern of knowhow companies is shown in Figure 20. During the first 'consultant' phase the company rarely creates any financial substance. Most of the value added is ploughed back into the development of the knowhow capital or consumed immediately by the professionals. The investor should steer well clear of companies with this kind of phase one business idea.

In phase two, the high growth phase, the investor can make a fortune. It is risky because the transition from one business idea to another is one of the most dangerous adventures any management team undertakes, but it can be highly rewarding too – just the sort of mixture good, self-confident venture capitalists love.

A knowhow company that survives phase two enters a period of lower growth and lower risk. It tends to become more like a service company. The capital-intensive knowhow companies tend to approach a situation similar to that of a bank where less-educated staff replace the key people. The knowhow has been institutionalised and embedded in routines.

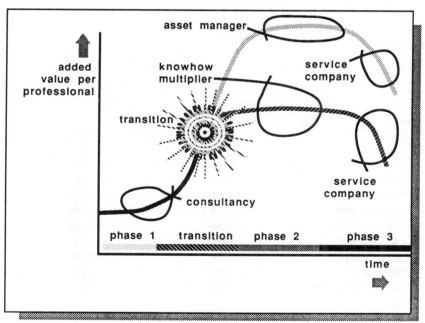

Figure 20   Most knowhow companies start as consultancies. They may retain this business idea indefinitely and grow organically by adding more professionals and becoming knowhow multipliers, or they may increase their leverage by changing the business idea and becoming asset managers, for example.

Phase one may last indefinitely. It is the decision to leave the organic growth path which leads to the transition to phase two. Phase two is usually brief, rarely lasting more than one or two years. When phase two growth levels out into phase three the company enters another stable period. When the company eventually becomes an ordinary service company it is likely some of the key people or new, eager professionals will 'spin-out' and start a phase one company.

The most critical point is the transition between phases one and two. The two cases of Cergus and Centrum-Invest discussed in Chapter Ten illustrate some of the problems and some of the opportunities that can arise when business ideas are changed.

SUMMARY

• All companies must **grow or die**. The **methodology of growth** for knowhow companies must be based on the organisation's **core knowhow**.

• The entrepreneurial leader must appoint **project champions** to drive new business development.

• Business development cannot be administered from the outside. It is the spontaneous result of a creative environment.

• It is possible to export knowhow.

• Growth is the expansion of the **knowhow capital**.

• There are three types of growth: organic growth, merger and acquisition and combining financial capital with knowhow.

• Organic growth is the most natural but may be too slow.

• Mergers don't work: problems of management and culture arise.

• There are three phases of growth: consultancy; high growth; low but stable growth. The critical point is the transition from consultancy to high growth.

12

• Investing in Knowhow

• The value of knowhow

It is clear that stock markets impute quite different values to employees depending on what kind of company they work for. The differences can be enormous. Some employees appear to be 'worth', according to stockmarket valuations, less than £30,000 whereas each IBM employee seems to be worth about £150,000 (summer 1987). The reason is not hard to find. Each IBM employee produced about £20,000 to £30,000 worth of profit in 1985 and 1986. Investors throughout the world are willing to bet similar sums on employees in other knowhow companies in the computer industry, the emerging biotechnology industry and in other 'glamour' sectors. The price-tags are justified on the grounds that employees in these companies can generate high profitability and rapid growth for their shareholders.

• Investing in a knowhow company

Potential investors in a knowhow company should consider their investment carefully. The questions they should ask themselves, and the company, are very different from those appropriate for traditional industrial companies. We have seen many examples of the risks run by ignorant investors in knowhow companies. A common mistake is to try to transfer methods, strategies and objectives from the conventional industrial company to the knowhow company. The investor who is ignorant of the relatively minor role financial capital plays in a knowhow company will lose money and the company manager who fails to grasp the basics of knowhow management will be thrown out. These are unnecessary risks.

Prospective investors in a knowhow company should first ask themselves two questions: **'do the company's managers understand knowhow management?'** and **'does the company need financial capital?'** As we have seen, financial capital is of secondary importance from management's point of view. Investors have every reason to ask themselves and the management the question: 'are we really needed?'

Companies seeking risk capital list their shares on the stock exchange. The exchange has two roles: to act as a source of capital and to be a marketplace for shares. **Companies with no need for risk capital need no listing.** Indeed, to seek a listing would be tantamount to an attempt to defraud investors. Consultancy-type companies need no risk capital unless they are entering phase two of the three growth phases we encountered in the previous chapter or are in transition from consultancy to 'knowhow multiplier' or 'asset manager'.

Even if a consultancy firm claims it needs money to expand through acquisitions, the investor should be wary. Saatchi & Saatchi appears to have been successful, for a while at any rate but, as we have seen, the mergers and acquisitions growth strategy is beset by problems. There is no evidence that Saatchi & Saatchi's prodigious acquisition-led growth has been matched by equally rapid knowhow growth.

- **Capital intensive knowhow companies need money**
  Knowhow companies like merchant banks, fund managers or high-technology firms need capital from outside shareholders but they must abide by the rules of knowhow management if their investors are to make money. The latter should always remember that there are **no quick profits** from such investment and that without patience and sympathy there are no long-term profits either.

- **Routine intensive knowhow companies may be good investments**
  Knowhow companies in which a few key people act as 'knowhow multipliers', transferring their core knowhow into routines, systems and software which can be run by less knowledgeable staff, are more robust. They need capital to invest, mainly in computers and working capital. The few key people remain very valuable however because it is their knowhow which determines success or failure in the marketplace.

- **Assessing risk**
  It is very important for the investor to arrive at a proper judgement of the risks associated with each investment. The risks of industrial company investment can be divided into:

  1. Operational risk: the inherent risk of the market in which the company operates. For example, shipping has a greater inherent risk than food manufacturing.
  2. Financial risk: the stability of the company. In the manufacturing industry the relationship between debt and equity is the most important measure of stability.

  With a knowhow company investment the picture is very different. **The operational risk is normally low but stability is usually a problem.**

The financial risk in the knowhow company usually appears to be low but **the visible balance-sheet does not show the true position**. The invisible balance sheet provides the real clues to the stability or otherwise of the knowhow company. Unfortunately, as we have seen, traditional accounting methods and legal reporting requirements are far from adequate measures of the strength of the invisible balance sheet. From the point of view of the outside investor the stability of a knowhow a company will have to be taken very much on trust until such time as researchers can provide ways of accounting for knowhow.

The special risk that needs to be assessed might be called '**Knowhow risk**', i.e. the risk of knowhow leakage because of inadequate R&D or the departure of key people. We call the asset on the invisible balance sheet that is at risk in this sense the 'knowhow capital'.

The investor can get quite an accurate picture of the risk by using the key indicators referred to in Chapter Five.

• The value of a professional

What is the value of a professional? It is important for investors to get an impression of the profit potential of the company they invest in. The key to future profit is **the profit potential of the individual professionals**. The investor should thus be willing to pay a certain **price per head** when putting money into a knowhow company. As we have seen, the added value of a professional varies from the short, high-peak performance of a Diego Maradona or a Björn Borg to the steady increase of a Henry Kissinger.

The potential of a professional depends on the market and the business idea. If we compare similar companies the average added value per professional does not vary much. The law of big numbers tends to even out individual differences between professionals who work in teams. The differences that exist between companies can be interpreted as the differences in managerial knowhow.

It is the knowhow of the individual professionals which adds the value clients pay for. This **knowhow must be maintained with R&D and education**. Equipment and support services for the professionals must also be paid for out of added value.

One must also consider **the professional life-cycle**. Very old and very young professionals tend to be less effective than the experienced, middle-aged ones. The professionals must also be given pensions and opportunities to shift careers. These costs must also be paid for out of added value.

A certain level of R&D and other costs are also needed to expand rather than merely maintain the knowhow capital of the company. These are policy decisions but the money for them must come from the added value of the professionals.

What remains after all these costs is the added value from which the investor and the professionals take their cuts. The value of the professional can then be calculated as the discounted present value of the added value produced by the professional over his or her active life – say 40 years.

But this is the value for society. The investor who acquires all or part of a knowhow company must come to terms with the fact that **the professionals will take the lion's share** of what they produce. The norm is between 70% and 80%. This is, incidentally, the average share of value added claimed by employees in all industries throughout the western world. A worker in a traditional smokestack industry will receive at least 60% of the added value he or she produces. In many cases the share is much higher, reaching well over 100% in some loss-making companies.

The investor should also consider some of the key ratios for knowhow companies described in Chapter Five. One important ratio is **personnel turnover**. An investor must consider the numbers of years each professional is likely to stay with the company. An annual personnel turnover of 10% indicates an expected employment of ten years per professional which is a very long time indeed.

The discount factor should **assume no more than 10 years**. In many young companies even five years, indicating an assumed personnel turnover of 20% a year, may be too long.

Since the productivity of a professional varies according to experience, the **average age** and the **age mix** of the company's professionals are also useful indicators of potential profitability. In practice profitability will tend to follow the pattern indicated in the chart below.

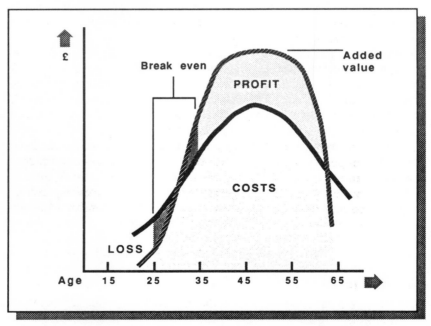

Figure 21 The ability to create profit out of the added value varies from industry to industry and depends on the cost level of the business and the remuneration of the employees. Young professionals are normally loss makers. The most profitable professionals are mostly in their 40s.

Young professionals are unlikely to produce a profit at all. They are not as skilled as their older colleagues, they cost more in training and supervision and will be unable to bill customers sufficiently to cover their salaries. But within a couple of years young professionals begin to produce added value in excess of the costs they incur. A year or two later, the cumulative breakeven is reached. It may thus take as long as three to five years to recover the investment made in the recruitment of a young, untrained professional. It is no wonder then, that most consultants prefer to recruit older, more experienced consultants who can earn their keep immediately. The breakeven level is not the same everywhere of course. It varies with the market and the managerial skills of the knowhow company. These rules of thumb would be accurate for the mature consultancy or accountancy firm.

But in the overheated capital markets of 1986/87 the new recruits in the banks and brokerage houses were profitable almost from day one, a fact that was vividly and notoriously reflected in the starting salaries of many City 'whizz kids' during London's 'Big Bang' in the autumn of 1986.

The professional's most profitable period is normally between the ages of 35 and 45. This is the period when the early training has matured into skill and proficiency and when the professionals confront their greatest challenges.

The slope of the profitability curve is very individual, of course. In a situation where the professionals can claim most of the value they add in the form of their own remuneration, the profit they generate for the company will be modest even during their most productive years.

In the latter part of the life cycle, professionals tend to become less profitable, largely because their remuneration continues to rise as their real productivity declines. One reason for this may be that the older professionals are also often members of the management team.

The chart below shows the added value curve of one of Sweden's largest auditing firms.

Owners of knowhow companies must understand that **the value of their investment depends largely on what the professionals and managers are willing to share.** The power of the former to claim the lion's share of value added varies, of course. Generally speaking their bargaining power, though still considerable, is somewhat lower in capital-intensive knowhow companies.

• The 10 success factors for the investor

One of the core concepts of this book is that **the balance of power between knowhow** (the professionals) **and capital is shifting**. The capitalists are no longer in control and their position can only weaken further. The 'knowhow revolution' is approaching in many companies. As soon as the professionals realise their power the traditional financial capitalists will be thrown out of what they had thought were their own companies. What can they do to prevent this?

For the reader of this book it should be evident by now that in knowhow companies it is the capitalists who have to adapt and make concessions – not the other way round. It is up to them to find a way to win equal status with the professionals.

The solution lies in our 10 success factors for knowhow company leaders. The owners of capital-intensive knowhow companies are members of the management team and must try to understand what that involves. They must **abide by the rules of knowhow leadership.** A business idea which relies on a combination of knowhow and capital must be managed as a knowhow company, not as an industrial company. If investors refuse to accept this they will quickly find themselves at loggerheads with their company.

Let us look at the 10 success factors again – this time from the perspective of the owner of a capital-intensive knowhow company. He should:

1. TAKE AN ACTIVE PART IN MANAGEMENT   Owners must be there in person. The position of an absentee leader of a knowhow company is soon undermined. One of the main causes of the failure of Cergus was that the majority shareholder failed to appoint an acceptable representative. Its decision to keep a low profile was a clear strategic mistake.

And the capitalists should not be so pre-occupied with other projects that they fail to keep an active eye on their investment. Many investors in knowhow

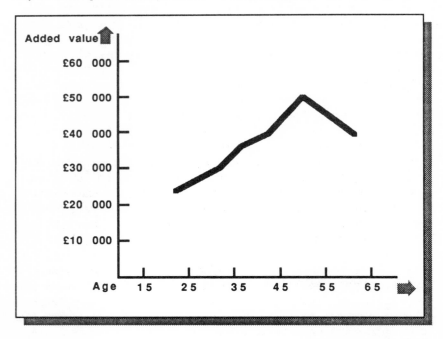

Figure 22 This shows the actual added value pattern of a big firm of chartered accountants in Sweden.

companies have bitterly regretted their haste to make other deals. The knowhow company demands and rewards interested and patient investors.

2. CONCENTRATE ON KNOWHOW AND HELP TO DEVELOP IT Owners must concentrate on the professional content of the business idea, not on the capital. They must develop existing knowhow and acquire new knowhow. Such expenditure is traditionally treated in the accounts as a profitability-reducing cost. The capitalist must recognise that the 'costs' of research, education, travel and creative breaks are really investments.

3. PUT KNOWHOW BEFORE CAPITAL Knowhow must be the main focus of management attention even in capital-intensive knowhow companies. This can be quite a difficult perspective for financiers to adopt since *their* objective is to generate a high yield on the financial capital. It is easy to forget, when large tranches of capital are involved, that the core of the business idea is not the money but the yield-generating knowhow, be it in portfolio management, analysis or asset planning.

Financial capital plays a subordinate role even in capital-intensive knowhow companies. Financiers must resist the temptation to put their money before the professional knowhow. The capital-intensive knowhow company must invest resources in R&D, education and personal development and must ensure the professionals are represented in top management.

Thus the financiers of knowhow companies must recognise that the best way to maximise the long-term return on their money is steadily to increase the knowhow capital.

4. COMBINE PROFESSIONALISM AND MANAGEMENT Investors in the capital-intensive knowhow company should see it as their prime task to help to build an organisation that can survive in the long-term. The professionals tend to forget how important it is to make the organisation robust. It is here where the financiers can become their natural complement.

In business start-ups at the beginning of the century it was the capitalist who took the responsibility of developing the organisation and managing the company. The inventor concentrated on product development and production. This division of responsibility remains valid today. The difference lies in the way in which the partnership operates and thus in the way in which investors must discharge their responsibilities.

5. LEARN THE CULTURE As personalities investors and professionals are often poles apart. The former tend to be more action-orientated; the latter more intellectual, analytical, creative and, above all, impractical. Conflict is never far away when such contrasting qualities are combined. The investors must try to understand the professional culture. Their success depends on it. They cannot and should not try to change the culture but should rather try to understand its strengths and weaknesses and to complement it. And they

should always remember that until they have earned the respect of the professionals they will be powerless to change anything.

6. CONCENTRATE YOUR INVESTMENTS   Financial capitalists should focus their money and, more importantly, their time on a few selected investments. This is true of any manager or businessman – success comes from focused effort. It is especially true in knowhow companies because it takes a great deal of time and effort to get to grips with the company and to learn how to manage it. Money is merely an input into a knowhow company. As such it can never be an instrument of power but it can be a management tool.

Investors must choose their companies carefully, spend as much time as they can with them and, above all, they must be patient. **The 'deal maker' is the worst kind of owner** for a knowhow company because he has no time to create the mutual understanding and confidence needed to survive a crisis.

7. FIND WAYS OF KEEPING THE KEY PEOPLE   Investors invest in people. If they lose them they will lose money. It is thus in their own interests to be generous with the key people. They must acknowledge that the knowhow capital riding on the shoulders of the key professionals is more crucial to the success of the venture than money and should be rewarded accordingly.

8. HELP TO DEVELOP THE EMPLOYEES   Owners should try to contribute to personnel development perhaps with job-swapping arrangements with other companies and knowhow areas in their networks. A fund for personnel development and research is useful. The important thing is for the investor to see personnel development and research as key ways of sustaining and developing the knowhow capital. It is a necessary 'cost' of investment in a knowhow company.

9. HELP TO ARRANGE FOR THE SUCCESSION   The key people in the capital-intensive knowhow company are in no better a position to arrange for their own succession than their counterparts in any other kind of knowhow company. Owners may have a very important roie here – they may even be the only ones with a real interest in ensuring orderly and effective succession. The education of crown princes and princesses and the transfer of knowhow to others in the organisation require procedures the professionals and managers of knowhow companies are seldom able or inclined to develop themselves.

The succession is so important that the investor should try to make a start on it from day one.

10. HELP TO DEVELOP A STRUCTURE   A firm organisational structure is a key long-term survival factor so it is in the interest of investors to help develop such structures by any means at their disposal. With a general managerial background they should be able to make particularly valuable contributions to the development of the two 'firm' structures, the legal and accountancy systems.

Financial capital is important in the capital-intensive knowhow company, by definition. Money is a cornerstone of the organisational structure. The capital itself provides some protection against the walk-outs that are such a threat to more people-intensive businesses because it may be possible to manage the assets after a walk-out, for a while at least, by hiring more expertise. And there will still be invoices being processed by accounting personnel which is, itself, a structure of sorts; a sign that corporate life goes on.

But the capital is not enough on its own. Investors must work with the culture, the office environment, accounting systems, agreements and so on. They are often better at such things than the average professional and success in these areas can aid capitalists in their most important task of all – earning the respect of the professionals.

• Dividing the spoils

The profitable, capital-intensive knowhow company contains within it a burning question: **how should the value added be divided between the suppliers of knowhow and the providers of financial capital?** This is amongst the most fundamental of all the questions addressed in this book because the capital-intensive knowhow company is a microcosm of what, in restrospect, will be seen as the historic struggle between the financial capitalists of the industrial society and the knowhow capitalists of the information society. For the present it is sufficient to note that premonitions of this struggle make this a practical question of great delicacy.

The normal way of calculating profitability assumes all the profit is distributed to the capital owners. We argue in this book that this is fundamentally wrong and that those who persist in this anachronistic view, be they investors or analysts, are going to make serious mistakes. Many capital-intensive knowhow companies distribute only 10-20% of the value added to the professionals; the rest goes to the capital owners. This balance of reward and effort will not be possible for much longer.

In knowhow companies – capital-intensive or otherwise – it is the knowhow that gives leverage to the capital, not the other way round. In a company which combines financial capital and knowhow, a reasonable distribution of the surplus, acceptable to all those involved, must be worked out. This involves departing from the accounting methods and traditions of the industrial society.

An investor who just supplies financial capital should not receive more than **a normal yield plus a premium for risk**. This risk component may be quite large in phase two but otherwise it can be kept low.

Only foolish investors extract high dividends or heavy 'group overheads' to assist other companies in their portfolios. The inevitable result of such exploitation is that the personnel in the knowhow company soon start to question the role of the capitalist. 'What good is he' they ask, 'if all he does is take money out of the business?' The professional staff of the knowhow company, unlike their counterparts in the industrial company, can become very troublesome indeed if they are dissatisfied or feel hard done by.

The knowhow capital has a prior claim on any surplus for its maintenance and expansion. This does not mean that most of the value added in a capital intensive knowhow company must be distributed as remuneration to the professionals! The professionals should have part of the profit in the form of shareholdings and salaries but **the rest must be allocated for the development of the knowhow capital**; to R&D, investment in education, computers, software and other equipment, as well as to employee development, research trips and so on. If the management does not permit such spending the knowhow capital of the company will drain away.

But it is equally irresponsible to allow the professionals levels of remuneration exceeding 70% of the added value. The result is the same: for lack of nourishment the knowhow capital leaks away. Only weak managements allow personnel to receive remuneration on that scale. Lazy or inefficient professionals, as well as knowhow of low quality, must be rewarded accordingly.

• Knowhow industries compared

The Affärsvärlden group of Sweden has built a database of knowhow companies which includes advertising agencies, computer consultancies and management

Table 3   Knowhow Companies in Sweden 1985

	19 Advertising agencies	19 Computer consultancies	14 Management companies
Sales per employee			
SEK '000	46.8	496	786
Added value per employee			
SEK 1000	300	271	389
Profit per employee			
SEK '000	46	36	31
Salaries & Insurance per employee			
SEK '000	254	214	314
Sales & Insurance in % of			
added value	77%	81%	85%
Profit margin	8.6%	7.5%	3.7%
Growth 85 over 84	8%	30%	48%

Unweighted averages
Source: Affärsvärlden data base

consultancies. Some of the key ratios are summarised in the table above. None of the industries seem particularly profitable; in the typical unquoted knowhow company most of the added value is distributed among the employees.

Added value per employee varies between SKr271,000 in the computer firms and SKr389,000 in the management consultancies. The added values differ only +/− 18% between the three industry averages. Profit margins are all well below 10%.

• The computer industry

That the computer industry is a typical knowhow intensive industry is evidenced by the fact that in computer companies most employees have university degrees. Computer companies are wholly dependent on their employees for their success, especially in software and computer consultancy.

In the scatter diagram below the points represent the 18 computer companies quoted on the Stockholm stock exchange in October 1986, a few UK companies, one French and one Finnish. All these are compared with the US computer industry as a whole.

Since computer companies are knowhow companies we would expect to gain a better understanding of them by analysing **key ratios about their employees** rather than about the financial capital. One revealing ratio is the market value per employee. This is the 'pricetag' implicitly hung round the neck of each employee by the market. It represents the sum investors are willing to bet on them per head.

As the diagram shows the pricetag per employee varies between £35,000 and £200,000. The large difference is because not all employees are equally productive. Profit per head ranges from £3,000 to £25,000. Investors are prepared to pay considerably over the odds for relatively efficient employees.

The chart shows the computer companies scattered in an oblong pattern sloping upwards from the bottom left to the top right. The most productive and thus the most 'valuable' employees are to be found in companies located in the top, right-hand corner. If markets were perfect the companies would all lie on a straight line representing the investors' demand for a return on their computer holdings.

A line representing a 15% return is drawn on the chart. The US industry is represented by two dots, one for the software industry and one for the hardware industry. The data for the US industry were compiled from Value Line and the data for the Swedish companies from the Affärsvärlden Investment Indicator. Profits were best estimates for fiscal 1986 made by the Affärsvärlden magazine and Value Line respectively.

The diagram may suggest profit-making opportunities to the investors among readers because according to our analysis, companies above or below the 15% line are over or under-valued respectively. But it is not our purpose in this book to give share tips. We shall restrict ourselves to three more general observations:

1. The stock market apparently recognizes differences in employee productivity.

2. There are limits to the profits that can be produced by each employee in a particular industry.

3. This analytical method can be used by investors for screening purposes.

In our opinion this approach to assessing corporate worth in knowhow intensive areas like the computer industry is **far superior to the widely used Price/ Earnings ratio**. It is vital for the investor to have a way to measure risk. Our analysis suggests, for example, that the investor should avoid those companies at the extremes of the chart. A more knowhow-orientated approach gives much more information to the investor than the old P/E.

It begs the question, for example, of whether it is likely the £200,000 employees will be able to continue to produce value added at the same rate in the future? And why invest in those companies in the upper, left-hand corner of the

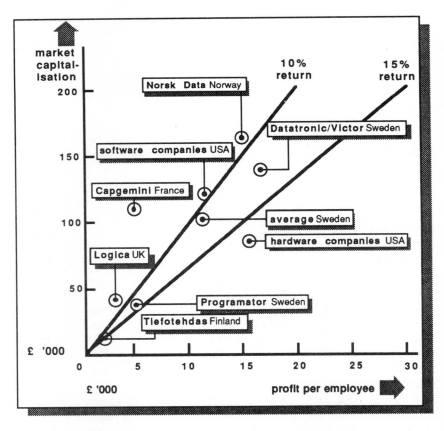

Figure 23   The value of professionals in the computer industry varies according to their ability to create profit, irrespective of nationality.

diagram that look distinctly overvalued by the standards of the industry as a whole?

The reader should bear in mind that the key ratios used in this analysis were calculated using the total number of employees as the denominator. According to the arguments we have put forward in this book a more appropriate ratio would, of course, be profits and market value per professional instead. The differences between the results of the two approaches would be particularly marked in industries where there is wide variation in the numbers of support, administrative and managerial staff per professional.

Many consultancy firms have professional/other ratios of 2 : 1 (twice as many professionals as other employees). Applying this yardstick to the consultants in

Table 4   Knowhow Companies in the UK

Company	Industry	Added value per employee	Profit per employee	Market capitalisation per employee	Total assets per employee
Addison Consultants	Advertising	23	5	103	49
Davidson Pearce	Advertising	31	11	95	50
Geers Gross	Advertising	30	-4	50	99
Valin Pollen International	Advertising	30	7	77	45
Saatchi & Saatchi	Advertising	34	7	82	15
Robertson Research	Consultancy	20	5	37	28
Seismograph	Consultancy	14	1	n/a	9
Dy Davis	Architect	19	6	91	36
Ricardo	Engineering consultancy	20	6	37	38
Micro Business Systems	Computer	17	-5	35	60
Logica	Computer	23	3	41	20
Electric Data Processing	Computer	19	4	n/a	-
Town Centre	Property	47	28	n/a	720
Rothschild	Merchant bank	64	50	n/a	720
Mercury Securities	Merchant bank	87	39	352	3208
Yorkshire Hospital	Hospital	15	5	25	34
Swindon Hospital	Hospital	14	1	24	49
JS Pathology	Consultancy	31	15	214	36
Biomechanics	Consultancy	78	-26	161	133

Source: Extel

the Swedish computer industry gives us a value per computer consultant in the range of SKr1m to SKr2m.

How does this compare with the international average? In the US the average market capitalisation per employee among the 15 software houses and 38 hardware companies followed by Value Line was SKr1.1m and SKr0.8m respectively in October 1986.

• Quoted knowhow companies in the UK

We also looked at 15 knowhow companies quoted on the London Stock Exchange in May 1987. They included advertising agencies, computer consultancies, an engineering consultancy and hospitals. The data are summarised in the chart below. Market value is the average for 1986 and profits per employee are for 1986. All data are from Extel.

The chart seems to support the general conclusions drawn from the computer industry. The 'pricetags' per employee are in the same range and so are profits per employee. (£1= SKr10). The slope of the curve is steeper than the one for the computer industry, showing investors to be more cautious about computer companies compared to other knowhow areas.

The investors have given us an answer. The value they impute to professionals or employees in knowhow companies varies according to their productivity and their ability to generate profits. In the knowhow industries we have analysed the value per employee seems to range from £100,000 to £200,000.

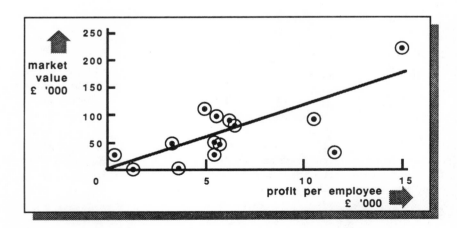

Figure 24   The companies in Table 4 plotted on a chart indicate that the UK Stock Exchange pushes up the 'price tags' of very profitable employees.

• The value of the capital intensive knowhow company

An interesting special case is the capital intensive knowhow company such as the stockbroking firm, the merchant bank, the property development company or the fund management group. In these companies financial capital plays a more significant role than in a consultancy firm for example. A typical consultancy firm's balance sheet seldom shows assets of more than £50,000 per employee, which is barely half the average for manufacturing industry.

As can be seen in Figure 18, employees in Swedish capital intensive knowhow companies manage substantial assets. A professional in a merchant bank may be responsible for as much as £5m. A 1% return on that amount is equal to the total annual profit of many consultancy firms which explains the high value attributed to portfolio managers by the stock market.

But here too the value of the professionals is intimately linked to the profits they can produce. In some cases profits per employee in 1986 were as high as £100,000. Mercury Securities, listed on the London Stock Exchange, is about average. Mercury's added value per professional in 1986 was £87,000, profit per employee was £39,000 and market value per employee was £350,000.

SUMMARY
- The prospective investor in a knowhow company should ask: **do the company's managers understand knowhow management** and **does the company need financial capital?**
- The investor must assess the risk involved, especially 'knowhow risk'.
- Future profit is dependent on the **profit potential** of the individual professionals.
- Professionals normally take a relatively low share of the value added they produce.
- Personnel turnover is a key ratio.
- Investment is not only a question of money: investors must take an active part in management.
- In valuing knowhow companies **key ratios about employees** such as **market value per employee** are far superior to the price/earnings ratio.

13

• The Worm in the Bud

• Generalising the argument

This book has been about the management of knowhow and about knowhow's role in corporate strategy and decision-making. In the interests of simplicity and clarity we have focussed our attention on what we call 'knowhow companies' – organisations more or less wholly engaged in complex problem-solving.

But the relevance of the knowhow-focussed strategy is by no means confined to this kind of organisation. On the contrary, practically all industries, manufacturing and service, contain within them larger or smaller areas of complex problem-solving activity. **Knowhow work is a pan-industrial phenomenon.**

And it is clear that many traditional industries in the Western world are **in the process of becoming knowhow industries.** Parts of the so-called service sector, such as banking and insurance, are in the vanguard of this change but signs of a steady and progressive process of knowhow enrichment can be seen practically everywhere. As we saw in Chapter Eleven, when describing the troubles Barclays Bank encountered with its new knowhow subsidiary BZW, the process of knowhow-enrichment can be difficult and turbulent for organisations unfamiliar with the problems of managing knowhow. Though the focus of this book is particular, the problems it addresses are general.

There is no escape even for traditional industries from the process of knowhow-enrichment, though so far it is mostly happening in those areas below the threshold of managerial awareness. The same is true for public sector organisations. Managers almost everywhere are finding themselves at war with important groups of employees without really knowing why.

A shift of focus away from the traditional perspective towards knowhow can make some of these problems seem less baffling. It becomes possible to visualise, if not actually to see, complex problem-solving in creative environments insinuating itself into almost every walk of corporate, commercial and administrative life. It must be recognised that such pockets of knowhow activity **cannot be managed in a conventional way**. All managers need to learn the rudiments anyway of knowhow management if they are not to be constantly ambushed by humiliating confrontations and mass defections.

• The pro-team

Within every company, large or small, manufacturing or service, there is a department, division, unit or subsidiary that is very different from the rest of the company.

It might be the General Electric Company's Hirst Research Centre, Jaguar's engineering department, Hanson Trust's corporate finance team, the securities division in Barclays Bank or the surgical unit in a large hospital. These special places all have one thing in common; **their working conditions are completely different** from those in the rest of the company or organisation. Research and engineering departments will be full of scientists and engineers talking together with great enthusiasm in a language quite foreign to employees elsewhere in the company. While the managers of Hanson Trust's operating companies get on with the business of making bricks, batteries or cigarettes the head-office corporate finance team are seeking out companies to buy and sell and planning bid strategies and tactics. As the manager of a Barclays branch in Oldham agrees a £500 overdraft limit a market-maker on BZW's equity pitch 'works' a block of three million ICI shares. Alongside the daily routines of a large hospital a team of highly motivated and qualified doctors and nurses, working under enormous time pressure, transplant a kidney. Such groups are special and they know it.

These 'pro-teams' should be seen as **embryonic knowhow organisations** operating and sometimes developing disruptively like worms in the bud within traditional 'industrial' companies. They keep themselves to themselves, have their own cultures – their own 'esprit de corps' – and tend to look down on the others.

Because of their cultural self-sufficiency and their cavalier attitudes to company rules and conventions they often cause problems. Their salary demands are rapacious and their manner with top managers is invariably disrespectful and often downright insubordinate, witness BZW's 'bearish' circular on Barclays Bank. When it comes to the 'prima donnas' of the pro-teams managers and union leaders are united. Both dislike them intensely. It seems quite wrong that the least loyal and least unionised employees should be paid the most.

The pro-teams of stockbrokers that have been brought into Britain's banks over the past couple of years demonstrate clearly the power such groups of professionals exercise in large organisations. Because the banks are in the vanguard of the transition into knowhow companies they lack the knowhow to handle the resentment, envy and disturbance created by the arrival of arrogant pro-teams.

• Management of pro-teams

The rise of the pro-team is **one of the symptoms of the developing information society**. Traditional companies must come to terms with them and the problems they cause. Managers will have to unlearn most of what orthodox theory has taught them. They must come to see pro-teams as opportunities rather than threats. The leader seeking enlightenment about pro-team management should look first at the successful knowhow companies – the professional organisations. As we have seen they require **a very different style of management** from that common in traditional industrial companies and they require a very different kind of leadership too.

The trouble is most manufacturing companies and what we call 'factory' service groups like clearing banks employ managers used to thinking in traditional terms. These organisations need to find new kinds of managers who understand and can handle pro-teams. Since they are in short supply in the traditional industries **they may have to be recruited from the knowhow companies**.

• Istel Ltd – from pro-team to knowhow company

John Leighfield began his working life at Ford in 1962, first as a management trainee, then as a systems analyst working in the areas of finance and stock control and finally as a project leader developing production and material control systems.

In 1965 he left to join Plessey as computer systems development manager in the telecommunications division. He was appointed company data processing manager in 1970.

Two years later he moved again to become engineering and manufacturing systems planning manager at British Leyland Motor Corporation (BL). He was appalled by what he found: 'There wasn't even a stock control system!' he recalled in an interview in *Financial Weekly*. He installed one similar to the system he had helped set up at Ford a decade earlier. Systems at BL were hopelessly fragmented and a dire shortage of good people was matched only by a surfeit of grandiose ideas. Staff turnover was 30% a year, intolerably high in an area where project life ranged from 18 months to two years.

But there was one improbably exotic feature of BL's mess of systems. A few years earlier a forward looking manufacturing engineer at Cowley, one of BL's main production sites, had become frustrated by the constant shuttling to and fro between Cowley and the other main centres in Birmingham and Coventry. He asked the Post Office to link the three centres with video conferencing facilities. When the PO was unable to comply with the request BL set up its own microwave communications network.

The communications emphasis was strengthened when the PO launched its pioneering Prestel videotext system. 'We asked if we could buy the software' Leighfield recalled, 'but they refused so we set up our own stock locator system and built Infotrac to support it'. The stock locator system of BL's volume car subsidiary Austin Rover, linked to distributors and suppliers through the Infotrac network, is one of the most advanced of its kind in the world and plays a key role in the group's day-to-day operations.

The environment for BL's systems pro-team improved markedly in the mid-1970s when the troubled, state-owned car company's top management, their minds concentrated wonderfully by the highly critical Ryder report, began to recognise the crucial importance of information technology.

Leighfield was still struggling at the time with the problem of how to recruit and keep good professionals. 'We had to pay market rates,' he said, 'and we had to create a culture for knowledge workers'. BL's own culture, saturated with failure and decline, was inimical. Leighfield began lobbying top management for permission to group the systems activities together in a separate company.

His efforts were rewarded following the arrival of Michael Edwardes (now Sir Michael), with a brief from the government to turn the loss-making BL round to profits. 'I met him just before Christmas 1977,' said Leighfield. 'Within 10 minutes he had agreed to the principle of separation.'

But BL's personnel department, fearful the unions would try to use systems as a wedge in pay bargaining, objected to the separation proposal vigorously. BL Systems Ltd., to be re-named Istel Ltd. five years later, was not finally created as a wholly-owned BL subsidiary until mid-1979. At the time it employed 930 people and was generating revenues of £20m a year, virtually all from BL. There was a little outside business but the freedom in principle to sell to third parties was not fully accepted until 1982.

Selling to outsiders was important to Leighfield but he admits that 'early on we didn't really know what we were doing. We were incredibly naive in the early years'.

Gradually the idea of 'focus' became important. 'Press an Istel man today' said Leighfield in November 1986 'and within five minutes he'll be talking about focus'. A clear strategy evolved. As Leighfield put it 'we decided to go for pre-eminence in the two things we were good at – advanced manufacturing systems and communications'.

The early 1980s was a period of heavy investment and low margins. In 1984 profits before interest and tax were only £1.2m on sales of £37m. The free-spending strategy aroused criticism elsewhere in the cash-starved company but it paid off. The following year margins swelled to 10% of sales which had grown to £50m. Thanks partly to the privatisation of BL's luxury car-maker Jaguar, which remained an Istel customer, sales to outsiders accounted for a third of the total.

The drive for outside business required another cultural change. 'In 1980,' said Leighfield, 'we had no salesmen. Now we have 60'. One of the keys to the successful transformation of a pro-team within a large group into an autonomous company capable of serving a wider market is **the development of a marketing culture**.

The car market was the obvious place to start. Istel counts Rolls-Royce, Jaguar, Ford and General Motors among its customers in addition to its two main clients Austin Rover and Land Rover. But Leighfield and his team were not content. They were confident there was a great deal of growth left for them in automotive manufacturing but they wanted to make Istel less vulnerable to the car industry's notorious cycles.

This was when their early work on Infotrac, a high-capacity communications network using lines leased from BT and supported by 64 access points throughout the UK, came into its own. The stock locator system was linked through Infotrac to car dealers all over Britain and therefore to a high proportion of the business population. 'We thought about travel agents,' said Leighfield 'they also need access to central information.' Today 60% of the members of the Association of British Travel Agents use Istel's network.

Other counter-cyclical areas identified by Istel were health and financial services. In collaboration with a financially-orientated knowhow company Istel launched Inview – a screen-based listing of low cost life-insurance endowment policies for the mortgage market. The Halifax, Britain's largest building society, was one of Inview's first users so it was not surprising that within a matter of months 29 of the 30 insurance companies supplying the endowment mortgage market had asked to become Inview information providers.

Istel has also established a small but promising foothold in the US market and has bought out a former partner in a computer disaster recovery company called Failsafe.

While Istel had been acquiring an enviable reputation for excellence in the converging computer/communications industry its still-troubled parent had been making its laborious way towards an exit from the public sector. Privatisation was in the air and since the flotation of Jaguar in 1983, piecemeal disposals had been on the cards. Istel was formally put up for sale in mid-1986 and is believed to have attracted a large number of bids. One bizarre suggestion was that the state-owned French systems company GSI was keen to buy and thus take Istel from the UK to the French public sector in one fell swoop.

But Leighfield and his colleagues, jealous of their autonomy and confident of their ability to survive and prosper as an independent company, began plotting a management buy-out. They knew the company intimately and were therefore in a better position than most to assess its worth. Its main weakness was that it was still dependent for about 60% of its sales on Rover Group (the re-named BL). On the other hand Leighfield's deft touch with professionals had reduced labour turnover to an impressively low 8% a year. It was unlikely that this figure would be given the attention it deserved in the accountants report on Istel commissioned by Rover Group's new chief executive Graham Day.

The management's bid was accepted in principle in late 1986. It is interesting to speculate what the company might have been worth had Leighfield and his professional colleagues walked out following the rejection of their offer.

- **Lessons to be learned**

The pro-teams, equipped with their specialist managers, **must be treated separately** and can, in some cases, be usefully turned into separate companies. But **pro-teams are seldom professional organisations in their own right** because, having been a part of larger organisations, they have not developed the ability to manage themselves. Unless blessed with leaders of Leighfield's quality a pro-team plucked untimely from its parental womb will not survive for long.

In any case the growth of management buy-outs is increasing the risk attached to the separate company solution, despite its obvious attractions. Once the pro-team has become a separate legal entity its **professionals will want more independence, perhaps even employee ownership** through a buy-out. John Padovan, head of BZW's corporate finance operations, was talking of a possible flotation of BZW from Barclays as early as December 1986, only six months after the company's formal creation. **Buy-outs can undermine an organisation's culture** by encouraging professionals and managers in other profitable parts of the company to ask for independence. If they have to be refused they will become demoralised and will probably leave.

Before leaving the buy-out it is worth exploring the implications it has for another of the main themes in this book – the shift in the balance of power from the owners of financial to the owners of knowhow capital. Managers like buy-outs because they can, thereby, become inordinately rich. The Nottingham University figures on buy-outs referred to in Chapter Three suggest a management team taking 10% of the equity in a £20m buy-out could be worth £6m between them within three or four years. That sum is a measure of their worth and thus of the disproportionate share of added value claimed previously by their parent company's shareholders.

The main weakness of the separate company solution for the knowhow-orientated parts of an organisation takes no account of one of the imperatives of the new management – the need to focus on knowhow. The lesson to be learned from the professional organisation is that pro-teams, from being seen as irksome pockets of unmanageability in large organisations, **can become windows on the future** – the weathervanes of companies – showing the way forward.

Pro-teams in large organisations represent the core knowhow and have the potential – if they can be regarded as prime assets rather than managerial liabilities – to exemplify a new business idea. Pro-teams can drive organisations but it is hard for them to be their servants.

• A strategy for pro-team management

Companies like AGA and Swedish Match in Sweden and Istel and Oxford Instruments in Britain, which have sold off or closed down peripheral activities accumulated during earlier periods, and have focussed on their core knowhow, have done well. Focus is one of the success factors.

There are other lessons of pro-team management that companies of all kinds can learn from the professional organisations. Again our 10 success factors provide a guide to the key points:

- Top managers in large companies tend to teach their young, ambitious potential chief executives that the higher up in the organisation they go, the more remote they have to become from the business itself. This is a very dangerous management style in a pro-team. **Managers must take part in the daily work**, be professional and be accepted by the professionals.

- Quality is a fashionable concept of the 1980s. It is a symptom of the growth of the information society. Not so long ago the idea of 'wear and tear' was all the rage. Now the demand for quality, in products ranging from bread to shoes and in services ranging from travel agency to health care, is on the march. **Pro-teams thrive on quality**.

- **Respect the knowhow** of the pro-teams. Give the pros ample opportunity for education, exploratory journeys and unusual careers. **Invest in knowhow** by engaging in 'in-house' R&D.

- Entrepreneurship within a company was once regarded as dangerous if not impossible. The idea of the **'intrapreneur'** – invented by Gifford Pinchot III and promoted by the Swedish Foresight Group – heralds a change in the orthodoxy. It suggests that large companies should **encourage internal entrepreneurs** and give them autonomy. The success of the idea is another sign of the advent of the information society.

- The pro-team develops a strong culture of its own. This should be encouraged, not destroyed. **Such cultures stimulate the development of professional expertise** and concentrate the focus on knowhow growth.

- **Focus and priority** are both important success factors. The success of Pharmacia's superheated Healon programme was the result of sharp focus. Healon is largely responsible for Pharmacia's success on the international capital markets in the last few years. Similarly Glaxo's decision to focus its research efforts on its anti-ulcer drug Zantac has paid enormous dividends for both the company and its shareholders.

  With the benefit of hindsight the selections of the Healon and Zantac projects seem obvious decisions but at the time they were each just one among several promising R&D projects at Pharmacia and Glaxo.

- It is extremely important to preserve the core knowhow of the organisation. **Do not allow key people to leave**. If necessary try to arrange unconventional inducements to stay such as allowing them to form their own companies, sending them on missions abroad or giving them more R&D resources.

- Develop the people in the pro-teams on their own terms, without reference to the larger organisation's rules and conventions. **Professionals must have their own careers**. It is wrong to try to turn a good professional into a bad manager as is the habit in the public sector.

- **Develop smooth change-over techniques**. The company must be able to change people in key positions without disruption, or the quality of the pro-team will be lost.

- **Create stable structures** which tie the pro-teams together and, through networks, link them to other parts of the group. These structures can be routines, understandings or formal agreements. Informal structures such as the personal relationships and networks between members of the pro-teams and their parent organisations are the most important of all.

• Top management is a pro-team

The top management of a company consists of a group of people with highly specialised knowhow in their respective areas. They can be seen as talented senior professionals who have progressed far in their own development. The management team might also be grouped in with the managers of divisions or subsidiaries who are also professionals in this sense. One can regard top managers as comprising their own pro-team in the middle of a large organisation. What can one do to maintain and develop the skills of the top management and thereby enhance the performance of the whole company? Let us try to answer this question by focussing on managerial knowhow and, once again, applying our 10 success factors.

1. The members of top management must work together and join each other in the day-to-day management tasks. The managing director should not withdraw to a separate office. He or she should act and work as a 'primus inter pares' (first among equals).
2. It goes without saying that top management, like all professionals, are constantly striving for quality in their own skills. But who monitors the quality of top management? Feedback consisting only of figures is seldom enough.
3. Focus on the knowhow – and develop it. For example, expose the financial director to new knowhow within his or her area. Insist they go to seminars even when they claim they have no time.
4. It takes high quality leadership to maintain and develop the knowhow of a team of top managers. They very rarely see themselves as a team, let alone as an organisation in its own right deserving of its own consideration.
5. Try and create a strong top management team culture which keeps it together. Have fun together outside the office.
6. Try to focus the work on the fundamental issues rather than the day-to-day routines. Try to avoid the endless flow of accounting information.
7. Try to keep the team together with carrots, golden-handcuffs, exciting projects and any other means you can think of.
8. It is important that the top management team should develop team methods. Playing management games together or studying and discussing how other successful management teams work can help.
9. Create a network of mutual respect and trust in each other. The personal relationships in the top management team are crucial. It is also important to ensure there are no rows about shareholdings and stock options.
10. Last but not least, organise the succession. Try to bring on the crown princes or princesses and avoid like the plague the temptation to build a monument to your own excellence.

SUMMARY
- **Knowhow work is a pan-industrial phenomenon.**
- Many industries are **in the process of becoming knowhow industries.**
- These pockets of knowhow – **'pro-teams'** – within large organisations **cannot be managed in a conventional way** and should be regarded as **embryonic knowhow organisations.**
- To survive on their own pro-teams must develop **marketing cultures.**
- The problem with making pro-teams separate companies is that **the professionals will want more independence, perhaps even employee-ownership.**
- Pro-teams often **represent the core knowhow.**
- Applying the 10 success factors to pro-team management suggests managers should: **take part in the daily work; champion quality; respect and invest in the knowhow; encourage internal entrepreneurs;** nourish the **culture; stimulate the development of expertise; establish focus and priorities; prevent key people from leaving;** allow the professionals **to develop their own careers; develop smooth change-over techniques and create stable structures.**
- It is useful to regard a group's top management as a **pro-team** and to apply the 10 success factors to the problem of managing top managers.

14

• Knowhow and the Future

• A paradigm shift in the information society

Our aim in writing this book was to provide the reader with some insight into what we believe is an extremely important and challenging new area of management and, above all, to equip him or her with a rudimentary set of tools with which to attack the problems of knowhow management.

This is first and foremost a practical book. Many of the problems we have discussed will be familiar to our readers. They are contemporary problems which have yet to receive, in our view, the attention they deserve in contemporary management literature.

But though pragmatism has guided our writing, theorising has seldom been far from our thoughts. We have asked ourselves what it all means and where will it end? We shall conclude with a chapter on the future. What are the long-term implications of our analysis for business? Does the advent of the information society herald a fundamental change in the way production is organised or merely a shift in emphasis? Can the new resource of 'knowhow' we have identified be accommodated by conventional theories? Is knowhow capitalism just a variant of orthodox financial capitalism or does it require a wholly new approach to the economics of the firm?

We argued in the previous chapter that knowhow organisations, be they knowhow companies, professional organisations or 'pro-teams' within large organisations, are spreading throughout the corporate sector. How far will this process go? Is it conceivable that complex problem-solving, the stuff of the knowhow business, will ever replace manufacturing as the driving force of economic growth and development?

In short, if the reader accepts the basic themes and concepts of this book, how much of the present economic and managerial orthodoxy will he or she be obliged to reject?

• Knowhow life-cycles

A particular knowhow has its own life-cycle. It is conceived, sometimes by an inventor, is born, then developed often over several generations and finally it becomes mature. Later it may be revived and stimulated into a new development phase. Re-visiting our farmer and his milk bottles will help to clarify the point.

It may be that the modern milk bottles or cartons on our breakfast tables represent the last phase of the life-cycle of a particular knowhow area. It is arguable that the farmer, in partnership with the organisational developments and research that have aided him, has developed his dairy industry knowhow over the last 100 years just about as far as it will go.

He and his helpers have together built up a sophisticated industrial organisation for crop cultivation, stock-breeding, animal husbandry, storage, processing, packaging and distribution. With the help of research, much of it state-financed, they have developed a vast managerial knowhow about how to exploit advances made in other knowhow areas like chemistry, genetics, biology, engineering and electronics. Armed with this knowhow they have vigorously pursued the goal of obtaining the **maximum volume of output per unit of capital and human resources**.

That the efficiency, measured in these terms, of the farming industry at large has grown prodigiously cannot be doubted. These days the 5% of the Swedish workforce engaged in agriculture produce more than twice as much as the 50% thus employed as recently as 50 years ago.

But the maximisation of output per units of capital and labour is no longer the only name of the game. The enormous success of the Campaign for Real Ale (CAMRA) in Britain during the 1970s, which forced the big brewers to re-think their strategies and rescued many small brewers from threatened extinction, illustrates the limitations of a single-minded drive for greater volume.

In common with many other Western countries a debate is raging right now in Sweden about food **quality**. It was sparked off by the revelation that Swedish wheat is no longer suitable for baking bread because its gluten content is too low. Most Swedes now admit that foreigners who complain about inedible Swedish bread have a point. The problem is partly to do with the climate but is also to do with the direction research has taken. The farmers have devoted their scientific efforts to a search for high-yielding crops at the expense, as it turns out, of baking quality. In our terms, the researchers, at the behest of the farmers, have concentrated the development of their professional knowhow on how to maximise the **quantity** of production by Swedish farms.

They have developed the same kind of knowhow in almost every area of food production. For example, Swedish chickens taste of fish because they are fed on blends of fish meal which encourage rapid growth.

Could it be that the development of all this modern knowhow has been based on an assumption that is no longer valid? Suppose the market to-day, less fearful of the threats of shortage and scarcity, has acquired a taste for **quality** rather than **quantity**?

A growing number of farmers and researchers have begun to experiment with other food production methods which require no additives to replace the 'goodness' modern, mass-production techniques take out. A line in a British television advert for bread spoke of the loaf 'with nowt taken out'.

Many of these experiments have been going on for years, against the wishes of the farming establishment, against the wishes of the authorities and sometimes even against the law. The 'new farmers' produce less food but of a tastier quality. Consumers express their preference for it in their willingness to pay a considerable premium for 'natural foods'. Some farmers are experimenting with new distribution methods too. Sweden's centralised meat distribution system is being challenged. Farmers are trying to free themselves from the network by opening their own butcher's shops.

It looks as if the food industry may have progressed as far as it can reasonably go in the accumulation of knowhow about how to maximise the quantity of food production. One might say that the knowhow area 'quantity' has reached its peak and is now moving into a period of maturity and decline.

The figure below juxtaposes two classically-shaped life-cycles. With our focus on knowhow we might detect the beginning of a new life-cycle, **the life-cycle of quality**.

To put it another way a new paradigm in the food industry appears to be at hand. The old paradigm, rooted thousands of years in the past, was that we must always try to produce the maximum quantity of food. It was once a laudable and appropriate aim. There are still those alive who remember the privations of war and the poor harvests which made starvation a harsh reality for many people all over the world.

Now, in the Northern hemisphere at any rate, the wheel has turned full-circle. We have butter mountains and wine lakes; Europe's granaries and abat-

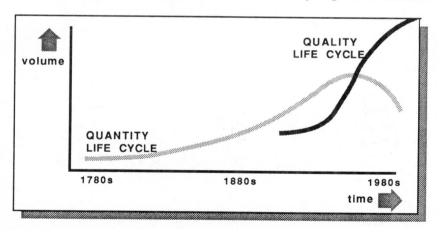

Figure 25   For hundreds of years farmers have concentrated their R&D efforts on how to produce maximum quantity per acre, increasing output every year. In industrialised societies customers are now demanding quality instead. Thus the knowhow of quantity production is being replaced by a new knowhow priority of quality.

toirs are bursting with produce. The volume maximisation paradigm has created not only large surpluses of staple foods but also an agricultural system that actively encourages surplus production. Since modern farmers produce more food than they can sell it is no wonder some of them have begun to think of how to produce what the market wants – quality food rather than mere food.

• A shift of paradigm

Knowhow is a living thing, always changing, developing, growing. It is essential for researchers in each knowhow area to keep open minds. The philosopher of science Thomas Kuhn coined the expression 'shift of paradigm' to describe the discontinuities that occur from time to time in scientific development. There are signs of such a paradigm shift in the food industry.

According to Kuhn the typical situation before a shift of paradigm is one where the Establishment knowhow is firmly embedded in government and the universities and where large institutions and bureaucracies, employing many people, have become dependent on the old knowhow. The emerging paradigm, because it poses a threat to the Establishment, is fought with every means at the Establishment's disposal. The heretics are persecuted by the collective force of the vested interests in government and research.

The law, designed to address the problems of an earlier age, will typically be recruited to frustrate the pioneers of the new paradigm. For example the 'new farmers' are unable to comply with the formal demands in Swedish law about hygiene in butchery. At the same time the big producer co-operatives are trying to price the small abbattoirs out of existence and are boycotting shops which trade with the 'pirates'.

According to Kuhn the new paradigm will only take over when the heretics reach critical mass – when they are so many that together they have the power to overthrow the establishment.

There do seem to be here some Kuhnian signs of an impending paradigm shift. The business establishment, including the financial markets, remains wedded to institutions and attitudes appropriate to a bygone age when the problems of shortage were paramount.

Changing patterns of demand, notably a greater revealed preference for quality as opposed to low price, are progressively invalidating the paradigm of scarcity. Many businessmen and entrepreneurs, amongst whom professionals are prominent, are responding to these changes. It may not be long now before the knowhow revolution achieves critical mass. No paradigm of business, however firmly established, can defy the customer indefinitely.

• Transition

The presumption in this book is that the knowhow professionals are, by and large, reactive players of the business game. We have tended to characterise the positions of the professional and the knowhow manager as static in the sense that both adapt to the existing situation.

But throughout there has also been the implication that the existing situation, already very different from that of a few years back, continues to develop at a rapid rate. There have been hints that the positions of the professionals and their companies are pregnant with further possibilities.

They still claim a relatively small proportion of value added. The kind of bargains they will be able to strike with financiers to-morrow may be very different from, and much more in their favour, than the bargains struck to-day.

Let us look at the case of the capital-intensive knowhow company we encountered in Chapter Eleven. It is interesting because here the nature of the trade-off between knowhow and financial capital is clearly set out in various agreements and in the ownership structure. Are there trends in these agreements that indicate **a change in the balance of bargaining power** that might, in turn, indicate an impending shift of paradigm? Are the knowhow professionals actively pushing for better deals or just accepting the status quo?

When modern venture capital began in Britain in 1980 the size of funds was small – £10m was big – and the stakes the fund managers had in the potential capital gains were meagre; rarely more than a few percentage points.

Nowadays deals between the managers and the suppliers of finance are sliced very differently. As the appetite of institutions and, stimulated by tax concessions, of individuals for investments in small, high-growth companies has grown, fund size has swollen enormously. There are several £30m + conventional funds and some management buy-out funds are larger still. The Electra-Candover fund has £260m to play with in the management buy-out market.

At the same time fund managers, those responsible for seeking out suitable companies to invest in, are demanding a larger slice of the action. We saw in Chapter Eleven how Lucius Cary, of Venture Capital Report, doubled his slice of fund management profits in three years. The norm these days is that of every £100 subscribed by investors the managers take £20. They normally have what is known in the trade as a 20% 'carried interest' in the capital gains – investors are obliged to give away 20% of their investment to the managers because if they don't others will.

Variations in the standard 'carried interest' percentage in venture capital are indications of a change in the balance of bargaining power between knowhow and financial capital. There may come a time when fund management knowhow companies keep most of the capital gains they make and merely rely on outside investors for loan finance.

But at the same time the relationship between the fund managers and their target companies is changing. Here they wear the hat of the financial capitalist and, particularly when investing in knowhow companies, they may soon find the balance of bargaining power shifting away from them just as it has shifted towards them in their relationship with their investors. They are competing for the good deals with other fund managers. If they don't improve their terms, others will.

It is instructive to compare the position of the venture capital fund manager with that of the management consultant. The bargaining power of the consultant is considerable though it varies somewhat according to the type of consultancy.

The problem with consultancy is that it is a service which can generate added value for the client that is out of all proportion to its costs. Good consultancy is a bargain.

It is therefore natural for consultants to wonder from time whether or not they might be better off working directly for their clients on a performance-related basis. Their knowhow would be much more highly geared in such circumstances than if they were to continue to work as the salaried employees of the consultancy firm and, in addition, they might have the opportunity to amass considerable wealth through stock options. There is, in fact, a constant migration of professionals from consultancy firms to their clients.

The consultancy firms are responding in various ways. Some of the smaller spin-out firms, very conscious of the dangers of defections, are trying to introduce gearing into their consultancy by taking small equity stakes in their clients in lieu of fees. This type of 'venture consultancy' provides a degree of 'performancing' not available with orthodox fee arrangements and also provides opportunities for consultants to accumulate wealth.

Another trend is the establishment of captive venture capital funds by some of the larger consultancies – Bain & Co., Boston Consulting Group and The LEK Partnership are just three examples. Investment strategies are based on the firm's specialist knowhow and capital gains are available for distribution to the consultants.

It is also instructive to compare the management consultancy firm to the top management group of one of the new breed of acquisition-led conglomerates. In some ways they are two aspects of the same phenomenon. Nigel Rudd and Brian McGowan run Williams Holdings, one of the most dynamic of Britain's young conglomerates. They could be seen as management consultants who have decided to leverage their management knowhow by buying companies rather than advising them.

• Imperfect markets

Venture fund managers, management consultants and the top management teams of certain types of companies are examples of professionals who are actively pushing the parameters of their bargains with the suppliers of finance. They show that there are imperfections in the professional marketplace, caused by the persistence of old conventions, which are still giving too high a return and too much power to financial as opposed to knowhow capital.

But these imperfections will be progressively ironed out during the coming decade or so. The old paradigm is already in retreat in some knowhow areas. The professionals are becoming conscious of their power. Soon knowhow start-ups will no longer have to cede control, as Cergus did, to the suppliers of finance when they decide to adopt a capital-intensive business idea.

And more generally the relative scarcity of knowhow capital, and a growing recognition of the need to focus on the invisible rather than the visible balance sheet, is likely to lead to a widespread re-structuring of companies and industries to suit the ethos of the professionals.

• The professional ethos

The ethos (Oxford English Dictionary: The prevalent tone of sentiment of a people or community; the genius of an institution or system) of the knowhow company is very different from that of the conventional, capital-intensive manufacturing company. We have learned a little about it in the previous chapters:

- management must be competent in the managerial *and* the professional areas.
- the importance of quality and quality control is paramount if the competitive position is to be preserved and enhanced.
- management must be intimate or 'hands-on'. It cannot operate effectively from the outside.
- the culture is precious and inherently fragile. It needs constant nourishment and re-inforcement. Cultural conflicts must be avoided at all costs.
- the business idea, though it can be changed from time to time, must never be confused. The focus must always be abundantly clear and acceptable to the professionals.
- the threat of walk-outs by groups of professionals is ever present. It is part of the climate within which managers manage. As the professionals' ultimate sanction it is enormously powerful for two reasons: it is plausible (walk-outs are frequent) and if implemented it can be fatal.

These elements of the knowhow company ethos conflict with the ethos of the old paradigm in several ways. **For a start they militate against size.** The dual competence and hands-on management requirements favour relatively small groupings of professionals and the importance of clear focus and cultural integrity make acquisitive strategies extremely hazardous.

They also favour **professionally-driven business ideas** and business development. It will become increasingly hard for 'conventional' managers to lead knowhow organisations when they begin to compete for talent with true 'professional organisations' as we have defined them.

There is much more, of course, which distinguishes the knowhow ethos from the ethos of the old paradigm but there is enough here for us to make a few predictions. As Sir Karl Popper, another eminent philosopher of science, has pointed out, theories that cannot be tested by 'falsifiable' predictions are not worth the paper they are printed on.

• Towards a knowhow future

We believe there is overwhelming evidence for the existence of the following 'megatrend':

THE BALANCE OF POWER IS SHIFTING FROM CAPITAL TO KNOWHOW.

We will now try to look further into the future by asking ourselves the question: If the above megatrend is a true description of what is happening what implications does it have for the business community at large?

We predict that:

- Knowhow workers, sometimes known as the 'gold-collar workers' or the 'cognitive elité', will become increasingly powerful at all levels of society.
- Their salaries and other remuneration will increase enormously in the coming years.
- The numbers of professionals will continue to grow as more and more people go through post graduate education.
- The prevailing attitudes in society will shift in favour of the professional and the intellectual so that art, architecture, literature and cultural values in general will be greatly up-graded.
- Traditional manufacturing industries will have to adopt knowhow-oriented strategies to survive.
- The unions will undergo a major transition following a review of their strategies inspired by falling membership.
- There will be a series of major upheavals in information producing companies as the demands of their pro-teams come into sharp conflict with the need to adopt industrial strategies for more routine services.
- Self-employment will increase as professionals try to maximise their share of the value they add.
- Managers of knowhow companies who employ methods derived from traditional manufacturing industry will constantly be running into trouble.
- Many of the new professional conglomerates recently created will demerge having realised that size confers no particular competitive advantage.
- Business ethics and the corporate culture will become key management tools because of the need to create structure in knowhow organisations.
- Federations of knowhow companies, their suppliers and customers will be formed to replace the traditional pattern of parent and wholly-owned subsidiaries. The concept of corporate ownership and of the company itself will be re-defined.
- Territorial control will cease to be an advantage, following the rapid build up of information networks and the flexible nature of knowhow capital. This will have important implications for the role of the State.
- The growing interdependence between countries will turn tax systems, civil law and economic policies into competitive weapons as each country woos the professional elite. Ergo, legal systems and economic policies will converge.
- Characteristics normally associated with the female, such as compassion, humanity, empathy and social skills, will grow in importance. This is because professional cultures are built on relationships between people.

- The new inequality debate will concentrate on the differences between those 'at the centre' (mostly the professionals), having access to all networks and information, and 'those at the periphery' who will suffer from a lack of knowhow capital.
- Hopefully the public sector, struggling with its ability to recruit and keep good people, will realise that many public service organisations are knowhow intensive and will therefore adopt knowhow oriented strategies.
- People of advanced years will be seen less as being 'old' and more as being 'experienced'. The West's obsession with youth will diminish as society realises the vast resources tied up in the wisdom and the networks of the older professionals. The retirement age will rise rather than fall as appears to be the current trend.

• Newspaper publishing

When Rupert Murdoch moved his UK national newspapers – the *Sun* and *News of the World* junk titles and the *The Times* and *The Sunday Times* qualities – from their traditional homes in and near Fleet Street to Wapping in London's docklands he was heralded by 'expert' observers as the industry's saviour.

He had solved the problems of the rapacious print unions and had thereby, in the words of the Newspaper Publishers Association, turned Fleet Street, albeit exiled to Wapping in this case, 'into an orthodox capitalist thoroughfare'.

But newspaper publishing is anything but 'an orthodox capitalist thoroughfare'. It is, on the contrary, a classic knowhow business teeming with professionals.

Murdoch's victory over the print unions, though it has earned him financial dividends in the short-term, has greatly enhanced the power of his journalists. And the Wapping move, though a 'coup' by conventional management standards, was a major strategic error by the standards of knowhow management.

The cultures of the quality papers in particular were seriously disturbed by the move. The professionals – the journalists – were forced, by the violent picketing of the Wapping site by angry printers, to take sides with Murdoch in an industrial struggle that had nothing directly to do with them. Though they liked the new technology at Wapping they disliked the place and were deeply hurt by the execration piled on them each morning as they crossed the picket lines.

And Murdoch made no attempt to win them over. There were no expressions of gratitude for their loyalty and forbearance, no substantial, compensatory increases in salary and no recognition that anything had changed in the relationship between the professionals and management. Many journalists left and the quality of the newspapers began to decline.

But the bargaining power of professionals, though inherently strong, requires appropriate market conditions if it is to be fully realised. Such conditions do not yet prevail. Though the owners have changed, the ownership structure in Fleet Street remains locked in the old paradigm in which the printing process, and latterly the struggle with the print unions, has been the key focus of man-

196 . MANAGING KNOWHOW

agement. For the moment a journalist leaving Wapping has little choice but to join another Murdoch-type operation.

This is changing. The launch of *The Independent* quality newspaper in the autumn of 1986 was a professionally-led initiative. *The Independent*, backed by City money and owing no allegiance to the publishing establishment, is developing a culture and a management style very much more in tune with the professional ethos. If it succeeds, and it is hard to over-estimate how difficult it is for a new entrant to break through in such a conservative market, it will add greatly to the bargaining power of journalists throughout the industry. Its launch and the launch earlier in 1986 of the rather less convincing *Today* newspaper have already shown that the new technology has dramatically reduced the barriers to entry in national newspaper publishing and, following the defeat of the print unions, made it potentially a very profitable business indeed.

Our predictions for the British national newspaper industry are as follows:

- As the widespread introduction of new technology allows the high inherent profitability of the business to be realised, journalists will begin to demand a substantially larger share of the added value. Their salaries, as one observer put it, 'will go through the roof'.
- The industry will become more competitive as barriers to entry fall and new entrants are attracted in. Margins will begin to narrow.
- Professional spin-outs of *The Independent* kind will become more frequent. Those that succeed are likely to become the dominant players because their professional origins make them better able to solve the problems of knowhow management we have discussed in this book.
- The Murdoch type of organisation will have to adopt the rules of knowhow management, and soon, or withdraw from the market.

• The advertising industry

Saatchi & Saatchi's phenomenal growth over the past one-and-a-half decades is seen by some observers as a sign that the business of advertising has changed fundamentally. They say it has ceased to be a profession and has become an industry, much like any other. That is certainly how the City sees it.

It is quite possible for this sort of thing to happen. The examples of fast-food chains like MacDonald's, Kentucky Fried Chicken, Wimpy and Wendy show how closely service companies like restaurants can come to resemble factories.

But is advertising like this? Has it become peopled by young, low-paid illiterates operating drawing machines and computers? Has the role of creativity in advertising been wholly subsumed into computer programs and administrative routines? In the Saatchi & Saatchi subsidiaries has management knowhow displaced professional knowhow utterly?

More to the point, do the professionals see it that way? Do they agree that because companies like Saatchi & Saatchi have succeeded in buying and selling agencies profitably their profession has thereby been transformed into an industry and they into factory workers?

The activities of Saatchi & Saatchi and of its emulators have given the advertising business the appearance of an industry but have done nothing to change its professional essence. Indeed, it is easier to believe that the professions of law and accountancy will ultimately be 'industrialised' than it is to believe that the fundamentally more creative business of advertising will be.

So how do we explain the Saatchi & Saatchi phenomenon? If large advertising groups are a flagrant denial of much of what advertising is, how have they come about? What has made it possible for this particular bumble bee to fly?

This is an important question. Part of the answer undoubtedly lies in the evangelism of the Saatchi brothers. Their victory over the hearts and minds of the City attracted a great deal of finance into advertising, subjected the putative 'industry' to traditional financial disciplines and criteria and, more specifically, armed Saatchi & Saatchi itself with the high share-rating it needed to pursue an aggressively acquisitive growth strategy.

But this financial respectability, though a necessary pre-condition for the emergence of the large advertising group, was not a sufficient one. The management problem had to be solved too. The professionals had to be persuaded that this was the way forward; that only in large groups could they develop their skills, hone their professionalism and advance their careers. If the professionals had objected to the Saatchi strategy; if they had seen it as predatory and contrary to the spirit of the business rather than, as they did until recently at any rate, a bold and exciting adventure, the Saatchi dream would have been still-born.

It is a measure of the genius of the Saatchi brothers that they were able to reconcile the apparently irreconcilable requirements of the City and of advertising professionals.

But the jury is still out on the Saatchi case. The fraternal jugglers are having to keep more and more balls in the air at the same time. If they drop one the chances are they will drop them all. The City's support is conditional on the continued good behaviour of earnings per share. This will be harder to deliver now that US profits have become so significant and while the US dollar is so weak.

And similarly the continued support of the advertising professionals is by no means assured. The fall-out from the Ted Bates deal has sent a frisson of unease round the group which, without skilful management, could lead to a substantial increase in the rate of knowhow leakage. If Saatchi & Saatchi begins to find it hard to recruit and keep good people it will be in serious trouble.

Our predictions for the advertising industry are as follows:

• Saatchi & Saatchi will fail in its attempt to win a 10% share of the world advertising market. (Though the largest advertising company in the world, its current market share is less than 5%.)

- The age of the giant agency will be relatively short-lived and will probably end well before the millenium.
- The naturally fragmented quality of the 'industry' will re-assert itself through an increase in the number of successful spin-outs.

• The hunger for growth

Two themes have come to dominate the strategic thinking of knowhow industry managers in recent years: 'globalisation' and the 'services supermarket'. Both are exemplified in the Saatchi & Saatchi strategy and were influential in persuading the City of advertising's investment merits. One fund manager recalled that 'I got intrigued by Saatchi when I read an article about their world strategy'.

These ideas of growth by territory and function have been common and respectable strategies in traditional industries for many years. Their application to professional services, including accountancy, consultancy, legal services, etc. as well as to advertising, are **a symptom of the growing power of managerial as opposed to professional knowhow** in these areas.

Knowhow companies and 'firms' have begun to address the problem of growth in increasingly competitive international markets and are borrowing growth strategies from the only source available – traditional companies and industries.

We have profound reservations about the long-term validity of these growth strategies for two reasons:

- we doubt the business assumptions on which they are based.
- they ignore the fact that knowhow companies are very different from the industrial companies from which they have derived their management style.

• Do the customers really want it?

When Maurice Saatchi told Saatchi & Saatchi shareholders in August 1986 that the loss of the RJR Nabisco, Warner-Lambert and Colgate-Palmolive accounts following the Ted Bates merger was 'a reasonable price to pay for the market position of great strength we have established' some might have thought that if this was the price of strength it might have been better to remain weak.

Initial 'conflict of interest' losses were inevitable, of course, but there was little sign of the promised 'widening the spread' gains which were the rationale of the acquisition. Saatchis would find it very hard to prove that in recent years the increase in its world market share has been the result of anything other than its acquisitive activity.

Likewise the international accountancy firms, put together in a hectic period of 'rationalisation' in the 1970s, have probably failed to improve the world market share of their constituent parts. Like Saatchis they have become bigger by adding pieces rather than by growing pieces at a faster rate than the market.

Wherein lies the virtue of Maurice Saatchi's 'position of great strength' if not in organic growth? Is it likely that sophisticated buyers of business services, who have a duty to their shareholders to spend wisely, will be persuaded by such arguments as 'never mind the quality, feel the breadth and width'?

And is it likely, given the problems of knowhow management we have discussed in this book, that the large groups will be able to achieve and maintain an above-average quality of service? Professionals do not like to be managed actively but active management there must be if large knowhow groups are not to be broken apart by centrifugal forces.

• Knowhow wars

• Soliciting for growth

In April 1987 John Wickerson, President of The Law Society, wrote to his members – Britain's 48,000 solicitors – asking them for their comments on a discussion paper entitled *Multi-Disciplinary Partnerships and Allied Topics*.

The paper focussed on the 'commercial challenge' facing the legal profession, particularly the increased competition from accountancy firms which, largely because of their move into management consultancy, had become the major employers of graduates in Britain, accounting for 10% of the annual total.

The paper said that 'compared even to the most sophisticated City solicitors' practices the largest international accountancy firms provide such a range of services as to be de facto multi-disciplinary firms'.

The rationale, according to the discussion paper, 'is said to be the desire of clients to have an 'all-in' service' though the paper expressed no view on whether or not such a desire existed in practice.

The dilemma as The Law Society saw it was that the commercial challenge of the multi-disciplinary firm conflicts with the solicitor's traditional role 'as an independent and impartial adviser of integrity enjoying a unique position as an officer of the Court'. Independence, which in any case some saw as 'a primary commercial advantage', comparable presumably, to the commercial advantage of the 'all-in' service, might be weakened, the discussion paper suggested, if a solicitor 'in serving the public . . . is in the employ of a non-solicitor, or his practice is owned wholly or in part by a non-solicitor'.

It might also weaken the power of The Law Society which was probably if not more, at least as much to the point.

But the discussion paper acknowledged that something would have to be done about the existing partnership model. The profession needed to respond to the competitive challenge; profit-sharing restrictions were making it harder 'to recruit and retain good quality non-partner solicitors'; partnerships were less tax-efficient than companies; there were serious insurance cover and personal liability problems and the impermanence of partnerships was causing difficulties with long-term contracts such as leases and pensions.

There was also a reference to the 'unreality of [the] partnership model being expected to manage and control a large solicitors' practice'.

Incorporation with limited liability, already permissible in Scotland, was a possible answer provided 'control and ownership did not pass from the solicitors managing the business'. It might allow the emergence of multi-disciplinary partnerships that could suppply a broader range of services, exploit 'economies of scale' and make it more easy for the profession to resist competition from accountants and financial institutions.

But The Law Society warned that if incorporation and multi-disciplinary partnerships were to be allowed its ruling Council 'might well only permit such partnerships to exist where solicitors were at least in majority control, possibly as high as 75% control'.

Elsewhere the discussion paper pointed out that the Institute of Chartered Accountants had recently decreed that if fewer than 75% of the partners of an accountancy firm are chartered accountants, or if chartered accountants hold less than 75% of the equity, they must practise under a different name from an associated accountancy practice.

Clearly the battle for the knowhow services market is about to be joined. Following the trail blazed by the advertising profession, lawyers and accountants are preparing to enter the fray with their own versions of the services supermarket, though both their governing bodies, jealous of their authority, are determined it shall be their members who hold the whip hand.

The scene for a bout of Saatchi-style mergers in the legal profession was set early in 1987 when two large City firms, Clifford Turner and Coward Chance, announced plans to unify their partnerships in a mega-practice to be called Clifford Chance. The rationale for the merger was that the specialities of the two firms complemented each other perfectly. Clifford Chance would acquire a position of great strength because of the unique breadth of its product line.

Shortly after the merger plans were announced a joke not in the best of taste was pinned to one of Coward Chance's noticeboards. It linked the merger with AIDS and read: 'The more partners, the greater the risk.' It gave voice to a disquiet on the part of associates, the legal profession's equivalent of the City's 'marzipan' boys, about the effect on their prospects of the increasing size of law firms and in particular about the effect on their partnership prospects of the formation of Clifford Chance.

One of the effects of increasing corporate size in any industry is to reduce the number of top jobs. In knowhow companies the professionals are not particularly interested in 'top' jobs of the managerial kind because, by and large, they are not attracted to management. But young solicitors are extremely interested in whether or not they become partners and they know that the bigger the firm the less chance they will have.

Between the years 1976-1986 the total number of solicitors in private practice, partners and associates, increased by 52%, from 26,000 to 39,500. During the same period the number of partners increased by 36% to 27,000 while the number of associates more than doubled to 12,500. The Law Society expects the trend towards fewer equity-sharing partners and more salary earning associates to continue because the more profit-conscious large firms rely for their profits growth on the leverage provided by salaried associates.

Mutiny in the ranks

The adoption by knowhow company leaders of growth strategies borrowed from traditional industries, though one of the most significant contemporary developments in the knowhow area, is likely, in retrospect, to be seen as a major mistake. The competent professional, in sharp contrast to the competent manager, sees no virtue in size for its own sake.

Professionals wish for challenging work, a stimulating environment and scope for personal development. They remain indifferent to the growth aspirations of their leaders and managers just so long as they do not interfere with their own needs and desires. As soon as they feel threatened or compromised by them, or as soon as the growth ethos disturbs the ambience of the working environment, they will leave.

Even the best managers and the most charismatic of leaders will find it hard to reconcile the exigencies of rapid, acquisition-led growth with the essential fragility of the knowhow capital on which knowhow companies depend. And even the most passionate supporter of the knowhow company breed would not claim they are presently over-endowed with good managers and charismatic leaders.

• Index

Page-numbers in italics refer to diagrams and tables